Motorcycling

Across

Wisconsin

Also by William M. Murphy

Motorcycling Across Michigan
Motorcycling Across Ohio
Motorcycling Across Indiana
Souvenirs of War

Motorcycling
Across Wisconsin

by William M. Murphy

Arbutus Press, Traverse City, MI

Travel/Motorsports

ISBN 10: 1-93326-20-9
ISBN 13: 978-1-933926-20-9

Manufactured in the United States of America
First Edition/First Printing

Photos are by the author unless otherwise noted.

Maps designed by Land Information Access Association, Traverse City, Michigan © Arbutus Press

Interior design and layout by Julie Phinney, Jericho, Vermont
   (802-858-9956 – mjphinney@msn.com)

"You see things vacationing on a motorcycle in a way that is completely different from any other one."

— Robert Pirsig, *Zen and the Art of Motorcycle Maintenance*

"Why think about that when all the golden land's ahead of you and all kinds of unforeseen events wait lurking to surprise you and make you glad you're alive to see?"

—Jack Kerouac, *On the Road*

Contents

Preface

WISCONSINITES ARE FANATICS. Before you take offense at my observation please let me explain. Folks in this fine state are absolutely nuts about motorcycles and motorcycling! As evidence, simply consider the number of residents who have a motorcycle endorsement on their license, and the higher than would be expected number of registered motorcycles. One assumes that states in sunny and warm southern climes such as California, Arizona and Georgia would have the highest per-capita number of motorcyclists, not a northern state like Wisconsin, which bears a striking semblance to the sub-Arctic for several months each year.

When I did the math, I found that my observations of motorcycling popularity in Wisconsin were in fact based on reality, not just an over active imagination. According to the Federal Highway Administration's 2006 Highway Statistics Report, they found that out of a population of 5.6 million, Wisconsin had 303,000 registered motorcycles. A 2005 study by the Wisconsin Department of Transportation discovered that there were 430,655 residents with a Class M motorcycle license. Compare Wisconsin's per capita percentage of motorcycle ownership of 5.4% to 1.9% for California, 1.4% for Texas, and 1.6% in sunny Arizona and you begin to see my point. These figures are remarkable and make obvious the love of motorcycling that exists in this part of the country. This phenomenon is further supported when you consider that other northern states also show a higher than expected percentage of motorcycle ownership as compared to southern regions.

So I stand by my comment that folks in this marvelous state are fanatical about their two-wheelers. And why shouldn't they be? Wisconsin and motorcycles go together like beer and bratwurst. This is a landscape and a system of roads custom-made for the magic of motorcycling. It is as if a century ago road builders decided that since these newfangled two wheeled vehicles were obviously making such a hit, then roads should be built specifically for the purpose of accommodating them. When one explores this state's roads, you cannot help but get the opinion that many were constructed with the motorcyclist in mind. They twist and turn and rise and fall across the countryside in a delightful fashion, precisely in the manner that bikers enjoy.

Motorcycling Across Wisconsin is the fourth in a series of motorcycle touring books I am writing about the Midwest. You see, I have long thought that this region has not received the proper level of respect it deserves as a motorcycling destination. So don't let Wisconsin's geographic location give you the wrong impression about its motorcycling credentials. All the things bikers want in their motorcycling wish list are here—twisting roads, wonderful scenery, lots of natural and man-made attractions, fascinating historical sites to explore, friendly people, rallies and motorcycling events throughout the riding season in all parts of the state, and so much more.

From the beginning, I have intended this book to be more than typical tour guides that simply provide the most efficient routes to a few popular destinations. I want to tell you about Wisconsin at the same time. There are thousands of fascinating stories, natural and man-made sites of interest, under-appreciated historical events, and just plain interesting things to discover while roaming across this state. I want to tell you the stories of the places you are riding through so that the land and the people who shaped it come alive, enabling you to appreciate the events and people that forged what we see around us today.

I believe that motorcycling is enhanced if you delve into the history and events that shaped the places you are visiting. Fascinating discoveries about our country are waiting out there to be revealed. This book will tell you about the Wisconsin that too many people don't see because they're rushing by the real stories on busy highways, oblivious to all the interesting things around them.

Perhaps we have to change the way we view motorcycling if we are to really enjoy all its facets. To that end, this book has two fundamental underlying principles: first, it is the journey that counts, not the destination; and second, that exploring the out-of-the-way places and learning about the little-known stories of Wisconsin on a motorcycle is a natural and enjoyable partnership.

You will find that the tours laid out in this book take you to a high percentage of the natural and cultural wonders that are located across the length and breadth of Wisconsin. This is accomplished by way of the best motorcycling roads; not the straightest or most efficient routes that a standard guidebook that has the automobile tourist in mind would utilize.

One of motorcycling's oldest dilemmas is encountered on almost every ride in Wisconsin: does a biker ride for hours on challenging roads through beautiful countryside just for the thrill of the ride, or does he or she stop frequently to enjoy the views and explore the many attractions? I will leave the answer up to you, but you will battle this inner conflict whenever you take advantage of Wisconsin's abundant motorcycling opportunities.

Why Wisconsin is an interesting and enjoyable place to ride…

Wisconsin offers riders a palette of motorcycling opportunities. These biking qualities are based on two factors: geology and roads. The geologic makeup of Wisconsin is unique and sets the stage for extraordinary riding opportunities. Wisconsin has five basic geographic regions. These diverse parts of the state offer different advantages and opportunities.

You will find virtually no straight roads in the southwestern portion of the state, the area known as the Uplands. Much of this locality also falls within what is known as the driftless area or the unglaciated region. A significant part of southwest Wisconsin (as well as small portions of northwestern Illinois, northeastern Iowa, and southeastern Minnesota) was bypassed by the Wisconsin Glacier that covered much of North America up to about 13,000 years ago. This 'island' of unglaciated landscape is unique in that it retained its 'natural' geology of rolling bedrock hills. Glaciers flatten and smooth out landscapes, as can be witnessed in southeastern Wisconsin, as well as northern Indiana, Illinois, and Ohio, and parts of southern Michigan. Southwest Wisconsin is unique in its natural wonders. If anything, the surrounding glaciers only served to accentuate what was already a work of art. The scenic coulee landscape of southwestern Wisconsin was carved down from above when glacial melt water caused the region's rivers to erode deep valleys in the high plateau that originally covered this region, resulting in a dramatic landscape for our viewing and riding pleasure. This part of Wisconsin has some of the most striking scenery in the Midwest with its river valleys flanked by hills of erosion-resistant bedrock. Interestingly, though Wisconsin has nearly 15,000 lakes, there are no natural lakes in the driftless area. If a person wanted proof of the connection between glaciers and the many lakes of the Great Lakes region, this lack of lakes in the unglaciated zone certainly tends to prove the point.

In the southeast quarter of the state the Eastern Ridges and Lowlands region provides the geologic backdrop. This unique district includes not only the Lake Michigan shoreline area, but also fascinating remnants left behind by the retreating glacier. These geologic features include hills, lakes, and rivers created as the ice melted. Winding roads wend through these features in places like the Kettle Moraine State Forest. The Niagara Escarpment, which forms a giant inverted 'U' from southeast Wisconsin, across the Upper Peninsula of Michigan, the Bruce Peninsula of Ontario, then southeast to Niagara Falls and the Finger Lakes region of New York, runs through this region. This marvelous Jurassic component adds its own scenic charms and provides a strong and enduring feeling that transcends the ages and man's changes to the landscape. Moreover, it is not possible to adequately describe the wonder and beauty of Lake Michigan and the impact it has on this region as one stands on its shore gazing across the fresh water sea, imagining its size, its history, and its impact on who we are as a people.

The Central Plain may not have high hills but it has stunning rock outcroppings and river valleys carved out of bedrock that delight us with their beauty and recreational opportunities. Features such as the Wisconsin Dells are a part of this landscape. Castellated crags rising above the trees make for fantasy settings in stone that are a delight to behold. It is also fascinating to realize that the castle-like rock outcroppings that soar high above the ground have been here for eons, and they survived the glacial period because they were located on the edge of the ice sheet, which was very shallow in these locations. These rocks jutted above the ice fifteen thousand years ago the same way they rise above the trees today.

The Northern Highlands is part of a great geologic feature that stretches from northern Wisconsin north all the way to Hudson Bay in sub-Arctic Canada. This is a landscape of ancient bedrock and glacial moraines. It is also a region of thin and poor soils more suitable to forestry than crops, thus it is the region of the Big Woods; a wild land where wolves and black bear wander freely, and where we are the visitor. The Highlands is a varied area, with large expanses of land that is quite flat even though much of it is over 1,400 feet in elevation. (In comparison the shorelines of Lake Michigan, Lake Superior and the Mississippi River at St. Croix are 634, 671, and 780 feet above sea level respectively.) The region is interspersed with hills that are nearly 2,000 feet in elevation. Timm's Hill, located in Price County, is the highest point in the state at 1,952 feet above sea level.

The last geologic region in Wisconsin is called the Lake Superior Lowlands. This is a narrow strip along the shoreline of this majestic lake that is a world unto itself. Here you will find the rugged water's edge where bedrock cliffs meet crashing waves, and where majestic waterfalls and white water rivers tumble through rocky canyons in a rush to join the cold waters of Lake Superior. The Lake Superior region is like no other place in North America, and Wisconsin's piece of this craggy and ruggedly striking region is an unforgettable destination for anyone that ventures there.

In addition to the regional geologic differences, being surrounded by water on three sides by the Great Lakes and the mighty Mississippi River delivers a large slice of maritime geography and culture to enjoy. Wisconsin has more than 500 miles of Great Lakes shoreline and the state's cultural evolution is wedded to these inland seas. Its location has resulted in a unique history and traditions, impacted by explorers who used these waterways in both ancient and modern times to discover the region's wealth and beauty. Wisconsin residents and motorcyclists alike are fortunate indeed to be able to enjoy all that the Great Lakes and the mighty Mississippi River bring in the way of nautical attractions not usually found in the middle of a continent.

Many of the most desirable destinations and unique things to see and do are located in Wisconsin's State Parks. These natural and cultural wonders are thus available to the public and protected for future generations to see and appreciate. Whether it is a one-of-a-kind museum, historic re-created villages, lighthouses, unique geologic formations, or just a good camping spot or beach where you can relax, you will not want to miss out on the many wonders and opportunities found

A group of Patriot Guard Riders gather to honor a fallen soldier, just one of many causes that bring the motorcycling community together.

in Wisconsin's state parks and recreation areas. Wisconsin also has many dozens of county and local parks and campgrounds and all are very popular as Wisconsinites are outdoor-oriented folks who enjoy being close to nature. Camping in state parks is in high demand so you are well advised to make reservations if you wish to camp or reserve a cottage. Contact the Department of Natural Resources at wisconsin-stateparks.reserveamerica.com, or 1.800.372.3607 to make a camping reservation at any of the state's 95 state parks, state forests, trails, or recreation areas. Contact the DNR at 608.266.2181 for generic information about the state's parks and recreation program. On a related note, I recommend purchasing a state park entry permit at the beginning of each year so that it's on your bike when the riding season starts, enabling you to enter all facilities where an entry permit is required. To make this process easy a person can even purchase the vehicle sticker via the Internet. Simply go to www.fwsp.org/stickers_passes or the DNR's main web site. They make great Christmas presents—truly a gift that keeps giving for the entire year.

Why we ride...

I can truly say that my more than thirty-five years of riding, and the associated experiences that I have enjoyed, have given me great happiness and have broadened my knowledge and appreciation of this land, its history, and its people. In short, motorcycles and motorcycle riding have enriched my life immeasurably. I truly cannot imagine what my life would have been like without this adventurous component. It would have been less complete and much less stimulating, for sure.

Because of fewer distractions, riding affords time for reflection as well as simply losing yourself in the wide-open world. There is certainly no doubt about the fact that you can see and appreciate the world around you much better on two wheels than on four. There is something liberating about being out of a car and on two wheels that allows a closer rapport with the world and people around you.

Most riders just love to be on the road simply enjoying the ride, the companionship of biking brothers and sisters who share the same love of motorcycles and riding, and discovering what's over the next hill. Others might spend time deep in thought, contemplating the meaning of life. For some of us non-gifted folks it is a chance to sing our favorite songs aloud without offending anyone.

For me the motorcycle has been a ticket for escape and freedom for decades. I can't adequately describe to a non-enthusiast the visceral level of enjoyment these machines, and the wide-open spaces one rides through, have brought me. As any citizen of this world must do, I have spent my life working and doing all the things required of a responsible person for the sake of family and community. While some may find a fishing boat, the opera, rock climbing, or the golf course as their means of escape, for me it has been motorcycles. The adventure and happiness I have experienced aboard my faithful horses of steel is beyond measure.

Motorcycling puts riders in touch with the world around them as few other motorized activities can. We can never isolate ourselves from our surroundings nor do we want to; rather we willingly immerse ourselves, which is of course part of the attraction. In fact, the essence of motorcycling not only includes the mechanical aspects—the leans, the power, the acceleration, the feel and sound of the machine and so on—it involves being part of the environment around us. Motorcyclists want to be part of the real world. We know we will get cold, wet, hot, or whatever the conditions are around us, and that's fine. We accept it because the occasional discomfort is a small price to pay for the immeasurable enjoyment we receive year in and year out by riding these marvelous machines.

Being part of a family that we know we can count on, no questions asked, is an unspoken but fundamental part of the lifestyle. I'll help you, knowing that you'll help the next rider in trouble is an article of faith that doesn't need to be in writing because it is firmly established by a tradition developed over several generations of riders.

In addition, it has not escaped my notice that when talking with fellow motorcyclists it is time and again the misadventures that are remembered. It is as if the perfect day on the road is soon forgotten, but when we were caught in the sudden storm, got lost, or had the flat tire—we remember those days—and after the passage of a little time, those incidents become the fond stories we tell.

Wisconsin roads—where it all begins...

Motorcycle touring depends on roads. Our wants, however, are different from what most users wish for in a road system. Long distance truck drivers and mini-van pilots want highways that are very dissimilar from what most motorcyclists' desire. They simply want an efficient and smooth roadway to get them to their destination as effortlessly and quickly as possible. For motorcyclists the *road itself* is the destination. We do not just drive *on* a road; we become one *with* the road. The road, not a destination, is often the underlying reason a motorcyclist ventures forth in the first place. We judge roads not by how efficient they are but by their character. We want roads with sex appeal, soul, and spirit, roads that dip, climb, twist, and turn; roads that excite the soul rather than deaden the senses. In this regard, Wisconsinites are fortunate indeed.

Ribbons of lightly-traveled asphalt beckon motorcyclists across Wisconsin's rural landscape.

The state's roads take maximum advantage of it geography and offer everything that most riders want—curves, hills, narrow pavement, and light traffic in a scenic montage that changes as a person rides from one part of the state to another. Many roads in Wisconsin follow streams. These roads often date back to a time when rivers were a critical part of transportation and commerce, and it was natural that roads and towns were built next to them. Today these roads provide unparalleled riding enjoyment for motorcyclists. Wisconsin has about 12,000 permanent rivers and streams of all sizes, totaling approximately 32,000 miles in length. This means there are tons of meandering streamside roads out there for our biking amusement.

This state also has a riding resource that locals know well and take advantage of at every opportunity—that is, its county primary road system, usually simply called the alphabet roads. These roads provide better motorcycling enjoyment than state highways. They are often in better condition due to less traffic overall and far fewer trucks, they have more character than main roads because they tend to follow the natural lay of the land and thus have more hills and curves than state and federal roads, and, importantly, they are very easy to follow. All primary county roads (usually alphabet roads) are well marked. They have signs in advance of an intersection that provide adequate notice that a county designated road is just ahead. This fact alone makes traveling on these roads much easier than in many states where the county road system is not well marked and a person often passes a road they want before they know it is there.

For roads to make it into this book as recommended for motorcycle touring they have to meet several criteria: First, they have to be paved, with the pavement in at least reasonably good condition so that a large touring bike or sport bike can navigate the road safely and without difficulty. Second, the road and area must have some scenic appeal. Traffic on the roads can't be oppressive, and the general touring area must have something to offer in the way of interesting scenery, history, land cover, geologic features, or other attractions. By intent, you will notice many natural, historical or cultural points of interest along selected routes. Third, the road must have character: that is, curves, hills or other qualities that make it an enjoyable riding route. If you are like me and find yourself unconsciously leaning into curves even when driving your family car, then you know the kind of roads to which I am referring. You will find that almost all of the rides depicted in this book are great for just kicking back and relaxing. The traffic is lighter than on main roads, and the roads themselves are generally narrower and more interesting. High speed or maximum efficiency is not what it is all about on these routes.

A noteworthy aspect of riding the roads I have identified herein is that you will find fewer tourists, large trucks, and road-clogging RVers on the majority of the roads I recommend. A feature that I really appreciate in Wisconsin is that, unlike many other states, there are still numerous waysides, or roadside parks, where a person can pull off the road to take a break, get out of the weather, use the toilets, or have a snack and drink under the shade of a tree. I find that I sorely miss this feature when riding in other states and I am forced to pull off at fast food restaurants or gas stations to take a brief respite from the road.

Badger bikers are blessed in several ways in regards to management of the state's roads. First, local transportations officials have obviously had a policy in place for some time to pave as many roads as possible—even most rural township roads are hard surfaced. This makes motorcycle touring a real joy. Another notable feature concerning motorcycling roads involves the Rustic Roads program. The state legislature created this program in 1973. It is a laudable effort to preserve and highlight those rural roads that by their nature have special qualities and characteristics that set them apart from busier roads and highways. Most residents appreciate and want to protect Wisconsin's rustic rural heritage. Rustic Roads preserve a part of history and Americana that it is important we not lose.

The majority of the state's designated Rustic Roads don't happen to be included in the various tours described in this book because they're fairly short and localized. However, by no means is that an indication they are not worthy of consideration. The only reason I don't discuss many of them is that they do not happen to fall where needed to complete a loop or arrive at an attraction I wish to discuss. By all means, get out and enjoy these roads, many of which are paved and make great short rides on a sun-drenched Wisconsin afternoon.

The state currently has one hundred seven designated Rustic Roads extending over 600 miles in length. They are in every part of the state, found in 56 of the 72 counties. In line with Wisconsin's motorcycle-friendly approach, the state even has a special award program for motorcyclists who ride these scenic byways. Provide photographic proof of having ridden ten of the roads and you qualify for a special motorcycle tour patch. Ride at least twenty-five and you receive a certificate. A photograph showing you and your bike, or just your bike if riding solo, in front of the numbered Rustic Road signs will qualify you for the program. It is a fun way to encourage riders to get off the main roads and explore these scenic trails.

If you wish to participate, send your information and pictures to:

Wisconsin Deparatment of Transportation
Bureau of Transportation Safety
Motorcycle Safety Program
P.O. Box 7936
Madison, WI 53707-7936
Call them at 800.368.9677 for more information.

All motorcyclists have taken road maps and tried to lay out enjoyable trips utilizing main highways that appear interesting on a map. Most of us would like to avoid busy state or federal highways and find suitable local roads to take trips on, but there is much uncertainty. Unless we know an area well, it just is not possible to be familiar with where each road goes. How many times have you followed a country road while out on a ride only to have the pavement or the road itself suddenly end?

Even when one has up-to-date and accurate maps, the many roads still have to be hooked together to create a tour across several counties. But it's just this kind of research, and a great deal of riding on back roads and knowledge of local lore that is necessary if one wishes to organize interesting and enjoyable rides with the intent of keeping off major roads as much as feasible. I think you will find that this book accomplishes those tasks for you.

There may be some hesitancy about riding on rural roads for safety reasons: perhaps fearing that you would be stranded should mechanical problems occur. I have found just the opposite. On major highways, many of the other motorists are either out-of-towners themselves who are unlikely to stop and help, or they are local folks going about their busy lives, and they assume that the police will be by to help a stranger. While there is definitely less of a law enforcement presence on county and local roads, I have found that people who travel these roads are much more likely to stop and lend a hand than drivers on busy highways and expressways.

While we all enjoy riding open roads with great biking character through scenic grandeur, there is also much to be said about slowing down and exploring and viewing our world from a totally different perspective—that of learning about and appreciating the unique history and culture of an area. Exploring the colorful history and the natural and man-made attractions of a region one is riding through adds a completely new component to motorcycling. We are all familiar with the old adage that advises us to slow down and smell the roses. Well, I think an equally apt philosophy for motorcyclists is to occasionally slow down and read the inscriptions on the many granite markers and historical monuments that dot Wisconsin's countryside, visit local attractions, and get back in touch with the people and places that the modern lifestyle has caused us to bypass. The state is best seen from its back roads and in forgotten small towns to be really appreciated and enjoyed. Wisconsin has many small cities and villages that still offer the kind of qualities many people yearn for in this rapidly urbanizing world where neighborliness has been replaced with anonymity.

All motorcyclists have some favorite local riding roads they escape to when they have an opportunity to take a quick ride. I've found it more difficult to find 'tours' close to home, and one or two day rides that aren't part of a longer trip to distant points. With this in mind, I have identified nineteen tours of various lengths that are within the one to seven-day ride category—with time figured in to enjoy the various attractions found on each ride. In fact, what may seem like a one-day ride in many cases is a two-day tour because the average speeds are well below the mile-a-minute rate we're all used to, and there are many sites along the way that call for exploration. These tours are located in all regions of Wisconsin. I am a firm believer that good motorcycling is found no matter where one lives—a person just has to be curious and take the time to explore to find the riding gems that are located in every county in the state.

The majority of these trips are round-trip tours so that a rider doesn't just go from point A to point B, having to figure out a way back home. Over the years I've noted that many of my rides are 'circular' and start and end at a common point—either home, or some other base of operations such as a campsite or motel. With this fact in mind, I lay out round trips that include scenic and enjoyable roads for the entire distance, ending up back at the beginning without doubling back on the same road.

I will no doubt expose some secret riding roads of long-time Wisconsin residents. Unlike other undisclosed places—perhaps a favorite trout fishing hole, which can in fact be ruined by over-fishing, or an undiscovered golf course that a player hopes doesn't get popular and crowded—I don't think having more motorcyclists enjoying our great riding roads will harm the experience or make these roads somehow less enjoyable for current users. I have learned about some of my favorite roads by talking with other motorcyclists, often at a gas station or restaurant. I have observed that bikers like to talk about great riding roads that they have discovered, and they are generally more than happy to share that information with others whom they know will find similar enjoyment.

In fact, a fascinating phenomenon that only occurs when traveling on a motorcycle is the number of total strangers—people that wouldn't pay you a moment's notice if you were another car driver—that will go out of their way to talk to you about where you're from, where you are heading, how the trip is going, and so on. It is a very interesting statement on how people view us. I am constantly amazed that folks from young kids to great-grandmothers will make it a point to talk to bikers at a gas pump or restaurant. I think even those who wouldn't get on a bike on a dare are still fascinated by the sense of adventure that motorcycles, and those crazy enough in their minds to ride them, represents. Indeed, I believe it goes beyond simple interest and even fascination. I have come to the conclusion that many people derive vicarious enjoyment from talking to riders about their motorcycling adventures. For a variety of reasons these folks can't or don't wish to ride themselves, but gain a very real sense of adventure by talking with us about the experience.

Rides described in this book cover all parts of the state and 6,985 wonderful miles are detailed in the nineteen tours outlined herein, taking riders to innumerable extraordinary places on fun-filled roads. I have little patience with travel writers who only extol the most obvious places or roads. There are many areas in Wisconsin in addition to the well known that deserve coverage because they too have great roads and attractions, and splendid stories to tell. I think you will find that I cover not only the obvious places that are already well known, but the lesser-known destinations as well.

You will note that I try hard to keep bikers off expressways. These super highways have their place in this modern world, but I do not believe that expressways are the realm of motorcyclists. Besides, most of us have to drive them every day in our four-wheeled cages, so what is the attraction? I also avoid the Interstates because I do not believe you find America on or along them: we find America in those places where people can interact with one another, be it in large cities or small towns. Since this book focuses on rural Wisconsin, we are going to look for America along country roads where friendly smiles and waves are part of the scenery. Kids on bicycles, farmers in pickup trucks, clerks at small stores or gas stations—they all have a ready smile or wave and are happy to make small talk with you, asking about your motorcycle, your trip, and your adventure. This wonderful slice of the American pie still exists but we have to put ourselves in those places where it can be found—and that is not in the fast lane of an expressway.

Hurtling down a superhighway at seventy miles an hour, unable to stop to enjoy the scenery, take a picture, or just stretch one's legs is not pleasurable riding in my mind. Being assaulted by the visual blight of billboards and riding not to appreciate the natural world around us but rather to stay out of harm's way or riding simply to arrive at a destination isn't what motorcycling is meant to be. Moreover, you certainly will not find adventure and exploration on expressways. The further off the beaten path you venture the more adventure and enjoyment you will find.

As Charles Kuralt said: "The Interstate Highway system in a wonderful thing. It makes it possible to go from coast to coast without seeing anything or meeting anybody. If the United States interests you, stay off the interstates."[1]

A word about safety…

While writing about individual routes, I found myself referring to safety issues such as deer, Amish horse-drawn buggies, and agricultural equipment that share Wisconsin's back roads. Rather than sound like I was repeating myself, I thought

---

[1] *A Life on the Road*. Charles Kuralt © 1990. G.P. Putnam's Sons, New York, NY.

I would discuss these realities just once.

The summer population of Wisconsin's state wildlife animal, the Whitetail Deer, stands at more than 1.6 million animals and they are located in every county, no matter how urban the landscape. In 2007, there were approximately 18,000 reported vehicle/deer accidents according to the Wisconsin Department of Transportation. Incredibly, deer accounted for the third most common cause of accidents in Wisconsin!

Ride accordingly, especially early in the morning or in the late afternoon. Most accidents involving deer occur between dusk and dawn. I try to avoid country roads at sunset or daybreak, or at least ride very cautiously if I am out. Remember, deer seldom travel alone. If you

Deer are beautiful and dangerous. Awareness of potential threats results in a safer and more enjoyable riding experience.

see one, there are almost certainly other animals nearby. This is especially true with does in the summer. If you see a female deer near the road, the chances are very good that there are a couple of fawns hiding within a few yards of mom.

There are other large critters on the loose, including many black bears and even elk in the northern portions of the state. Throw into this mix the occasional farm tractor pulling wide agricultural implements, cows, horseback riders, bicyclists, and other unexpected road travelers and the need for common sense and caution becomes obvious. The farming season and motorcycling weather coincide, of course, and that means that farm equipment is going to be using the same roads we enjoy riding. Even more potentially dangerous than the tractors and grain trucks is the mud they leave on the pavement. These chunks of clay turn as hard as bricks when dry, but even light rain turns the clay into mud as slippery as ice. If your riding experience is primarily limited to urban areas, this reality could pose a danger if you are not mindful of it. In addition, some of the most scenic areas in Wisconsin have large Amish populations. These temperate hard-working folks are often seen on primary roads on bicycles or in horse-drawn buggies. Give them a wide berth. Spooked horses are a danger to both the motorcyclist and buggy passengers.

Miscellany

Many years of hanging around with motorcyclists has taught me that as a group we are far more appreciative of mechanical things than the average person is. We care about how things work and how power is created and transferred through gears and shafts. We appreciate the look of finely crafted metal parts and the heft of iron and steel much more than we do imagining electrons flowing through silicon computer chips. Because of this kind of mechanical aptitude and appreciation, I will point out places and events you are likely to be interested in such as car shows, railroad museums, steam locomotives, aircraft and maritime museums and so on when they are on a particular tour. Any time motorcycle shows or events are pertinent I will of course highlight them as well.

Before hitting the road, I have just one more suggestion for you back road travelers. That is, experience not only the road, the scenery and the local lore but the other things that make up what Wisconsin is as a state. Food, for instance, is always high on any motorcyclist's list of priorities. Make fun and memorable eating part of the overall experience. I appreciate the convenience of fast food establishments but it is so much more interesting when you avoid the clown, the king and the pig-tailed girl and enjoy real food with an ethnic or local flavor. I find that eating in the many hometown restaurants that can still be found across the state adds an additional sense of discovery when on a trip, as well as allowing one to meet some wonderful small-town folks who still serve up home cooked food.

In many of the tours I note the presence of biker-friendly restaurants or taverns. These are places where a rider will get a warm welcome, and in fact will doubtless see other riders also stopped for food or conversation. I list biker-friendly taverns because they typically are great places for large portions of good food and enjoyable company, where you are likely to meet fellow bikers. Alcohol and motorcycles do not mix, however. My personal stance is that even one drink is too much when riding and that is the code I choose to follow. You may choose differently.

If you intend to ride after the stop I recommend a coffee or Coke rather than an alcoholic drink. Save the cold beer for the end of the day. It will taste better and you can enjoy the drink without jeopardizing your safety and possibly that of a riding partner. A glass of locally produced wine or a beer from one of Wisconsin's many microbreweries is a great way to end a fun day of riding.

I hate to admit it in this book, which after all is dedicated to motorcycle touring, but these tours make great automobile trips as well. If I were king for a day, I would issue an order declaring that most of the roads I write about in this book be restricted to motorcycle use any time the ground was not snow covered. If a person must drive a 4-wheeled vehicle, however, these tours can make that burden a little more enjoyable.

You will find that each tour has a mileage chart accompanying it with distances between certain points on the ride and a running mileage total, as well as an accompanying map. These charts and maps are meant to provide a quick overview of the trip so you know what's around the corner.

In calculating mileage for the circular tours I had to choose a starting point and also whether to go in a clockwise or counterclockwise direction. You may well choose to make the trip in the opposite direction and use different starting points, so don't feel bound by the charts and maps—they're here to help you plan the trip, give you an idea of what towns and roads await you and where, and give a graphic representation of the layout and geographic location of the tours.

I have tried hard to give enough detail in the rides so that if you wish you can plot the tours in your GPS unit. In recent years even I, a person who has always taken a minimalist approach to motorcycle travel, have begun utilizing a GPS unit on lengthy trips. If your riding style is such that you use interstate highways to travel long distances then a GPS unit might be a waste of money. Use those dollars for other motorcycle accessories! However, if you ride many local and county roads a GPS will not only make these adventures more fun it is also safer. Glancing down frequently at a map in the plastic sleeve on your tank bag is dangerous. Too many of us succumb to the dangerous temptation of trying to read a map while riding. A GPS unit—mounted near eye-level—offers a safer alternative. Whether you utilize a GPS unit or not, I suggest purchasing a map book of Wisconsin counties and plotting the rides on the pages of the map book. (By the way, I don't recommend the popular DeLorme county map books. The print used to label roads is extremely small and impossible to read at a glance and the differentiation between a small dirt township road and a primary paved county road is so slight so as to be virtually nondiscernable—they're all just red lines across the pages. Get a map book that in a quick glance, through the use of different colors, tells you whether the road in question is gravel or paved, and whether it's a county, state or federal road. Most county road departments print maps that have very clear legends to define the category of roads and these maps can often be obtained for free or at very low cost by contacting the county road department or WisDOT).

The first thing I do when I buy a book of county maps for a state is to tear out all the pages so I can fold them and carry the desired pages with me. I still do this even with a GPS unit on board. In my opinion, the utility and value of paper maps will never fade away.

In an attempt to provide riders with helpful information, I list many phone numbers and other contact information in the appendices. These include information for all Sheriff Department and State Patrol offices, plus numbers for motel chains and emergency numbers for lost or stolen credit cards. I also provide a lengthy list of motorcycle dealers and independent repair shops for virtually every brand of bike out there. I know of no other similar compilation, and in fact, this listing is probably the most comprehensive list of dealers and repairs shop now available. I know I did not locate every dealer or repair facility in the state but that wasn't my intent. I wanted to list as many as possible in all parts of the state so that in the event you encounter mechanical problems on the road, you will be able to find a nearby dealer or repair shop for assistance. I include many independent shops because it has been my experience over the years that these folks are the ones most likely to be able to help a stranded biker when the major shops are closed for the night or on Sundays and holidays.

It is my intention that this book not only provide the basis for years of motorcycling exploration and enjoyment, but that it also serve as an aid to help riders enjoy trips with fewer concerns about some of the common troubles that can plague rides.

For a little fun, I start each chapter with a question about Wisconsin. It is an enjoyable way to learn a bit more about the state without having to get too serious. Answers are provided at the end of each chapter.

As one motorcyclist to another, I truly hope that you enjoy reading this book, especially on a cold winter's night when the riding season is but a distant desire. It is also my wish that the information in here will enhance your motorcycling experience, and help you gain an appreciation for the marvelous opportunities that are here for us to enjoy.

May traffic be light, car drivers courteous and alert, the scenery magnificent, a blue sky overhead, and the road beneath your wheels smooth and never-ending.

Ride safe and I hope to meet you on the road.

The Formative Years

I begin the heart of the book with this section because like the first miles of a long tour, or the first pages of a new book, these three rides take us to the beginning, to a time when Wisconsin was just starting on its epic journey through history. They carry us to places where we can discover a bit about our past and ourselves as we enjoy the thrill of motorcycling down lightly traveled and enjoyable roads that seem designed with motorcyclists in mind.

While exploring early Wisconsin on two-wheels we can learn to appreciate the courage and faith it took to leave it all behind and start a new life in the untamed frontier. The cold reality of war, the struggles of life in the wilderness, and immigrants in boomtowns scratching a living from the earth; these stories and places await our return. We can also use our mind's eye and imagine what life was like for young soldiers carving the Military Road across a hostile and difficult wilderness while we trace the route of the Old Military Road from Green Bay to Prairie du Chien.

These rides blend the joy of motorcycling with the sense of wonder and fulfillment that we get when we explore the world around us—both in the present and past tenses.

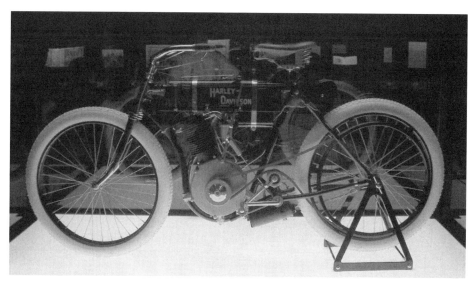

1903 Harley Davidson original.

Riding Through History

Helmet Hair Quiz

What Hall of Fame baseball player began his career with the Milwaukee Braves and ended it with the Milwaukee Brewers?

BEING ON A MOTORCYCLE puts things in perspective for a rider. There is something about exploring our world on two wheels that makes the proper scale of things more obvious. It helps separate the important from the trivial. Because of fewer distractions, riding affords time for reflection as well as simply losing yourself in the wide-open world. Most riders love to be on the road merely for the sake of enjoying the ride, the companionship of good friends who share the same love of motorcycles and discovering what's over the next hill. Others might spend time deep in thought, contemplating the meaning of life.

This particular ride is one that I hope causes reflection on your part. As you ride through Wisconsin's bountiful rural landscape and small towns in the southern part of the state it's my wish that you consider how very fortunate we are to have the ability, good health, resources, and freedom to ride these roads in this wonderful land without limitation or hesitation.

There will be much to reflect on: mounds and effigies built a thousand years ago by a civilization that has vanished from the land. A wilderness fort, and a battle site where two cultures—one fighting desperately to maintain centuries-old ways of life and the other pursuing its manifest destiny—clashed with deadly results. You will explore sites where early settlers literally dug a livelihood out of the hard earth for sake of their families' futures, and mull over how their hard work ultimately led to what we have today. The establishment of Wisconsin as a state, and all the work and thought that went into what we think of as a given state of affairs will be there for our consideration. Finally, the very land itself, and the work of human hands and minds, are to be contemplated and enjoyed. This is a wonderful ride through our shared history and one that I believe demonstrates the ceaseless struggles of humanity to achieve and overcome difficult odds.

This tour in the south-central part of the state includes some of the region's best natural and manufactured attractions. It is a ride on wonderful biking roads that will take you on an unforgettable tour of discovery.

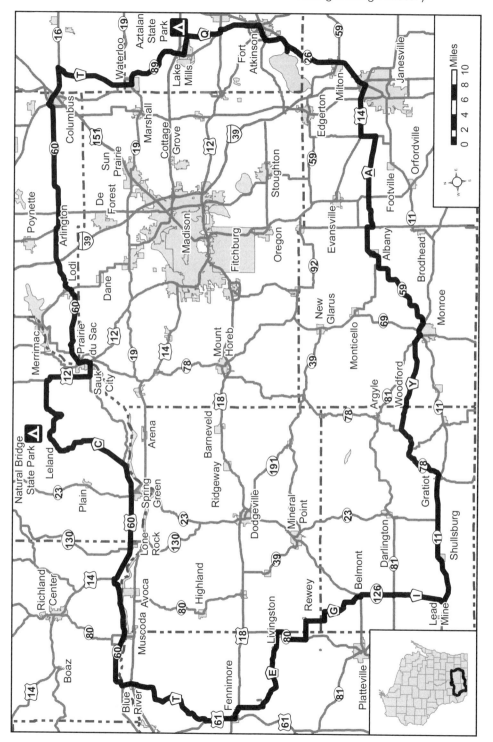

Miles	Destination	Total
	RIDING THROUGH HISTORY **318 MILES**	
0	Fort Atkinson	0
20	Janesville / U.S. 14	20
22	State Route 59	42
20	Monroe / Route 81	62
26	Gratiot / Route 11	88
30	Belmont	118
33	Fennimore	151
25	Eagle Cave	176
28	Spring Green	204
36	Sauk City	240
39	Columbus	279
29	Aztalan State Park	308
10	Fort Atkinson	318

I recommend that this 318-mile ride be a two-day tour. There is just too much to do to try to squeeze it all into one day.

We begin our tour in the city of Fort Atkinson, located in Jefferson County on the Rock River. This town of 12,000 is a pleasing community surrounded by some of the state's most productive dairy and crop farms. The city derived its name from General Henry Atkinson, a veteran of the War of 1812 and commander of U.S. forces during the Black Hawk War of 1832. It was at the height of the Black Hawk War that General Atkinson ordered construction of a fort at the confluence of the Rock River and the smaller Bark River (which many years ago was called the Peelbark River). The fort was originally called Fort Koshkonong due to the presence of a large marsh about six miles away of the same name (today's Lake Koshkonong). The name was later changed to Fort Atkinson. Frontier forts of that era served two purposes—prosecution of war, and protection of settlers.

The city of Fort Atkinson developed when the fighting ended and what was once a wilderness military outpost soon became a bustling frontier town. The original fort was a few blocks east of Main Street, marked today by a monument and plaque. Take Milwaukee Avenue east from Main Street to visit the site. During the Depression of the 1930s, the WPA (Works Progress Administration) built a replica fort on open parkland located on the west side of town perhaps a mile from the original site. The location of the original fort had become a developed part of the city in the century since it had been built and all traces of that original structure had long since disappeared. Even though you are not seeing the real thing I recommend stopping at the site of the replica fort. The stockade construction is interesting to see and gives the viewer a good feel for how they were built and what it would have been like being a lowly soldier based in a fort on the frontier. It was they, after all, who cut and trimmed the trees, dug the holes, and placed the tree trunks in the holes to construct the stockade. This would have been backbreaking work in a mosquito-infested environment.

Speaking of the replica fort, I have to go off on a tangent to discuss a pet peeve. Over the several decades that I have been diligently exploring the country on a motorcycle, I have been flabbergasted and frustrated at the number of times that I found it very difficult to find a local attraction. These sites could be anything from a unique geologic formation to a historic battlefield, or a museum, an old stagecoach inn, and anything in between that you can imagine. Some local municipalities are woefully negligent in providing signing for these attractions. I find this puzzling because these are precisely the sort of tourist destinations that could be an economic shot in the arm for communities and the small businesses located there. The first time I tried to locate Fort Atkinson, in the city of Fort Atkinson, I assumed it would be a piece of cake. After all, the city was named after the fort, and its street signs depict the fort in proud acknowledgment of the town's history. I rode all around town, however, and did not see a single sign directing me to the fort. I stumbled onto the monument and brass plaque at the original fort site, but found no evidence of the replica fort. With all the male DNA code in my body screaming in protest I admitted defeat and finally stopped at a gas station to ask directions. That act in itself testifies to my frustration! The attendant gave me directions and of course I then easily found it, but it was yet one more of countless frustrating similar instances that have occurred over the years.

Come on, local officials! You may assume that everyone knows where the sites of interest in your towns are located, or you may assume that nobody cares about such things. Well, you would be wrong on both counts. The aggravation I have experienced trying to locate various out of the ordinary sites has of course been experienced by many others with the same interests. Just one sign would do the trick!

To save all of you from having to stop to ask directions, the replica fort is in Rock River City Park located on the west edge of town on state route 106—also known as Riverside Drive.

I recommend starting the tour with a breakfast stop at Fat Boyz, at 219 Main Street. This motorcyclist friendly restaurant serves quality and reasonably priced meals, and for you late risers their breakfast menu is available until noon on weekends. Their dinner offerings range from burgers to New York Strip Steak, and you will always feel welcome. They are located four blocks south of 106 and two blocks south of the river.

Before riding west to the fort an interesting stop in Fort Atkinson is the Hoard Historical Museum, located on US 12 / Whitewater Avenue about a half-mile south of the river in town. This museum has permanent exhibits on topics ranging from wildlife to Native American life. It also has a room dedicated to Abraham Lincoln's experiences as a soldier in the Black Hawk War in Wisconsin.

Route 106 intersects with route 89 two blocks north of the Rock River. Turn west onto 106 and follow it about a mile along the river. Be attentive as you are riding and you will see a plaque documenting the site of the Panther Intaglio, the outline of which Native Americans dug into the ground about one thousand years ago. The panther outline is about 125-feet long and dug roughly two feet into the ground. This is the last known intaglio in the United States! The ravages of time and development have quite severely affected the intaglio, and today it is surrounded by homes. If you look closely the details can still be made out, however. There were several of these structures in this area at the time of settlement, but all but this one succumbed to the plow or bulldozer.

Wisconsin has a rich heritage of Native American antiquity sites, most in the shape of effigy, conical, and platform mounds built close to a thousand years ago by a civilization connected with other Mississippian cultures located further south in the Mississippi River Valley. Intaglio can be considered as reverse effigy mounds—carved into the earth rather than built above it. Unfortunately, early settlers destroyed many of these sites during the rush to convert the land from wilderness to farms and cities. In fact, the Fort Atkinson Panther Intaglio very nearly met the same fate. It was only through the determined action of the local DAR chapter that the site was ultimately preserved. A fascinating article in a 1920 newspaper tells the story of how the landowner was only 24-hours away from clearing the site and plowing it under if the DAR did not make an immediate payment of $200 to continue a lease agreement. There were originally eleven intaglios near Fort Atkinson—nine in the shape of panthers and 2 that resembled bears. Even the tail of this last remaining antiquity was damaged when somebody constructed a driveway across it many years ago.

The replica of Fort Koshkonong is on route 106 just a few blocks west of the intaglio. Turn into Rock River City Park and the fort will be quickly visible.

When finished exploring what Fort Atkinson has to offer leave town via route 106 west as it meanders next to the river to route 26 on which we ride south. Our journey on 26 is short lived, however, because soon after starting south you will see a sign for Old 26 and the Koshkonong Indian Mounds. Follow Old 26 and the signs to these mounds. They are located in a small park just east of Koshkonong Lake. If you reach the country club and golf course on the lake, you have gone a couple of blocks too far.

These effigy mounds are in various shapes. Though not very large, the eleven mounds that survive are well preserved and make for an interesting stop. There is also a segment of an Indian trail that dates back to pre-settlement times preserved in the park.

When done exploring the mounds head back to Old 26 and go south the short distance to new route 26, taking it into Milton. Conveniently located right on our road in town you will find the Milton House—a complex that includes a stable, log cabin, and the old stagecoach house itself. This National Historic Landmark is a very cool stop. The hexagon-shaped building was built by Joseph Goodrich, a man who is best described as one of those rare renaissance men who had skills and visions beyond most of us normal mortals. The building was originally a stagecoach inn that served travelers after it was built in 1844. It replaced a smaller wood frame house that had served as both family home and a travelers' inn since 1838. The building is the oldest poured concrete structure in the United States. Mr. Goodrich was an active abolitionist and his inn was a stop on the pre-Civil War Underground Railroad. A tunnel connected the inn and a nearby log cabin that is still there. Runaway slaves would enter the cabin and access the tunnel via a

History runs deep in Milton. This cabin was part of the underground railroad, and a young Abraham Lincoln camped nearby while serving as a scout in the military.

trapdoor in the cabin floor. They would then follow the tunnel to the basement of the Milton House where they would receive food and shelter until they could continue their journey. The stable that served the hotel's guests is still located across the street.

Building the inn, running a successful business, and helping runaway slaves wasn't enough for Mr. Goodrich, however. In 1844, he also created Milton Academy, which morphed into Milton College, a prestigious private institution that was Wisconsin's oldest college until it closed in 1982, after 138 years, due to financial problems.

Milton got its name originally as a tribute to English poet John Milton. It seems that one of the original settlers was bemoaning the fact that when he left his home in the east it felt like 'paradise lost'. However, when he discovered the beauty and potential of southern Wisconsin, he said it felt like paradise regained. In that philosophical moment, he suggested naming the new community in honor of Milton, who had penned *Paradise Lost* almost two hundred years earlier.

General Atkinson and his army camped at nearby Storrs Lake in 1832. A historical marker across the street from the Milton House notes this occasion and describes the role that young Abraham Lincoln served in this military mission as a scout in the Illinois volunteer militia. Lincoln was mustered out of the military before Atkinson's army engaged Chief Black Hawk in several skirmishes across southern Wisconsin.

The city as it exists today is quite new, having been formed in 1967 after two adjacent towns of similar names—Milton and West Milton—merged into one community. Present day Milton is unique in that it still has what can be described as two downtowns. If you take Madison Avenue (located adjacent to the Milton House) west a bit over a mile it will deliver you to old West Milton, and its distinct downtown area. The main attraction here is the Liberty Station restaurant and small railroad museum. The building is the old depot and is a popular stop.

We continue south on route 26 a short distance to route 14 where we turn west. We will avoid most of the urban Janesville area in this manner. After seven miles on route 14 you'll come to CR-H. There is a very large natural gas pipeline facility and storage tanks on route 14 just prior to reaching CR-H.

Turn left on H and take it two miles down to CR-A, at which point turn right and continue west. County Road A is delightful. It is a rural road through bucolic countryside with just enough flowing curves and small hills to make it an enjoyable as well as scenic ride. Traffic is almost nonexistent but smiles on the faces of riders will be profuse.

All riders can recall with great clarity certain rides, roads, or places where they had an especially memorable trip. Sometimes those memories are not always positive. I will always remember CR-A as the road on which I attempted to outrace a massive and severe thunderstorm for several miles, before it finally overtook me with winds and rain worthy of a hurricane. It was quite a day; one of those where better judgment would have served me well. 'I can get to my destination before those clouds in the west turn into anything serious', I told myself. Infallibility will never be one of the qualities that folks who know me would grant me, and that day showed how error-prone I can sometimes be in my cerebral performance!

But you know what? That's all part of the fabulous motorcycling experience! Even the less than wonderful things that we do, or that happen to us while riding, is what it's all about. Perhaps there is even a little pride involved in knowing that we can face adversities without quitting. Rain? No problem. Stop to put on raingear and keep going. Or stop and wait out the storm under an overpass or a pavilion at a park or rest area sharing stories and small talk with other bikers who have sought similar refuge. If we didn't want to be part of the natural setting we'd drive a four-wheeled cocoon and be comfortable, and disconnected, at all times.

We get to enjoy CR-A's many charms for about twelve miles when it dead-ends at state route 104. Turn right onto 104 for less than a mile to SR-59, where we once again commence our westward ride nineteen miles to the small city of Monroe. Route 59 is a decent ride as it stair steps its way southwest to Monroe. It runs through typical farmlands and has light traffic and a good road surface which courses over hills through rustic scenery, especially west of Albany.

Route 59 will end at route 11 on the east side of Monroe. At this major intersection turn onto route 11 / 81 and continue west. After just about a mile there will be signs for Business 11 and route 69. I suggest a trip into downtown Monroe at this point to see the impressive Green County courthouse. This majestic building, built in 1891, is one of the more imposing courthouses in the state and it's worth the time to see the building and grounds.

Our trip carries us on 11 / 81 west another mile to where route 81 turns off to the north. Follow route 81 for just over one mile to county road Y, turning left. CR-Y will happily carry us many miles across beautiful countryside to the village of Woodford. The road is a delight to ride. It embodies those qualities we seek out for a fun ride in the country. For the last several miles, west of CR-M, the road narrows and has many challenging tight curves, so be at the top of your game in this section. The scenery is delightful and the riding is great as you lean left and quickly lean right in a wonderful rhythmic two-wheeled dance.

The village of Woodford is a town that has seemingly been kept in a time capsule. By all appearances not much has changed here in many years, which I am sure is exactly the way most locals like it. In town you will come to a stop sign where a right turn is required to remain on CR-Y. This road will deliver you

The hamlet of Woodford witnessed history at the bloody Battle of Pecatonica.

to the Pecatonica Battle Site, located in Black Hawk Memorial Park. This important battle took place in June 1832 and was one of several deadly skirmishes that occurred in Wisconsin during the Black Hawk War. Colonel Henry Dodge led his troops to a swampy site along the Pecatonica River where the battle, also called the Battle of Bloody Lake, occurred. All members of a band of Kickapoo warriors, who had killed several local settlers earlier that day, were trapped and killed in the engagement. Colonel Dodge went on to become territorial governor for the Wisconsin Territory. Interestingly, General Atkinson, who was overall commander of the Black Hawk War operation, faded into obscurity after the war.

Two signs in the park mark this historic event. The first is at the park entrance and the other is a plaque and small monument on the river floodplain close to the actual battle site. Follow the narrow park road into the interior of the park to see this plaque. The small monument marking the actual battle site was placed in 1922 by the DAR. To protect this important historic site the land was purchased in 1968 and made a public park. Camping is allowed in this quiet out-of-the-way park if that fits into your plans.

Each year on the first weekend of May the Yellowstone Flint and Cap Club holds the Bloody Lake Rendezvous. Participants dress in period clothes and camp in teepees.

County road Y ends at the park so you have to retrace your ride back to Woodford. At the main intersection again, turn right (west) onto CR-M. You will shortly ride past a farm with a large colorful mural painted on the entire side of their large barn, and through a rolling landscape punctuated with bountiful farms and rolling fields. Take 'M' to a somewhat confusing intersection where several roads come together. The first stop sign is at the juncture with CR-N, but you want to go about 50-feet further to the second stop sign, which is at state route 78. Turn left onto 78, which is a very agreeable ride as it meanders through an undulating countryside of farms and woods. The road is a bit rough in this stretch, not in the pothole sense but because it seems that the base has given way, allowing for small dips and cracks. Nothing serious, just ride accordingly. You will shortly come into the village of Wiota and as you do watch on your left for a mural on the side of a building marking the site of Fort Hamilton. This fort was one of many built for the protection of local settlers during the tumultuous period leading up to and during the Black Hawk War. Of interest is that the fort was named in honor of Colonel William Hamilton—Alexander Hamilton's son.

Continue on highway 78 back south to route 11 at the village of Gratiot and turn right. Route 78 between Wiota and Gratiot is another very nice biking road, but it has an abundance of tar snakes that cause occasional unnerving front wheel wiggles on hot summer days.

Follow route 11 eleven miles to the town of Shullsburg, Wisconsin's third-oldest community, established in 1827 by John Shull. Before being given this name it was locally known as New Dublin, because of the many Irish immigrants that settled there. Shullsburg was a mining town and the Badger Mine and Museum is a good place to explore the history of the town and its early residents. The museum has many artifacts from Shullsburg's nearly two hundred years of history, and touring the 19th-century underground lead mine will give you an appreciation for the lives of the miners who used picks and shovels to extract this ore from the hard ground. Watch for the sign on route 11, but if you miss it the museum is located at 279 West Estey Street at the corner of Galena Street, next to the high school athletic field. Their phone number is 608.965.4860 should you wish to call them. The museum and mine is open from Memorial Day to Labor Day. Admission fees are very reasonable and well worth the experience.

If you have an interest in mines and mining, just be aware that there are two closed mines two miles south of Shullsburg on CR-O. When you reach CR-W the large Calumet and Hecla mine, closed in 1979, will be off to your east, and the Mulcahy Mine, where eight men died in a 1943 cave in, is less than two miles to the west. This was Wisconsin's worst mining disaster. You really cannot see much from the road so I don't think it's worth the trip down to these two sites. This information is just FYI. In addition, a couple miles south of town on county road U is the famous Gravity Hill, where cars allegedly roll uphill. It is an optical illusion, not mysterious forces or magic at work.

If you wish to make this tour a two-day event, spending the night in one of two quaint and historic inns in Shullsburg is a memorable experience. The Water Street Place and Inn has four rooms for lodgers, and the Risken Lee Holiday House, built in 1842 and possibly the oldest building left in Shullsburg, has three upstairs rooms that are right out of last century—but with all the modern amenities today's travelers expect. Suites with fireplaces and whirlpools are even available.

I definitely urge following the signs off route 11 to Shullsburg's historic downtown district. In fact, if you arrive at lunch or dinnertime I suggest a stop at the

Miner Alley restaurant in the downtown district. This is the kind of restaurant of which there is only one, but that on the other hand has 'twins' in towns and cities all across America. Miner Alley is a hometown staple, about as far removed from national chain restaurants as you can get. Memorabilia and artifacts spanning many decades of time cover the walls. Numerous pictures and newspaper articles highlight their school's athletic teams, both boys and girls, for several decades. The folks here are obviously proud and supportive of their children. Antique baseball gloves and mining gear share wall space. It has the usual friendly small town atmosphere and local people all greet one another as they walk in the door. History runs deep here; a framed 1927 newspaper tells about the town's centennial celebration.

Sitting at a table in Miner Alley one September Saturday afternoon, shortly after a parade and pep rally to cheer their high school football team on to victory over a nearby small town foe, I had time to muse about things while waiting for my food. Listening to the friendly banter that surrounded me, looking at the various pictures and reading the many newspaper accounts of life in this close-knit community, it struck me—this is what it is all about. This represents the best of America. Looking around it occurred to me that this is what untold thousands of American men and women, over countless generations, have gone to war to protect. This is worth fighting for! Of course you don't have to be in small towns to see this kind of interaction. However, I think it is so much more obvious in places like Shullsburg on a sunny September afternoon. I left the restaurant with a full stomach, a light heart and in good spirits; life is good.

When you are done exploring the various attractions in Shullsburg, continue west on route 11 six more miles to CR-I, making a right turn to the tiny burg of Lead Mine, a disappearing small town. About all that is left are a church and an old tavern, surrounded by a handful of small houses.

Take CR-I north eight miles to route 81. CR-I becomes a fun ride as it gets increasingly hilly the further north you ride. About midway between Lead Mine and route 81 you will crest a hill and in the distance will be *Belle Monte,* the high tree-covered hill from which the town of Belmont derives its name.

At route 81 jog west just a block and continue north on state route 126 to Belmont, the state's first capital. Route 126 ends in Belmont so you will continue north on U.S. 151 a few blocks to the north edge of town. Turn west onto CR-G and ride this county road northwest to two interesting attractions; Belmont Mound, and the first capitol building.

It was early French explorers who gave the name *Belle Monte*—beautiful mountain—to the nearby high wooded hill that overlooks the surrounding countryside north of the city of Belmont. You will want to be sure to pull into the park

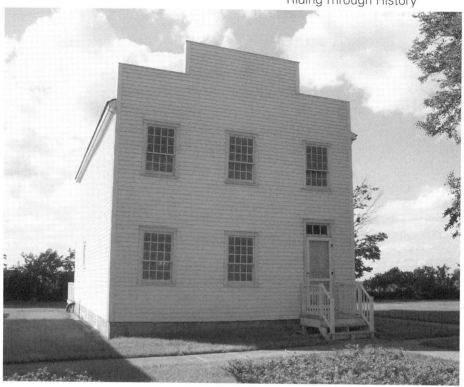

The territorial capitol, located in the wilderness, is a far cry from the current capitol building in Madison.

at Belmont Mound itself. It is located on your right as you travel north on CR-G. A winding blacktop road corkscrews up the mountain, ending at a small parking lot at the top. From there, an approximately forty-foot lookout tower takes the climber above the trees for a truly breathtaking view of the surrounding country-side. You don't want to miss this attraction! A tip of the hat to the local Lions Club is in order for their help in maintaining this park.

A bit further up the road is a small park housing the state's first capitol build-ing. Territorial Governor Dodge called together a session of territorial legislators in the winter of 1836 in this building to lay the groundwork for Wisconsin's first territorial government and its ultimate admission to the union twelve years later. Wisconsin's current capital, Madison, existed only in the dreams of James Doty, a territorial judge and land speculator when this first legislative session was held. Doty purchased 1,200 acres of wilderness at present-day Madison and at least in part due to pressure he applied, Governor Dodge and the legislators decided that his wild strip of land between Lakes Mendota and Monona would serve in the future as capital of the new state.

After enjoying Belle Monte and the First Capitol park, continue on CR-G as it makes several easy to follow jogs west and north, ultimately meeting CR-A at the tiny crossroads village of Rewey. Turn left onto CR-A and take it the less than three miles to state route 80. Turn north on eighty, following it up to the town of Livingston. Turn left onto CR-E in Livingston and enjoy the fine motorcycling character of this rural road as it heads west. In the tiny burg of Stitzer turn right onto CR-F and go north about three miles to U.S 18, then left on 18 the short distance into Fennimore.

This pleasant city of 2,500 souls is a nice stop on the trip, especially if you enjoy unique railroading equipment and history. The Fennimore Railroad Museum is located downtown on U.S 61. What makes it special is that this display is all about a short-lived railroading phenomenon—narrow gauge tracks and equipment. These 36-inch tracks served areas that were difficult to access with larger equipment, and in situations, such as logging operations, where the tracks were meant to be in place for only a limited operational period. Economy of operation was the bottom line in most instances. The Fennimore narrow gauge system was used to provide rail connections in the rugged landscape west of town where sharp turns and short but steep inclines made standard gauge rails and equipment impractical.

Fennimore's narrow gauge train operated from 1878 to 1926. All other narrow gauge train systems had been taken out of service long before 1926. Because of the small size of the engines and cars used on these 36-inch rails, folks gave the name Dinky to the engines. Years ago, standard and narrow gauge trains exchanged their passengers and freight at a nearby depot. There were daily runs between Fennimore and Woodman, the tracks meandering 16 miles through the Green River Valley and serving as a key link to other railroads. The line was famous for a horseshoe curve that made it possible to climb a steep slope west of Fennimore.

The museum has an engine and tender on display outside on tracks, a water tower, and several other large pieces. There is also a miniature train on 700 feet of 15-inch gauge rails that enthusiasts can ride on weekends for mere pocket change. Inside the adjacent museum is other railroading paraphernalia that I think most folks will find interesting. A steam engine that uses compressed air to show how all the moving parts work is especially intriguing.

There is also a doll and toy museum in Fennimore that might be of interest to some of you. It is located on Lincoln Street in town and has a unique collection of antiques that collectors or aficionados would enjoy perusing.

An interesting story about Fennimore involves its founder—John Fennimore, who had settled on the nearby Old Military Road. The unfortunate Mr. Fennimore disappeared in 1832 during the Black Hawk War and his fate was never determined.

From Fennimore we will ride U.S. Route 61 less than four miles north to CR-T and turn right. I think if someone asked me to recommend one stretch of road that a person could navigate to see the best of southern Wisconsin's mix of farm and forest, and hills and valleys, it would be this road. CR-T is a marvelous stretch of blacktop. The first time I rode it was at daybreak on a magical June morning. Recent rains resulted in fog-filled valleys, with the forested crests of hills rising above the ephemeral mists in a magical kingdom setting. Along this road, you will see picture-perfect fields with windrows of cut hay, or rows of corn curving across green hills like works of art created by skilled artisans. On frequent occasions it will be cows or horses that dot the hillsides with a variety of colors; now black and white, now brown, now almost red. They fit as if they were born to live their life on the verdant hills of Wisconsin.

I often think of Ireland when in this part of the state. The similarities are just too great to overlook. In both places you will find a green hue the depth of which just doesn't exist in most other places. Farmers who love and respect the land affectionately care for it. The landscape is one of rolling hills and wooded river valleys where cold-water streams have worked their magic in the shade of stately trees that have seen the passing of many generations. I think the lads of the Auld Sod would like it here.

County Road T rises and falls across the landscape in an enjoyable manner, allowing you to surf the asphalt with the road an ever-changing wave beneath you. Traffic is very light and scenery is pleasing to the eye. The last two miles just before reaching the small town of Blue River are especially nice as the road winds down the face of a bluff to the broad floodplain of the Wisconsin River. Mindful of the stop sign at CR-T and SR-133, at this point you might want to make a brief side trip east a couple miles on 133 to see an interesting display of old motorcycles and related bits and pieces. A local resident has perhaps two dozen old bikes, and an assortment of motorcycle paraphernalia displayed in his yard and adjacent field. I'm not sure what it's all supposed to mean, but it's interesting to see.

To go on with the trip we will continue north on CR-T at Blue River across the Wisconsin River, turning right onto state route 60 on the other side. The next recommended destination is Eagle Cave, which we will find on Eagle Cave Road, about two miles east of where we turned onto SR-60. Eagle Cave Road is a narrow road that becomes very scenic after the first half-mile. It is paved, though not recently, and traffic is almost nonexistent. Eagle Cave itself is at the north end of a narrowing valley that this road traverses. It is a privately owned site that includes a small store and campground. Camping here would virtually guarantee a relaxing and quiet night in a natural setting far from the clamor of cities or highways.

The tour commences by pointing your front wheel toward the rising sun on route 60. The stretch of sixty between Blue River and Gotham is wonderful. In places, the road is wedged between a rock wall on the north and the river just a few yards away to your right. It is tree-lined, hilly, and meandering, making it enchanting to ride.

East of Gotham everything changes suddenly. The road becomes straight and flat. For the first five miles east of this village, the road takes us through woodlands. The remaining six miles to Spring Green, however, is through intensively farmed flat and fertile terrain.

Our tour has us bypassing Spring Green, remaining on route 60 about six more miles to CR-C. The flat lands are left behind us as we ride east of Spring Green. At the intersection with county road C there is a sign pointing north toward Natural Bridge State Park, our next destination. Turn left onto C and follow this excellent biking road as it snakes north and northeast for an exhilarating ride through about thirteen miles of the best of southern Wisconsin. Much of this stretch of road was recently paved making it especially smooth and pleasurable to ride. There will be almost no other vehicles on the road and the landscape is picturesque with the mix of field and forest so common in this part of the state. A fun ride is guaranteed as you work you left foot and right hand in a mesmerizing cadence conducted by the beat of the road.

Unfortunately, there are no warning signs for the entrance of this small and lightly visited park and as you come around a curve the sign pointing to the park driveway looms quite suddenly. The park is about one mile east of the tiny village of Leland so use that as your guide.

Once in the parking lot a footpath is visible heading across a small open meadow to the woods beyond. Take this trail into the woods and I recommend taking the left fork when it splits. The trail in the forest is normally a loop with the stone bridge at the apex. Major rainstorms in the spring of 2008 washed out the right side of this loop, however, and I suspect it will be awhile before it is repaired. It is a relatively short hike to the stone arch formation but well worth it. The site has a long history, with thousands of years of human activity having taken place there. Just seeing the ancient arcing stone overhead is quite a thrill even if one ignores the archeological record of the place.

Upon leaving the park the fun continues for several more miles as we motor east on county road C. The road ultimately straightens out as it heads directly east towards its junction with U.S. 12, where we turn right toward the twin towns of Sauk City and Prairie du Sac. State route 60 joins U.S. 12 at the north edge of Sauk City. We ride on both and turn left staying on route 60 just prior to the bridge on which U.S. 12 crosses the Wisconsin River at the south end of Sauk City.

Thousands of years in the making, stone bridge formations are a rare sight in Wisconsin.

SR-60 will angle northeast along the river for two miles in Prairie du Sac, eventually crossing the historic waterway and commencing its easterly journey to the town of Lodi. In the native tongue Lodi meant peaceful valley, and today the town's claim to fame is being known as the home of Susie the Duck. Mallard ducks became the city mascot in 1948 when a hen nested in a masonry flowerpot in the heart of downtown. When her eggs hatched this duck family became a tourist attraction as people came from near and far to observe them. The police chief's granddaughter named the duck Susie, and a legend was born. Ducks apparently nest in the downtown location each year, and in return, the city hosts an annual Susie The Duck Day each summer. Attendance is mandatory; don't try ducking out.

Route 60 is our host all the way east to Columbus. The first half of this section, to the village of Arlington and the juncture with U.S. 51, is enjoyable with good pavement and mild curves in a varied and scenic landscape. Have your brain in gear at the point a short distance further east where U.S. 51 curves south, parting company with SR 60. It is very easy to just follow the curve and end up on 51 unintentionally heading south to Madison. I have to admit that this might have hap-

Christopher Columbus is honored in his namesake city.

pened to me once or twice. A left turn is required to remain on route 60 when route 51 turns south.

East of Arlington the road straightens out and heads to Columbus in a business-like manner. Not bad riding, but not great. Columbus is a town whose founders and early residents must have been fixated on the fame and fortunes of one man, the stalwart mariner himself, Christopher Columbus. The town is named in honor of the explorer, and the stately city hall was built in 1892, to honor the four hundredth anniversary of his discovering the New World. As you enter the city from the west, keep your eyes open for a statue of Columbus on the right side of route 60 just west of the route 151 interchange. On the opposite side of town, on Whitney Street, is an antiques mall and museum filled with items related to the wandering Genoan. Of most interest are pieces from the 1893 Chicago World's Fair, which was also in large part a celebration of Columbus's discovery of America.

I recommend a short tour through Columbus, especially east and west on Ludington Street and route 73, as well as along route 60. There are many stately historic mansions from the mid and late nineteenth century that have been carefully maintained in town, many of which can be found on these mentioned streets.

Our voyage out of Columbus takes us east on route 60 less than four miles to CR-T. Turn right onto 'T' and quickly you will cross the bridge spanning the Crawfish River. At the east end of the bridge turn right and you'll find yourself in front of the Danville Mill. Though this old mill is privately owned one can park along the small street adjacent to the river and get an excellent view of the historic mill building and dam.

Continue the journey south on CR-T and eventually it will merge with state route 89 on the north side of Waterloo. CR-T is quite nice. It crosses a rolling landscape of tidy farms and woodlots, with very little traffic to interfere with your daydreams as you ride through the appealing surroundings. Route 89 carries us through Waterloo and then to the pretty and historic city of Lake Mills, situated on the eastern shore of Rock Lake. Lake Mills is a laid-back town with a downtown commons area where many events are hosted, or where folks just hang out as the temptation strikes. At the south edge of town, take county road B east three miles to visit the Aztalan Museum and nearby Aztalan State Park.

Ceremonial mounds in Aztalan State Park leave visitors in awe.

The state park contains one of Wisconsin's most important archaeological sites. It is an ancient village and ceremonial complex that thrived between 900 and 1200 A.D, built by a sophisticated civilization that experts call the Middle Mississippian Tradition. Archaeologists believe that the occupants of this city may have had cultural ties with Cahokia, a large settlement near East St. Louis, Illinois. Founders of Aztalan built large, flat-topped pyramidal mounds and a stockade around their village. Though many Native American cultural sites were destroyed over the last 150 years, the very impressive platform mound and reconstructed stockade in this popular reserve are protected for all to gaze upon. The Native Americans who lived in the village hunted, fished, and farmed along the Crawfish River. Viewing the complex leaves one with a sense of awe that people could build such mounds with nothing but their hands and bone or stone tools. Most extraordinary indeed! The site also speaks to the political, spiritual, and technical complexity of civilizations that lived here a thousand years before us. Many centuries after they were built Native American effigy and ceremonial mounds still have the ability to create wonder and inspiration with each new generation of viewers. I think that a large part of my fascination with them is that they will always be enigmatic to a large degree and the answers as to the what and the why behind these mounds will never be completely understood.

The Aztalan Museum, located just north of the park, is operated by the local historical society and includes 19th-century buildings, as well as artifacts of pioneer and Native American life. If you have not yet visited Aztalan, now is the time.

The land around us becomes more open and the road straighter as we do the final stage back to Fort Atkinson. I hope you enjoyed this fascinating journey of discovery and that it gives you a renewed respect and interest in the history, people and places of this marvelous state.

Helmet Hair Quiz Answer

Hank Aaron

Trolls and Badger Holes

Helmet Hair Quiz

The figures of two men are shown on the state flag; what occupations do they depict?

THIS ENTERTAINING AND EDIFYING tour of discovery begins in the small town of Mt. Horeb, just west of Madison. The city obtained its unusual name in 1861 when the first postmaster, who also happened to be a church minister, chose the name from the Bible. He felt that the name reflected the natural beauty of the area, and of the nearby-forested hills known today as the blue mounds.

It seems that most successful enterprises, including cities and towns, need something to set them apart from everyone else. Some people may call these unique features gimmicks, though others would say that they are the successful implementation of a good idea. Mt. Horeb has a couple such claims to fame. The first is the presence of carved trolls located throughout the town. The second is the international mustard museum; an unlikely business enterprise for tourist dollars, but a successful one just the same.

Mt. Horeb's Main Street is called Trollway because over the last couple decades a variety of these creatures have been carved and placed in front of businesses and on street corners. Local sculptor Michael Feeney is responsible for this phenomenon. He began carving trolls out of tree trunks years ago, starting something that the city capitalized on and that has drawn tourists from near and far.

The city, and in fact the entire region, has a strong Norwegian flavor due to immigrants from Norway settling here last century. As a result, several local attractions and restaurants retain a Norwegian flavor. Go ahead and have your picture taken next to any one of the many trolls that line the street—they won't mind and there aren't many places where you can find subjects like these for some amusing photographic pandemonium.

The Grumpy Troll restaurant and brewery is a fun place to end the day with a delicious meal and unique brew. The restaurant, called The Grumpy by locals, is located in the old Mount Horeb Creamery building. The owners turned it into a restaurant and brewery in 1996. The Grumpy has full lunch and full dinner menus

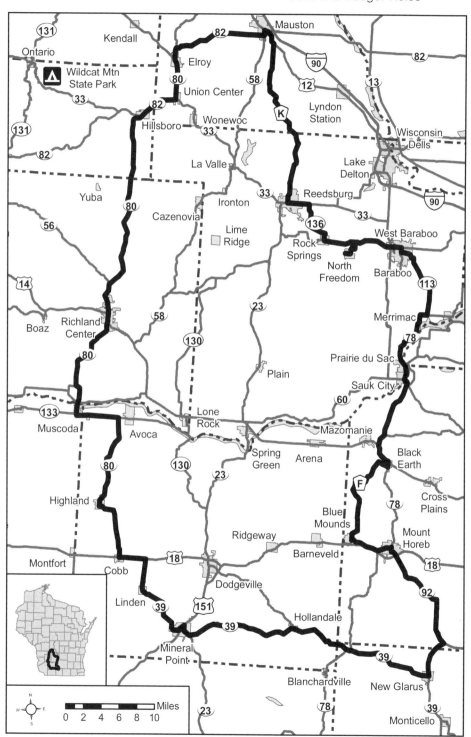

TROLLS & BADGERS 233 MILES		
Miles	**Destination**	**Total**
00	Mt. Horeb	00
18	New Glarus	18
31	Mineral Point	49
37	Muscoda	86
22	Rockbridge	108
25	Elroy	133
33	Reedsburg	166
37	Prairie du Sac	203
30	Mt. Horeb	233

and its on site brewery features twelve beers on tap. Brewery tours are offered free of charge.

Let's put our gear on and thumb our starters to get underway. Begin by riding south on route 92, leaning left and right and rising and falling on our iron horses as we chase Deer Creek, which shadows the road often just out of sight as we ride. Route 92 is a double yellow line road most of the way from Mt. Horeb south to route 69. In motorcycling parlance, following streams and double yellow lines translate into great riding.

After a few miles on route 69 we find ourselves in the village of New Glarus at the intersection with route 39. If Mt. Horeb had a Norwegian flavor, New Glarus is unabashedly Swiss. In fact, the city is named in honor of Glarus, Switzerland. In 1842, when the mother country was in the grips of desperate economic strife, the government devised a program whereby volunteers were sent to America. This emigration helped relieve social pressures in the homeland and resulted in a Swiss colony in southern Wisconsin that proudly bears the name of their ancestors more than one hundred fifty years later. There are signs of Swiss culture everywhere one looks, from the many chalet style buildings, to the cheese industry and brewers of Swiss style beers. If you want to explore the Swiss culture and history further, be sure to visit the Swiss Historical Village, located at 612 7th Avenue in town. Call them at 608.527.2317 or go to swisshistoricalvillage.com for more information.

This is a great town to sample authentic Swiss food and drink. There are many establishments where you can accomplish this objective, including the award-win-

Photogenic trolls pose for pictures along Mt. Horeb's main street.

ning New Glarus Brewing Company (their Spotted Cow ale is my favorite, though if you prefer a darker unfiltered beer give their Fat Squirrel ale a try), the New Glarus Bakery (reportedly one of the best in the state), and the New Glarus Hotel. Swiss immigrants built the hotel in 1853 and today its restaurant is legendary for fine Swiss cuisine, thanks to its in-house Swiss-trained chef. Authentic specialties include offerings such as Wiener schnitzel, Swiss sausage platter, daesechuechli, and beef fondue bourguignonne; items you just will not find on most menus! You most assuredly will not find food like this at any of the fast food joints. The hotel also hosts polka dancing on Friday and Saturday nights. The Glarner Stube restaurant, located on 1st Street, is another New Glarus destination that serves fine Swiss and American food and spirits. In addition, you might be lucky enough to hear their in-house bottelier making music by 'playing the bottles' in the bar. Toffler's Bar and Grill, on 5th Avenue, is also a favorite stop. A tavern has been at this location since 1880, and in addition to food and drink, live music is a common feature at Toffler's.

Even if you don't stop at any of the many attractions in New Glarus it's fun to ride around town to see the unique architecture. Painted cows found at various locations add to the charm and pastoral character of this village, and of the ancestral homeland of many residents.

We depart New Glarus westbound on state route 39, traversing the rural and attractive countryside of northwestern Green and southeastern Iowa Counties. Route 39 winds across the land primarily on hilltops, providing bikers with countless beautiful vistas as far as the eye can see. This is a delightful stretch of road to kick back and enjoy a relaxing and unchallenging, but yet enjoyable, ride.

The historic town of Mineral Point is our next stop. Situated as it is in rolling hills that were left untouched by the last glacier to cover much of the northern U.S., minerals at the surface of the land were readily discoverable and relatively easily mined. Prospectors, skilled and unskilled, swarmed the hills and many lived in their mines, giving the appearance of "badger holes", from which Wisconsin got its nickname: The Badger State. The discovery of lead gave rise to the first "mineral rush" in the United States and Mineral Point grew to be the largest, most important settlement in the area. Hastily built stockades were built in the lead mining region in 1832 with the onset of the Black Hawk War. In Mineral Point Fort Jackson was constructed in the city to protect local residents and outlying settlers if it became necessary. Fortunately, the need did not arise and the fort was dismantled shortly thereafter.

In the 1830s, news of lead mining opportunities reached Cornwall, England, and the Cornish miners and their families started arriving in Mineral Point. These immigrant Cornish miners brought advanced hard rock and deep mining skills along with a distinctive stone building tradition to the area. The Cornish character of the community remains prominent to this day, in large part because of the many limestone and sandstone buildings constructed by these early immigrants.

Mineral Point was fundamental to Wisconsin's early economic development. Founded in 1827, the city's population by 1830 was more than that of Chicago and Milwaukee—combined! It was here that Henry Dodge was sworn in as the first governor of the new Wisconsin Territory on July 4, 1836. This cool history-filled town continued to impress, and in 1971 Mineral Point became the first city in Wisconsin listed on the National Register of Historic Places.

I find it interesting that until 1834, when the lead mining industry was beginning to boom, the fur trade was still Wisconsin's major economic industry. John Jacob Astor's American Fur Company took over the fur business in this part of the country after the British were expelled following the War of 1812, making him one of the richest men in the country. Two hundred years of over harvesting fur

One of the well dressed bovines that greet visitors in New Glarus.

bearing animals in the Great Lakes and upper Mississippi region had made such an impact by the 1830s that fur traders had to move further west to find ample supplies of beaver and other animals whose fur was still desired by Europeans and the well-to-do in large eastern U.S. cities.

Pendarvis, located on Shake Rag Street, is a collection of rehabilitated homes and buildings that had originally been built by Cornish miners in the mining boom days. Shake Rag Street got its name from the habit of wives waving rags from their front doors to catch the attention of their husbands mining on the nearby hill, letting them know that lunch was ready. Pendarvis is one site in Mineral Point that should be a stop on any visitor's agenda. The renovation and preservation began in 1935 when two residents observed the town's history decaying in front of their eyes. They began to preserve the stone houses built by the early immigrants, as these buildings were Mineral Point's most evocative symbols.

Following the Cornish tradition of naming each house, these two gentlemen named their first restored house Pendarvis, after an estate in Cornwall. In the Old

World tradition they also gave other restored buildings uniquely Cornish monikers, including Polperro and Trelawny, their next two preservation projects. Following these successful efforts, they then acquired and restored a rowhouse on a nearby hill. Preservation work of course not only involves hard work, it takes a lot of money. To support their work on the restoration the two men established the Pendarvis House Restaurant, specializing in Cornish pasties—a meal popular throughout the upper Midwest, especially among miners in Wisconsin, Michigan and Minnesota. A pasty is a self-contained meal consisting of meat, potatoes, and vegetables (plus various secret recipe items added by inventive housewives and chefs) that the men could carry into the mine and eat with their hands. Whenever you see authentic pasties offered at restaurants in the Great Lakes region I encourage you to try them—they are truly delicious and guaranteed to keep your stomach from growling for several hours!

This authentic ethnic restaurant was very popular while it existed, but was eventually closed when the owners retired. The Wisconsin Historical Society acquired these properties in 1970. This organization runs the restored village as a historic site interpreting the history of this Cornish settlement and Wisconsin's vital lead-mining period.

I suggest that you ride through the historic downtown section of Mineral Point, located along State Street just a few blocks southwest of Shake Rag Street and Pendarvis. The buildings in this part of town will make you believe you have been transplanted to a village in old England or Wales. And of course this is no accident, as it was immigrants from the British Isles that built those stone buildings over a hundred fifty years ago in the same style as they had been building structures in their home villages for generations. Today many of these old buildings house restaurants, antique shops, or small offices. Located at the bottom of the hill at the south end of downtown, the Mineral Point Railroad Depot museum is another place you may wish to visit. Wisconsin's oldest depot and the oldest surviving structure of the Milwaukee Road, the Mineral Point Railroad Depot operated from 1856 to 1984. After a six-year restoration project, the former depot opened in 2004 as the Mineral Point Railroad Museum. The two-story limestone depot houses a collection of items that tell the story of 150 years of railroad history. Exhibits detail the depot's function from its early development with the Mineral Point Railroad Company to the late twentieth century. I find railroading museums to be fascinating not only because of their obvious attraction to gear heads, but also because they do such a good job telling the story of past times, people, and events.

Looking east from the old depot one sees a stone cliff. At the base of this cliff is a sign that states that it was at this spot where minerals that led to the lead mining boom were first discovered.

Restored stone cottages bring old world charm to the streets of Mineral Point.

Depart Mineral Point northbound on route 39. For many miles we have nothing to do but ride and enjoy the sound of the engine, the scenery, and the ride itself. What more could a biker want? In fact, as the miles roll by this may be a good opportunity to slip away from the ride a bit to ponder motorcycling and motorcyclists. Two-wheeled vehicles have fascinated me from my very earliest years. My first bicycle was a ticket to freedom that struck a chord deep in my soul. A feeling that has never left. I loved the feel of riding on two wheels. I enjoyed the quick turns and off-road capabilities; limited though they were. Suddenly places that were too far away to walk to became a day's adventure by riding there, alone or with friends. And it grew from there. The addition of a motor of course changed everything.

In a way, I regret that so many people just don't get motorcycling. Some folks are of the opinion that bikers must be antisocial. After all, they reason, why would we voluntarily participate in this dangerous and rebellious activity if we weren't? We may never be able to convince everyone that motorcycling is neither excessively dangerous nor a sign of rebellion, but slowly the message is getting out. It is hard to maintain a negative view of an activity that has become so commonplace that ones dentist, lawyer or pastor may well be an enthusiast.

Is motorcycling's vestigial outlaw image part of its charm? I believe so. It is fundamental to the American spirit to want to be at least a bit of a nonconformist or iconoclast; to have some part of our life that separates us from the crowd and that makes a statement about who we really are. In some cultures there is a social axiom that holds that a nail that sticks out gets pounded down. Here it is just the opposite, with individuality and personal tastes respected and even honored. Bikers value this creative freedom as much as any group in the country.

For the majority of us being a motorcyclist is much more than just owning and riding a motorcycle. It is a way of life. It is a manifestation of our desire to find freedom and adventure in a world of expected behaviors and commitments. Being a part of this lifestyle means associating with out-of-the-ordinary people who share a desire for adventure and personal freedom.

I believe that enthusiasts have certain traits and qualities that make us different. We are willing to accept an increase in potential danger and discomfort for the adventure and independence that are its rewards. It doesn't matter who we are when we aren't riding. All that matters is our passion for the sport and the happiness it brings us. Personally, I don't much care if everyone understands us or knows why we ride. If you are reading this you know, and I know, and that is all that really matters.

◄◄◄◄◘►►►►

Ride north on route 39 to U.S. 18, taking this main road west a short way to state route 80. Turn north on 80. This road will be our partner for many miles, across parts of Richland, Vernon and Juneau Counties. South of U.S. 18 route 80 is only fair riding, but it's a short stretch, and north of U.S. 18 things noticeably improve (except for a short stretch of congestion at Richland Center where 80 and U.S. 14 intersect).

Going north from Richland Center the land is beautifully rolling and a mixture of farm and forest. Route 80 follows the Pine River resulting in the usual delightful partnership of road and stream. At the tiny village of Rockbridge there is an interesting attraction that you do not want to miss. As you come into town from the south there is a small sign pointing left to Pier Natural Bridge Park. Follow the narrow paved drive back toward the rock cliff and eventually you come to a tunnel in that cliff wall that was formed over thousands of years as the river changed course from one side of the escarpment to the other. A person can walk through the tunnel to the opposite side. Though degraded by graffiti it is an out of the ordinary sight and the park is a good place to take a break from the road.

About ten miles north of Rockbridge, and a couple miles west of 80 on county road V is the Blue Highway Motorcycle Lodge. This camping and lodging facility is for and by motorcyclists, and offers everything from rustic campsites to cozy cabins and beds. If your riding schedule works out so you can spend the night at this lodge it will be a wonderful enhancement to an already fun ride. Call the lodge at 608.489.4131 for more information. They are located west of route 80 at S2669 County Road V.

Our ride keeps us on route 80 all the way to the small town of Elroy where we turn east on route 82 toward Mauston. For half of the way to Mauston 82 crosses rolling and wooded land, and then things open up as Mauston gets near.

Some of you may think of Mauston as that congested area at exit 69 off I-90/94, but we will avoid that mess. In central Mauston route 82 intersects with route 12. Turn right on 12 and follow it east out of town. You will pass the St. Patrick's Cemetery and a short distance further is CR-K. Turn right on K, which will take us south to Reedsburg. The first two miles are straight and flat, but then things quickly change for the better. CR-K is a charming road of curves and hills, through a wooded backdrop. Traffic is light and the road surface is in very good condition, providing miles of smiles right to the city limits of Reedsburg. Remain headed south through Reedsburg, through the first stop sign, and then turning left at the second, which is state route 33.

Like all towns, Reedsburg didn't just happen. There is usually a series of events that take place first that are determinative of whether a spot on the land became a town or remained unsettled. Reedsburg's history dates to the mid-1840s when timber prospectors discovered iron and copper outcroppings. This led to others coming to the region and in 1848 David Reed and a partner set up a sawmill that produced wood for the early homes built in what became Reedsburg.

The town is noted for very different things today. The Museum of Norman Rockwell Art, located at 227 South Park Street, houses about 4,000 works of art by this famous American artist and illustrator. Call the museum at 608.524.2123 for more information. Reedsburg is also home to the little league baseball tournament every August. This tradition dates back to 1951 and today involves more than eighty teams.

We depart Reedsburg on 33 east three miles to route 136. Turn right onto 136 to our next destination and as you do you will pass through what's called the North Range, a series of geologically unique hills that encircle Baraboo. These hills are formed of a particularly hard and resistant form of Quartzite that has resisted

Railroading history is alive and well at the Mid-Continent Railway Museum in the village of North Freedom.

erosion for the last 350 million years. To the south of Baraboo these hills comprise what's called the South Range, and together they formed the Baraboo Range which a few years ago (like about one billion) was as tall as the Rocky Mountains.

The boundary between the driftless glacier-free uplands area of western Wisconsin and the glaciated central plains lies between Reedsburg and Baraboo. The Baraboo River has carved a channel through the South Range at Rock Springs—a pathway also followed by route 136.

Follow 136 beyond Rock Springs to CR-I, turning right to the village of North Freedom and the very impressive Mid-Continent Railway Museum. If you visit only one railroad museum in the state it should probably be this one. It has an outstanding exhibit of a variety of rolling stock that is accessible for up close viewing. Train rides of approximately one hour round trip are available in cars from circa 1900. You can also arrange to ride in a caboose; how many of us wanted to do that as kids?! North Freedom is just a couple of miles south of 136 and this is a highly recommended part of the trip.

When you are ready to resume the tour ride east again on 136 and when you get to U.S. 12 continue straight across this busy intersection into the city of Baraboo. We are going to follow the signs on route 113 to the Circus World Museum on the riverbank on the east side of town. This state historic site is the original wintering quarters of the Ringling Brothers Circus in the late 19th and early 20th centuries. I have never been to this museum but it looks like a fun place to visit if you are into circus events and rides.

Continue south on 113 with the next stop Devil's Lake State Park. This natural wonder is nearly 10,000 acres in size and is perhaps the most popular park in Wisconsin. The reasons for this popularity will become immediately obvious when you view such marvels as 500-foot cliffs, or the Devil's Doorway rock formation towering high above Devil's Lake. There are also effigy mounds located throughout the park. This geologically unique recreational area is also part of the Ice Age National Scientific Reserve, and the Ice Age National Scenic Trail runs through the park.

Devil's Lake Park is located in the South Range and as one rides down route 113 it's easy to see where this range ends. A steep downhill just south of the park signals the end of this geologic phenomenon.

Conditions flatten out and become more open when the park and hills are left behind. Route 113 joins route 78 onto which we'll make a right turn toward Prairie du Sac and Sauk City. Route 78 is a fun route, but with rough pavement. It's unlikely that the state will pay to repave the existing roadway as there are plans to dramatically "improve" route 78 with a new road. As part of the abandonment of the Badger Army Ammunition Plant, land has been given to WDOT for a new SR 78 corridor. You can be sure that any new road will be flatter and straighter than the current route, which still curves across the landscape in an enjoyable manner.

Stay on route 78 as it crosses the Wisconsin River in Sauk City. Crossing over the river brings us into western Dane County, the home of several more intriguing attractions. The first is just a couple miles south of Sauk City on route 78—the site of the 1832 Battle of Wisconsin Heights. Following the June 16, 1832 battle of Pecatonica, Chief Black Hawk and his followers, including many women and children, moved north with soldiers from the Michigan Territory and the Illinois state militia close behind. On July 21st the militias under Colonels Henry Dodge and James Henry caught up with the Indians as they were preparing to cross the Wisconsin River. At this point in time Chief Black Hawk was said to be prepared to move his band back across the Mississippi River and end the hostilities but the militia did not know of his intentions. Occasional hostilities kept the fires burning and tensions high.

Upon seeing the militia approaching, Black Hawk set up a blocking action to divert attention away from the civilians escaping across the river. The tactic was successful though the price was high, with at least forty killed in the skirmish. Many were feared drowned in the dangerous crossing, in addition. Even with these high casualties most historians view this as a tactical victory by Chief

Black Hawk as it allowed his band of followers to make their way west toward the Mississippi. They had no way of knowing that the fateful and disastrous Battle of Bad Axe lay in their future.

The Battle of Wisconsin Heights is listed on the National Register of Historic Places. It is also managed and protected as part of the state's Lower Wisconsin State Riverway reserve. A series of trails take hikers through the battlefield to several sites where the various skirmishes actually occurred.

<<<<●>>>>

Continuing south on 78 will deliver us to the village of Black Earth. A sports bar on the north edge of town called Rookies is a biker-friendly place to eat.

Six blocks south of the railroad tracks in Black Earth we turn right on CR-F, also known as Blue Mounds Trail. This very enjoyable road will take us south to three attractions—Blue Mounds State Park, Cave of the Mounds, and Little Norway.

The Blue Mounds are a series of beautiful tree-covered hills located west and northwest of Mt. Horeb. They are scenic to look at and add a definite charm to this region. Blue Mound State Park's 1,153 acres protects the highest hill in southern Wisconsin, rising to a height of 1,716 feet above sea level. Two forty foot high towers perched on the hill offer a marvelous panoramic view of this beautiful part of the state. The Cave of the Mounds is located just east of the park and offers an underground tour of a cave accidentally discovered in 1939 during an explosion to remove rock in a limestone quarry. The million year old cave's presence was made known when the blast removed a wall of stone, and as they say, the rest is history. The cave is open for tours every day between Memorial Day and Labor Day. The constant 50-degree temperature in the cave is a welcome relief on a hot and muggy summer day.

A fun and out of the ordinary way to see the Norwegian influence in the Mt. Horeb and Blue Mounds area is to visit Little Norway, a fascinating collection of authentic Norwegian buildings. The site is in an idyllic valley near the scenic Blue Mounds. Simply go east from the cave on County Road-ID for one mile, to CR-JG and turn left, following the sign. The Norwegian village is just a mile up the road.

Little Norway has another more authentic name, that chosen by its founder Isak Dahle. Nissedahle, or valley of the Elves, is an ethnically appropriate name that sounds like it could also have been conjured up by J.R.R. Tolkein in his *Lord of the Rings* trilogy. The buildings are authentic Norwegian architecture, simple yet made durable to withstand the inclement weather found in both Wisconsin and Norway. One has a growing sod roof and another is peaked with three cupolas. Even the colors used on the buildings are typical Norwegian hues so the trolls and gnomes will feel right at home.

Because the landscape of southwest Wisconsin reminded him of Norway, it was in this lovely valley that Osten Olson Haugen from Telemark, Norway settled with his family in the mid-1800s. This started a wave of migration from Norway to this region, and the Norwegian flavor is retained to this day.

After you have soaked in all the fascinating attractions of the Blue Mounds region it is time to take the very short trip east on CR-ID back to Mt. Horeb. That completes this marvelous ride, one that I am sure you will be talking about with your friends for a long time.

Helmet Hair Quiz Answer

A sailor and a miner.

The Old Military Road

Helmet Hair Quiz

What two drinks is Wisconsin most famous for producing?

CALL ME STRANGE, but I find old roads and trails used by early explorers and settlers in the frontier to be fascinating things to explore. Moreover, the routes do not have to go back to the earliest days of exploration to pique my curiosity and get me wondering what it would have been like to be an early traveler on such a trail. The Allegheny Pike, The National Road, The Natchez Trace, The Santa Fe and Oregon Trails, The Lincoln Highway, and yes, even Route 66—they all awaken the same feeling of a voyage into the unknown. These roads evoke a sense of awe as one considers the adventures and hardships of travelers on the very same roadway a hundred or more years ago. The early versions of these roads were the opposite of what it is to travel on today's roads in our tamed and civilized western world. They were pathways to discovery and adventure for early travelers, and they can be the same for us.

These roads and trails are an important part of our history. Even if they no longer exist, in their day they played an incalculable role in the formation of our country. We no longer drive on the Santa Fe and Oregon Trails, but I don't think anybody today questions their impact and importance to the opening of the west a hundred fifty years ago. Some of the early trails evolved into major highways (The National Road, The Lincoln Highway, The Grand Army of the Republic Highway, The Detroit & Chicago Military Road, to name just a few), while others were abandoned and nearly forgotten. The abandonment part is understandable as these trails were replaced over the years by newer and better roads, but the forgotten aspect is unfortunate. They are a part of our collective history that we should remember.

And so it is that in a book about motorcycle touring I'm writing about a road that in large part hasn't existed for well over a century. However, motorcyclists are a curious and intelligent group that appreciates there is more to our sport than simply putting gas in the tank and riding the bike down the road. Different

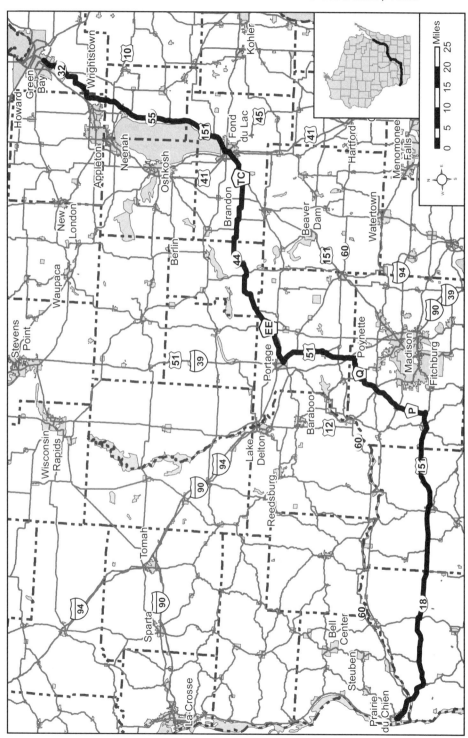

Miles	Destination	Total
	THE OLD MILITARY ROAD **249 MILES**	
00	Green Bay	00
27	Sherwood	27
32	Fond Du Lac	59
40	Kingston	99
33	Poynette	132
39	Mt. Horeb	171
49	Fennimore	220
29	Prairie du Chien	249

motorcyclists want different things but I think two of the common goals are exploring the world around us and immersing ourselves in new experiences as part of our biking repertoire. So what do you say we partake in a bit of Wisconsin's history by exploring the route and history of The Old Military Road, which played a vital role in history, even if just for a relatively brief period time?

We have to transport ourselves in our imagination back to the early 1800s to really understand why the road was built in the first place. The War of 1812 had only recently ended, and to the surprise of many the war had been brought to the upper Great Lakes and the upper Mississippi River by the British. Suddenly the land that a young America thought was securely its own was put in jeopardy. There was a need to stake a claim on America's sovereignty of this region, and to enhance exploration and protect early settlers who braved the wilderness. Fort Howard, built in 1816 on the Fox River at present day Green Bay, and Fort Crawford built at Prairie du Chien following the loss of that battle a few years earlier to the British, were built to help secure the area. Another fort was later built in Portage in 1828 to help secure that vital link in the crucial Fox / Wisconsin Rivers water highway.

In 1830 the U.S. Congress authorized a road from Fort Howard to Fort Crawford and over the next decade soldiers from the three forts constructed a crude road that was called the Military Road. Its function originally was as a means of getting supplies to the three remote forts, and of course to move troops rapidly if the need should again arise.

The trail followed the east shore of the Fox River south to Lake Winnebago, then along the east shore of this lake where it swung west through Fond du Lac to Portage, then southerly to Poynet and the Blue Mounds area, where it swung west, crossing the Wisconsin River at present-day Bridgeport and finally to Fort Crawford. This tour will follow the original route of the road as faithfully as we can given the changes that have taken place over these many years.

We begin our ride in Green Bay. Of course there are many things to see and do in this vibrant city, much of which could be centered on the Packers. If you aren't a local it's fun heading over to the stadium and walking around the grounds at Lambeau or strolling

Traces of the original military road still exist after 170 years of change.

through the Hall of Fame. While still west of the river I also recommend spending time at the National Railroad Museum. See General Eisenhower's command train or marvel at the world's largest steam engine. The large collection of railroading technology and history at the museum will amaze you, I guarantee. The museum is located near the river at 2285 South Broadway just north of route 172 and west of the Fox River. Check them out at nationalrrmuseum.org.

On the east side of the river, where we begin our ride, you will find Heritage Hill State Historic Park. This is living history museum with many replica buildings and presentations that explore the development of this part of the state over several centuries. The park is bounded by route 172 on the south, route 57 on the west, and Webster Street on the east. Entry to the park is from Webster Street.

We leave town via route 57, along the east side of the Fox River, just as the original trail through the wilderness did. Just south of town route 57 veers off to the southeast and route 32 goes southwest—we want route 32. After three miles watch carefully for Old Military Road heading off southwest from thirty-two. The intersection isn't well marked, but it is three miles beyond the 32 / 57 divergence, and across the road from the Rockland Township office building.

Old Military Road is a county road that will take us down to Wrightstown Road (in the 1830s there was a village in the wilderness in this vicinity called Wrightstown that the military road went through). Old Military Road "Ts" at Wrightstown Road, so we turn right, heading west less than two miles to a "T" intersection at the Fox River and CR-ZZ. Turn south on ZZ and ride this very nice road as it closely follows the curves of the river. After six miles CR-ZZ turns southwest and you will see CR-GG heading straight south. At this point we want GG, which after a few miles has a name change to Old Military Road again. South of highway U.S. 10 Old Military Road turns into CR-M—no turns necessary, just keep going straight ahead, only the name of the road changes. CR-M delivers us to the town of Sherwood and route 55. Ride south on route 55, which will be our partner for many miles, then continuing south along the sunrise shore of Lake Winnebago to the city of Fond Du Lac on U.S. 151. Route 151 angles off northeast of Fond Du Lac as an expressway, and our road becomes Winnebago Drive as we approach Fond Du Lac along the shoreline from the northeast. Stay on this street into downtown where it turns straight west as Scott Street, and then soon intersects with Main Street—the main north / south street in Fond Du Lac. Go south on Main a bit more than a mile to Western Avenue (there is a park on the northwest corner of this intersection). Turn right on Western Avenue, taking it three-tenths of a mile to Military Road, where a left turn is made. Follow Military Road through the southwest portion of the city, and soon you will go through the busy interchange at U.S. 41, and our road magically becomes old 151 again, heading southwest through the countryside outside of Fond Du Lac. Mark your odometer as you pass the U.S. 41 interchange, because six miles beyond that point on Military Road / 151 there will be a sign for CR-TC, onto which we turn right. CR-TC will go basically straight west, make a short northerly jog on CR-M, and then west again into Brandon. Just before the town of Brandon, however, there is a historical marker on the north side of CR-TC marking the site of the original military road, which in that vicinity became known as Raube Road, in recognition of the family that owned the land years ago. The actual segment of the Old Military Road is behind the historical marker, through a gate.

Continue west on TC into Brandon and onto route 49. Forty nine leaves Brandon to the west, and shortly becomes route 44. Ride forty-four west through the towns of Fairwater, Markesan, and finally Kingston. Route 44 becomes a very enjoyable riding road the further west we progress. This is a road that really doesn't get much traffic, is in good shape, and makes for fun biking as it becomes progressively more rolling and curvy. Probably the only concern about riding in this vicinity is the number of Amish that share the road with modern travelers.

A short distance west of Kingston is the small village of Dalton. Less than a mile west of Dalton route 44 will begin to head straight south, and CR-EE will angle to the southwest, continuing the course of the original road of our travels. Follow EE for several miles southwest across the good-looking landscape, and then at a stop sign the double-E will turn due west, and straight ahead of us across

These surgeons' quarters would have been a busy place during Wisconsin's dangerous frontier period.

the intersection will be Military Road. Just continue across the intersection and we're on our way once again. Military Road is custom made for fun motorcycling with its curves, scenic landscape, and very light traffic. It will take us all the way to route 33 and the city of Portage.

Just prior to arriving at route 33, however, is the historic Fort Winnebago cemetery. This cemetery was begun in 1835 and because the U.S. government never transferred the 2-acre cemetery to anyone else, it has in effect been a small national cemetery at which veterans from all wars from the Revolutionary War through World War I are buried. The cemetery, and its story, is just another fascinating bit of bygone times of which too few people are aware.

Portage is a geographic part of Wisconsin with a long and important history. As its name suggests, this is where travelers over many centuries made the portage from the Fox River waterway system to the Wisconsin River, and ultimately to the Mississippi. This strategic location was a natural place for the third fort in the chain that linked Lake Michigan and the Mississippi River.

Turn right onto route 33, and almost immediately there will be a historical marker on the right side of the road that you will want to stop at. This marker tells the story of Fort Winnebago, built in 1828 to ensure peace between Native Americans and settlers, following skirmishes a year earlier that came to be called the Winnebago War. Soldiers stationed here also saw some action in 1832 during the Black Hawk War. An interesting side story is that young Jefferson Davis served in Fort Winnebago as a lieutenant, and he helped build the Military Road between this fort and Fond Du Lac. Davis of course went on to become president of the Confederate States thirty years later.

Almost straight across route 33 from the historical marker is a collection of old buildings and displays, including the original 1834 surgeon's quarters for the fort. An 1824 house and a 19th century school are also part of this park, as well as a few military items from that era.

◄◄◄◄◉►►►►

When you are done exploring the history of Fort Winnebago continue west on route 33 for about two miles to routes 51 / 16. Turn left on this main road, following it south along the Wisconsin River dikes. Eventually route 16 will diverge and we will remain on U.S. 51 south to the town of Poynette, through which the original road ran. For a main road 51 has some quite good motorcycling credentials. It's not a bad ride. Just north of Poynette on the right side of highway 51 you may notice a blue cross, placed there many years ago by the Daughters of the American Revolution memorializing the Old Military Road.

Coming into Poynette you will see North Street—turn right and take it a half-mile to Main Street. Turn left onto Main Street and take it south a mile, where you will see CR-Q angling off to the right. This is our road. CR-Q runs south through the countryside 5.5 miles where it ends at CR-K, and our southbound road becomes Patton Road, after a slight jog to the east. Take Patton Road south, over the I-39 expressway, and then just over a mile to CR-DM. Turn right on DM, following it as it twists and turns into the village of Dane. The road takes on the name Military Road once you get near the town. Dane is another village that has a historic connection of the original military road passing through the village.

In Dane, turn right on route 113, taking it one mile to county road P where a left turn is made. We will be on CR-P for many miles as it angles southwest toward Mt. Horeb. It is a fun motorcycling road, with the exception of the intersection with highway U.S. 14 in Cross Plains, where traffic can be heavy. Immediately south of route 14 on CR-P keep watch for a roadside sign on the left side of the road explaining the story of Hainey Tavern, which served early travelers on the Military Road.

CR-P is a nice road for a motorcycle ride as it wanders across the mixed landscape of farms and woods, all in a nice rolling tableau. If you study local maps carefully, you will notice that there are segments of Military Road between Dane and Mt. Horeb. However, they do not compose a continual route and it would be

exceedingly confusing to try to follow these short isolated stretches.

We will stay on CR-P all the way
south to U.S. 151 / route 18. A few
miles before reaching U.S. 151 CR-P
will join forces with CR-S, and shortly
thereafter cross the Sugar River. A
small distance later CR-P makes an
angled turn to the left, while CR-S
goes straight ahead. It is an easy place
to end up going west on S without
realizing it. When you reach U.S. 151
turn west toward Mt. Horeb, though

*A retired cannon enjoying its golden
years in Prairie du Chien.*

we will bypass the town on 151. If you wish to visit Mt. Horeb you'll have to exit
and then get back on 151 to resume the trip.

Our next portion of the ride takes us west on 151 / 18 for many miles. The
military ridge hiking trail that runs just north of and parallel to the highway we're
on was built on an abandoned railroad line which was itself laid on the original
military road. Military Ridge is a geologic formation called a cuesta. These are
ridges comprised of erosion resistant rock that have a steep slope with exposed
bedrock on one side, and a long gentle slope on the other. There are several other
cuestas in southern Wisconsin that form a roughly circular belt around the southern half of the state.

After many miles (about 24) U.S. 151 will dip south and U.S. 18 will continue
straight west into Dodgeville. U.S. 18 is our road, and we remain on it all the way
to Prairie du Chien. But there is still much to see and do before reaching the end
of the road.

The history of Dodgeville reaches back to the lead mining boom of the late
1820s. Colonel Henry Dodge, who was to become the first governor of the Wisconsin Territory in 1836, led a contingent of miners and their families here in 1827
and started the settlement. Dodgeville became the county seat for Iowa County,
after years of wrangling with Mineral Point for that honor, and the courthouse
that was proudly built in 1859 is still in use, making it the longest serving courthouse in the state.

The Dodge Mining Cabin, built in 1827 is located on Fountain Street (take
route 23 south a few blocks from route 18 and follow the signs). If you are in town
in mid-July, and are a blues music fan, then you are in luck. The Blues Fest has
become a successful annual event. The show is held rain or shine in a large tent on
the courthouse grounds; and it's free, so what are you waiting for? Check them out

at dodgevillebluesfest.com. Interestingly, Dodgeville boomed until the late 1840s when many miners left for the California Gold Rush of 1849.

After Dodgeville we begin our long run westward on highway 18, passing through several small towns. One of these, Montfort, was known as Wingville in the 1830s and was built on the military road. Five-and-a-half miles west of Montfort, at the tiny burg of Preston and at a barely discernible dip to the south by route 18, Military Road continues as a straight road across the top of this slight curve. If you happen to catch this slight detour off highway 18 you will be traveling on the more historic alignment for slightly over a mile, when it joins route 18 once again. A person has to turn onto 1st Street for a block in Preston to access the old road.

In Fennimore route 18 takes a northerly jog on U.S. 61 and then resumes its westward journey. I talk about Fennimore in another tour, but if this is your only chance to be in town, I suggest exploring the small railroad museum in town. You will ride right past it while on highway 61.

West of Fennimore highway 18 becomes more enjoyable and scenic as the world begins to rise and fall around you. There are some delightful stretches where hills, curves and scenery combine to make pleasurable motorcycling. Providing a dose of the irony that makes life interesting, things flatten out again near Mount Hope. A few miles west of Mt. Hope, on the north side of the road, is a small roadside park and historical monument to the Old Military Road. This is a good place to take a break and read a bit more about this early trail through the wilderness. West of this small park route 18 remains an enjoyable road, and gets better the further west one rides. In the bluffs just east of the Wisconsin River riding conditions are very rewarding. The road takes a dramatic drop in elevation as it moves from the uplands to the river valley below, going from about 1,250 feet to near 640 feet at the river, according to my GPS unit. Cruising down this long and curvy downhill portion makes for a very enjoyable ride.

Across the river is the town of Bridgeport, which is mentioned in historic accounts as the place where the original military road crossed the Wisconsin River. Once across the river follow highway 18 into Prairie du Chien, turning left on West Broadway Street, taking it west six blocks to Beaumont Street, where a right turn will take you to Rice Street and the Fort Crawford Museum.

The original Fort Crawford was built in 1816 near the shore of the river, after Fort Shelby was captured and destroyed by the British. Floods in the 1820s destroyed that structure, however, so a second fort of the same name was constructed in 1829. This time it was built of stone and situated on higher ground about a mile south of the original fort. The nearby Wyalusing Academy stands today where Fort Crawford stood for the last time. Troops stationed at Fort Crawford took part in the 1832 Black Hawk War, and the fort was to have its brief period of fame when Chief Black Hawk surrendered to Colonel, and future president, Zachary Taylor there in 1832 to end the Black Hawk War. The fort and its garrison served a couple more decades in the role of keeping the peace between settlers and Native American tribes, before being abandoned in 1856. It reopened temporarily in the Civil War for use as a recruiting center and war hospital.

By the time Fort Crawford was closed in 1856 the Old Military Road was already an anachronism. A new and improved system of roads and the railroad network made this meandering trail through the wilderness pointless. But because evolutionary progress occurs one step at a time, even for a country's transportation system, the Old Military Road was a crucial part of Wisconsin's early history and it and similar historic roads in our country should be remembered and celebrated.

I hope you enjoyed this ride through history with the ghosts of those who preceded us—both the great and the small.

 Helmet Hair Quiz Answer
Milk and beer.

This impressive monument to Father Pere Marquette in Prairie du Chien commemorates his reaching the Mississippi in 1673.

Following the Great River

I LOVE IT WHEN MOTORCYCLING roads and rivers team up! All across America this partnership virtually guarantees the qualities we seek in our biking roads, and of scenic backdrops that are icing on the cake. Nature doesn't do straight lines, and rivers are perhaps the best proof of this fact. As a result, roads that follow rivers twist and turn and rise and fall in an intimate dance with the river itself. It's a marriage made in heaven.

An additional bonus when following rivers is the unique cultural and historic mix of the land and communities along the waterway. This is especially true of rivers such as the Ohio, the Missouri, and of course perhaps most of all, the Mississippi. The Illinois Tribe called the Mississippi River *Meschasipi,* meaning *Great River.* Three hundred fifty years ago French explorers and missionaries followed suit and named the river *Mitchisipi ou grand Riviere.* It is truly a grand river and a region with a long history and many stories to tell.

Towns on major waterways are different from those just a few miles inland. Their reason for being is special, and daily life in these communities moved to a different beat.

In this section, we will explore that part of Wisconsin that borders what has been called the father of all rivers, and the adjacent bluff country that was formed over the eons by the Mississippi and its various tributaries. It is a distinctive and uniquely beautiful part of the state, so fill up the tank and explore it in the best way possible; on a motorcycle.

The Heart of the Uplands

Helmet Hair Quiz

Name two foods of which Wisconsin is the nation's number one producer.

SOUTHWESTERN WISCONSIN is one of those regions that bring to mind images of splendor and adventure when mentioned. Nestled as it is in the driftless area with the mighty Mississippi to the west, forested land to the north, and hillside farmlands that have the unique qualities of being among the most beautiful and productive in America to the east, this is one spectacular area. My first motorcycle ride in this part of Wisconsin was about thirty years ago and I must say that the roads and scenery are as enticing to me today as they were all those years ago. Friendly people, natural beauty, great motorcycling roads, and loads of fascinating history make this part of Wisconsin a natural destination for what I like to think of as exploratory motorcycling.

This tour embraces the best of motorcycling. For pure fun, it takes the rider down some of the very best biking roads in the state. However, there is more. This ride also takes bikers through places whose history goes back to the very earliest days of the country's exploration and settlement. This is a land that was formed by the forces of nature and upon which the story of humankind has been boldly written. Though the tour is only 244 miles in length it is another of the several rides in this book that could be ridden in one day that really deserves two days to complete.

Embark on this tour of discovery in the small town of Cassville. The southwest lead mining portion of Wisconsin saw the earliest development while Wisconsin was still part of the Michigan Territory. It made sense that a port on the nearby Mississippi River was needed to efficiently handle the ore being mined in nearby towns such as Mineral Point and Shullsburg. Cassville would serve that need just fine. The town was begun in 1827, being named in honor of Lewis B. Cass, then governor of the Michigan Territory. The Wisconsin Territory was formed in 1836 after Michigan's status as a state of the union became certain. (Interestingly, the spelling was different in 1836, with the new name being Wiskonsan for a short time).

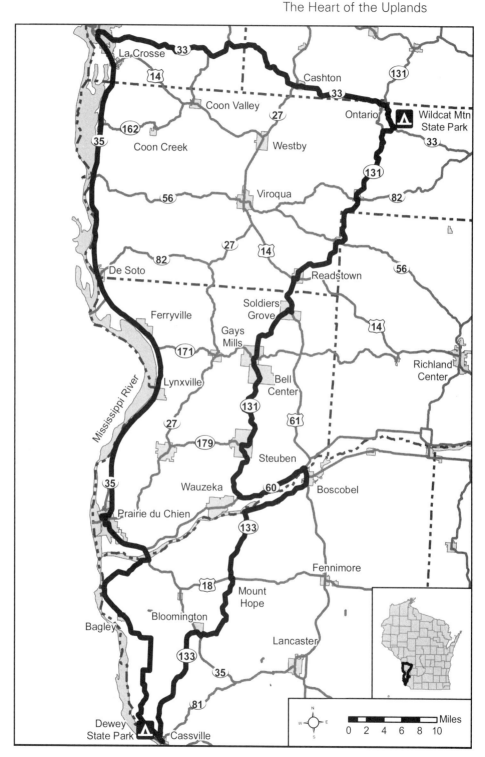

Miles	Destination	Total
00	Cassville	00
35	Prairie cu Chien	35
25	Ferryville	60
36	La Crosse / SR 33	96
28	Cashton	124
25	La Farge	149
18	Soldiers Grove	167
36	Boscobel	203
18	Mt Hope	221
23	Cassville	244

**THE HEART OF THE UPLANDS
244 MILES**

For several months, speculators felt confident that Cassville would soon become capital of the newly formed Wisconsin Territory due to its central location in the Territory (as it looked then). After Madison became the capital hopes were dashed and Cassville never became the metropolis on the river that investors had hoped for. When the first territorial legislature met in Belmont in 1836, Cassville received just one vote less than Madison as the place where the new capital would be established.

A site of interest in downtown Cassville that dates back to 1836 is the Denniston House, a large red brick hotel on the waterfront (commonly referred to as the Big Brick) that builders thought would one day soon house legislators and other officers of the territory in its new capital. The Denniston House stands vacant and for sale today on Front Street after serving for many generations as a hotel under various owners. It was listed on the National Registry of Historic Places in 1974. Across the street (and railroad track) from the Denniston House is a small but very nicely done veterans memorial located on the water's edge.

The riverfront area near Cassville is a prime bald eagle viewing area. This is true year-round, but especially in the winter months, though it's unlikely that most of us will be riding our motorcycles to view eagles in January!

After checking out Cassville go north on route 133 to the north city limits where you'll see county road VV going off to the left front. This is our road, which will very quickly take us to Nelson Dewey State Park, and Stonefield, a Wisconsin Historic Site.

Nelson Dewey was a Connecticut native, born in 1813, who migrated to the new town of Cassville as part of the wave of immigrants seeking to make their fortunes on the land and opportunities that were opening up in this region. Dewey became active in local, and then state politics, and was elected as the first governor of Wisconsin as a compromise candidate in 1848. Dewey was always a major booster for the Cassville area and he bought a two thousand acre estate just north of town that he named Stonefield. His dream home extended from the edge of the Mississippi River up over the bluffs and consisted of some cropland, orchards, and a vineyard. He also raised cattle and imported horses. By 1868 he completed a handsome mansion that was called a "palace in the wilderness." It must have been like heaven on earth; his realm amongst the magnificent bluffs, prairies and forests along the Mighty Mississip'.

Mrs. Dewey, however, did not enjoy living in what was in reality a wild and unsophisticated area, and when their daughter was ready for college mother and daughter moved to Madison and they never returned to Cassville.

On a snowy day in January 1873, fire swept through Dewey's dream home, and a financial panic that same year drove him into bankruptcy. He died a pauper in 1889 in the Denniston House, which ironically was part of the venture that first brought him to Cassville, and in which he had earlier invested heavily. Dewey's own home stood in ruins until Walter Newberry of Chicago bought the land and restored the house. Using the foundation and standing walls of the house, he had it reconstructed but in a significantly different style and size than the original. Today we can see Newberry's version of the Dewey mansion in Stonefield. The Nelson Dewey State Park and the Stonefield historic site sit on much of the land that was Dewey's estate.

If you're interested in antique farm equipment and the way of life of late 1800s and early 1900s rural Wisconsin, Stonefield is an enjoyable stop. It houses the state agricultural museum, with its amazing collection of farm machinery from a hundred years ago.

The first few miles of CR-VV are very enjoyable, though it straightens out when the road turns inland for a bit. Ride CR-VV north to the point where the road "Ts" at CR-A. Head west on A and follow this scenic road into the small town of Bagley. On the north edge of this village we pick up CR-X (Bagley Avenue in town) and follow it close to the riverfront as it winds its way north to the village of Wyalusing. The bluffs in this area are fabulous, especially just north of the burg of Wyalusing. Here, dramatic stone cliffs jut out at the water's edge,

Natural beauty and enjoyable roads make a wonderful partnership along the Mississippi River.

doing a serious impression of coastal Oregon. This entire area is very scenic and makes for great riding.

County road-X winds around the picturesque perimeter of Wyalusing State Park and then straightens out and goes east. After a short distance you'll see CR-C going north to U.S.-18, (just follow the Great River Road signs along this stretch, and watch for the Dew Drop Inn at this corner) and this is where we also want to turn.

After a short but nice ride on CR-C we finally arrive at route 18,where a left turn will carry us across the Wisconsin River, through the town of Bridgeport, and into Prairie du Chien, a city with lots of stories to tell, things to see, and history to share.

What might be considered the modern history of Prairie du Chien began on June 17, 1673. That's the day that Father Pere Marquette and Louis Jolliet floated down the Wisconsin River and entered the Mississippi River at this site. They were the first known non-native persons to see the upper Mississippi. The French gave the unusual name to the site because the Fox Indian tribe lived on the prairie at the juncture of the two rivers.

Prairie du Chien soon grew into a key trading post where voyageurs and Native Americans met to trade for furs and manufactured goods. The British took over the region following the French and Indian War's end in 1763. Following the American War of Independence, the Treaty of Paris of 1783, and then Jay's Treaty in 1794, the Americans took control of this region and other strategic forts and cities in the Great Lakes and Upper Mississippi River region.

The U.S. government built Fort Shelby to establish a presence and claim sovereignty of the area. The only War of 1812 battle in Wisconsin was fought at the fort in 1814. A force of British and Indians, under command of Major William McKay captured the fort, renaming it Fort McKay in what is officially referred to as the Battle of Prairie du Chien. The American force was organized in St. Louis, Missouri and moved north on the river under command of Zachary Taylor and William Clark. The British force came from Fort Mackinac located on Mackinac Island in the straits between Lakes Huron and Michigan, in what is now northern Michigan.

What I find remarkable about this battle is the distance and considerable trouble that both sides endured to hold this vital piece of real estate. The Americans and British both understood the strategic importance of the Fox / Wisconsin / Mississippi River water highway, and they certainly fully grasped the present and future military and economic consequences of losing control of the Great Lakes and Mississippi River to the other side. This vast region had to be controlled or the expectations of each country were in jeopardy.

The British did not want an emerging America to gain a foothold in the northwest, and the Americans did not want the British to hold Prairie du Chien as they could then easily launch an attack on St. Louis, which by then was rapidly becoming a major jumping off point for western exploration and settlement. The British victory in June 1814 was short lived, however, and the tide of the war turned following American victories in other major battles. The war soon ended with the Treaty of Ghent in December 1814, and American sovereignty in the Great Lakes and Mississippi River valley would never again be seriously challenged by a foreign power. The Brits burned Fort Shelby prior to vacating it in 1815.

Fort Crawford, another wood compound, was built at essentially the same location as Fort Shelby in 1816 but floods in the 1820s destroyed the structure. For a few years no soldiers were stationed at Prairie du Chien, but in 1827 Winnebago Chief Red Bird led a brief uprising which resulted in the death of some settlers, causing the federal government to once again send troops here to secure the area. A second Fort Crawford was constructed in 1829, but this time it was built of stone and situated on higher ground about a mile south. Troops stationed at Fort Crawford took part in the 1832 Black Hawk War, and it was at this fort that Chief Black Hawk surrendered to Colonel Zachary Taylor to end the Black Hawk War.

Fort Crawford's story is preserved in a museum located at the corner of Beaumont and Rice Streets, just west of route 18. Of the various displays at the museum, one that I find fascinating is a section of the actual iron bars that were on the window of an upper level room at the fort where prisoners were kept. Chief Black Hawk had been kept in that room after his surrender. In one of those events that proves what a small and intertwined world we live in, Lt. Jefferson Davis, who was station at Fort Crawford, was charged with delivering Chief Black Hawk to St. Louis, Missouri, where the Chief spent some time in custody. Davis of course would become president of the Confederate States of America less than thirty years later. It was at Fort Crawford that Jefferson Davis met and fell in love with Sarah Knox Taylor, the daughter of Colonel, and future U.S. president, Zachary Taylor. The Colonel never approved of the relationship, thinking that the life of an army wife on the frontier was too harsh for his daughter. Davis resigned his military commission and the couple married in Kentucky in 1835. Tragically, Sarah died only three months later from malaria. Her death hit Davis and her parents very hard, and they were bitter antagonists for several years. Davis ultimately reenlisted in the Army after remarrying in 1845. In an amazing turn of events he once again fought under Zachary Taylor, this time in the Mexican American War in 1847.

‹‹‹‹◉››››

Most of the fascinating history that occurred in Prairie du Chien was on St. Feriole Island. Immediately adjacent to the river, this locale was the base of the fur trade for many decades. This is where the Battle of Prairie du Chien took place, and it was the location of the first Fort Crawford. Ironically, it was a fairly large ancient Indian mound on the island that provided some high ground for the earliest explorers and soldiers.

To get to the island from the Fort Crawford museum continue west on Rice Street to Main Street, and turn right at this T intersection. Follow Main Street north, past historic Wyalusing Academy, across busy route 18, which carries traffic across the Mississippi River into Iowa, to Blackhawk Avenue and the entry of this island park.

Two attractions to see on the island today are Villa Louis, a mansion built in 1870 that became Wisconsin's first state historic site in 1952. Near Villa Louis is the Brisbois Store and Fur Museum. This stone building was built in 1851 by a fur trader and like Villa Louis is also on the National Register of Historic Places. The museum chronicles an important part of Wisconsin's early history.

Of interest to military buffs is the annual re-enactment of the War of 1812 Battle of Prairie du Chien on St. Feriole Island. Learn more of this event by calling 608.326.2721 or go to wisconsinhistory.org/villalouis.

When done exploring St.Feriole Island and Prairie du Chien, continue north on fabled route 35, aka The Great River Road. This road between Prairie du Chien and the LaCrosse area is nothing short of fabulous. It is a designated National Scenic Highway that won't disappoint. You want great scenery? How about forested hills and rock cliffs on your right, while frequent glimpses of the mighty Mississippi River offer enchanting views to your left! Want variety in terrain and road characteristics? Then hills and curves served up on smooth pavement with light traffic and as many motorcycles as four-wheeled vehicles to share the road with should keep you in high spirits! This is a destination road that bikers travel from far and wide for the opportunity to ride, so if you live close enough to ride it frequently consider yourself truly blessed.

A Corps of Engineers campground in Black Hawk Park near DeSoto offers a unique opportunity to camp on the river's edge if an overnight stop is in your travel plans. In this facility are also historical markers that tell the story of the bloody Battle of Bad Axe, the final battle of the Black Hawk War.

Several historical markers and scenic overlooks are located along route 35 in this vicinity and I suggest a stop at each to learn about the area's history and to marvel at its scenic and geologic wonders.

On the south side of LaCrosse U.S. 61 joins route 35 and takes us into this energetic city of 52,000. The city sprang up from humble beginnings in 1841 when a fur trader went upriver to set up his own fur business away from the crowded fur markets of Prairie du Chien. The geographic site had been named back in 1765 when Zebulon Pike explored the area. He gave the name Prairie La Crosse after seeing Native Americans playing a game (lacrosse) with sticks shaped like a bishop's crozier or cross.

This fertile prairie between the river to the west and high bluffs to the east was a natural place for settlement and development, and the fact that two rivers joined the Mississippi from inland Wisconsin further enhanced this young community's future as a major river port.

A couple fun things to do in La Crosse include checking out the S & S Cycle facility on Causeway Boulevard west from route 53 about a mile north of the U.S. 61 / 14 bridge to Minnesota. Along the riverfront, you will also see some paddlewheel cruise boats at the docks. Two companies at the port just north of the 14 / 61 bridge offer a wide variety of cruise opportunities—from multi-day trips up and down the river to short cruises of an hour or two. La Crosse Queen Cruises can be reached at 608.784.2893 and the Great River Steamboat Company at 800.815.1005.

We all have our "wish list" of places to visit or activities that we hope to do one day, and one of the items still on mine is a long cruise on a paddle wheeler on the mighty Mississippi. Over the years, I have watched these boats sailing the river from port cities as diverse as Natchez, Memphis, St. Louis, La Crosse, Minneapolis and more, but have never taken a ride on one. I intend to achieve this goal one day soon.

We depart La Crosse eastbound on state route 33, riding into the bluffs and beautiful rolling landscape located just east of town. Route 33 in town takes us through an older part of La Crosse and the many aged buildings speak to the history of this river port city.

If you ride a bike that takes premium fuel, I recommend topping off the tank before leaving La Crosse. The route we will be taking doesn't have a lot of gas stations, and my experience is that the few that are encountered sell only regular and mid-grade fuels. I'm not sure why this is the situation but that's what I have found.

The fact that a person climbs in elevation a significant degree from the floodplain of the Mississippi to the plateau tablelands to the east becomes very apparent with a long uphill climb out of the city. Route 33 is a bit rough in this stretch due to settling of the concrete, but it is a short ride on the uneven concrete. Once on the top of the ridge there is a scenic overlook with a marker explaining the geology of the area and of the formation of coulees so common in southwest Wisconsin. This is a nice place to stop to not only learn a little geology but also to gaze upon the marvelous vistas that surround you.

As we ride east on 33 the countryside opens up for a bit with lush farmland being the main feature. Our road follows the high ground in much of this area making for some very nice scenic views. As you ride through the village of St. Joseph, notice the striking Sisters of St. Joseph Abbey and the handsome stone grotto in front. A bit further east another fine-looking hilltop church is found in the crossroads village of Middle Ridge.

We continue east on this delightfully fun road as it dips, turns, and dances across the countryside. Traffic is light on route 33 as it isn't one of the main east / west routes for the region, and it carries mainly local traffic. Beware that the presence of Amish buggies increases as you work your way east on route 33.

East of the town of Cashton things really pick up. The countryside becomes noticeably more wooded, and the road even more enjoyable as it dips into a river valley and follows the twists and turns of Upper Brush Creek. However, this is nothing compared to the biking fantasy just ahead. Beyond the village of Ontario route 33 enters Wildcat State Park, and what is a fun road becomes fabulous. The narrow pavement twists like an out of control pretzel as it steadily climbs through the densely wooded landscape. It is the kind of road where many of us have been known to turn around and run it two or three times just because it is so enjoyable. If you like hairpin curves, you will love this portion of route 33!

Just as the road starts to calm down a bit, you will see county road F going off to your right. Turn onto F, a very nice biking road in its own right, and ride it west two miles to its junction with state route 131—yet one more of southwest Wisconsin's storied motorcycling roads.

Route 131 begins our southward portion of the trip. It's a ride through fabulous countryside on a road that one couldn't be blamed for thinking it was made primarily for the sport of motorcycling as it closely follows the meanderings of the nearby Kickapoo River. This delightful road is our riding partner all the way south to the Wisconsin River and route 60; and you won't find a disappointing mile between here and there. What with the curves, hills, great scenery, light traffic and wonderful overall ambience of the road, the only negative I can report is that the pavement is starting to get a little rough in spots. I hope that the state will do some repaving soon to make things perfect once again. In any event, just kick back and enjoy a wonderful ride for many miles. If you are feeling extremely hungry at this point consider a stop at the Rockton Bar, but don't go there for a light snack or low calorie left coast frou-frou. Their portions are generous and the quality is great (and you will get all the calories you will need to burn to get through the remainder of this trip). The restaurant is on 131 at a wide spot in the road not too far south of CR-F.

⋘◆⋙

About midway between Ontario and route 60 is Soldiers Grove. A historical marker there explains that this site was an encampment for soldiers pursuing Chief Black Hawk in 1832 and that the name of the town was changed in 1867 to reflect this history. Soldiers Grove has another story to tell that involves the Kickapoo River, which flows through town. Over the years the village has had a series of devastating floods. After the flood of 1978 the village essentially moved uphill a bit. Then in 2007 the largest flood ever hit the community again, but it flooded only open lands and parks, and the main part of the new town on high ground was spared.

Of course, there is an obvious lesson here that people seem to be unable to comprehend. That is—don't build on floodplains! Rivers flood—they always have and always will. What is it about this reality that we so-called intelligent humans don't seem to be able to grasp?

Interestingly, thirty years ago the dam builders thought they had the answer to the natural seasonal fluctuations of the beautiful Kickapoo. A dam was to be built upstream near Lafarge, and it was thought that this would forever tame this wild and scenic river. Public outcry over the idea ultimately killed it, even though the federal government had spent almost twenty million dollars on a dam that was never completed. Today this stream continues to wind in its deep valley through forested hillsides as it has for millennia. It remains one of the state's favorite canoeing rivers.

The Kickapoo received its name from the Indian tribe of the same name that occupied this part of Wisconsin prior to European settlement. It is fitting that this beautiful stream was spared being forever tamed by a dam. It is one of those wild and free rivers that shouldn't have to be controlled and diminished. We should instead learn to live with it. Many people have marveled at the beauty of the Kickapoo, but perhaps nobody else has penned a poem to its graces as eloquently as Reverend William Haughton did back in 1882. His words are as true today as when he fell in love with the river all those years ago. An excerpt follows:

> *O Beautiful Kickapoo*
> *When Heaven's creative hand was laid,*
> *Upon those gorgeous hills*
> *In emerald sheen and gold arrayed,*
> *And cleft by flashing rills,*
> *Is traced in beauty mead and dale*
> *With charms forever new,*
> *But left its blessing on the vale*
> *Where flows the Kickapoo.*
> *O favored land! No foot hath trod*
> *Through fairer paths than thine,*
> *Where hills uplift their crests to God,*
> *And speak his power divine;*
> *Where valleys breathe of peace and rest*
> *Fresh as the morning dew.*

Eventually we arrive at route 60, and while the Kickapoo joins with the mighty Wisconsin River at this point and the water flows west, we turn east on route 60. Because 60 is located on the flood plain of the Wisconsin River it has a different character than route 131. Gone are the sharp curves and hills, replaced by a gentler form of meandering. However, this is not to say that route 60 isn't an enjoyable motorcycling road; indeed it is. On the south side of the road the land is almost totally publicly owned, being part of the Lower Wisconsin State Riverway. As such, both sides of the river are protected from development encroaching into the river's natural course. The normal rise and fall of the river out of its banks and across the floodplain continues as it has since the time when glaciers covered the land just north of here and the Wisconsin River received melt water from the mile thick ice. To your left forested hills rise to form the broad river valley that contained all this water for the last ten thousand or more years.

Route 60 is a very enjoyable biking road, and the fact that this stretch has been newly paved makes the joy of two wheels even more complete. We cross over to the south side of the river on route 61, immediately entering the town of Boscobel—also known as the wild turkey hunting capital of Wisconsin. You will see a lot of wildlife all along this ride, especially in the low lands along the Wisconsin River, where turkeys, deer, and waterfowl are common.

From Boscobel we head south on state route 133. Not too far west of Boscobel is the small town of Woodman, which is of note because it was the terminus of the narrow gauge railroad that ran out of Fennimore called The Dinky.

Once we leave the vicinity of the river and travel south the land gradually changes from heavily wooded to mostly farmland. The ride becomes a pleasant trip through a part of Wisconsin that many of us find appealing—the appeal of open roads, rolling farm fields, blue skies stretching to the horizons, and a tranquil feeling that all is well with the world.

At U.S. 18 we take a very short jog to the east and continue south on CR-J into the village of Mount Hope. Continue south out of Mount Hope on J for five-and-a-half miles where it "T's" at CR-A. Turn right on A and ride it west four miles to the town of Bloomington. These two county roads are enjoyable rural roads where you will likely be the only vehicle on the blacktop. They wind their way through the hills and dales of attractive farms while following small creeks, which of course always adds to the scenic and riding qualities of a road.

In Bloomington we need to turn right onto route 35 for less than a mile where it joins with route 133. Turn left onto route 133 and let the fun continue as you ride back to Cassville and the end of yet another fun and enlightening ride through one of the prettiest parts of a state overflowing with beauty.

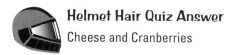

Helmet Hair Quiz Answer
Cheese and Cranberries

Pioneer Stories

Helmet Hair Quiz

Where is the Unidentified Flying Objects capital of Wisconsin?

IT IS IMPOSSIBLE TO GET TOO MUCH of the marvelous motorcycling opportunities found in western Wisconsin. Whether it's the coulee country of southwestern Wisconsin or the lakes and forests of the northwest, the entire region is nothing short of magical. This ride will prove beyond any doubt that western Wisconsin is where Courier and Ives depictions of beautiful rural America are mated with motorcycling.

Beginning in Fountain City on Old Man River, we will explore the beauty and marvelous byways of the Mississippi River valley, and then go inland to discover the charms of roads that wind through a montage of some of nature's most beautiful offerings.

We begin our tour in Fountain City, tight on the banks of the Mississippi. Fountain City is a logical place to begin as it is one of the oldest places on the river, first settled when others were just beginning to explore this region by water. A small group led by a hardy entrepreneur by the name of Thomas Holmes settled here in 1839 to trade with the local Indians and to cut wood that steamboats burned as they began plying the river. The site was initially called Holmes Landing, and in 1854 it was platted to create the village of Fountain City—because of the many natural springs found nearby.

Every person or community will capitalize on unique attributes or occurrences that happen to them, and this village is no exception. In 1995, a 55-ton boulder fell off a cliff onto a house 400 feet below. Fortunately, nobody was injured, but it did open the door of opportunity and the Rock In The House (as opposed of course to the House On The Rock) tourist attraction was born. The house is located on the north edge of Fountain City, where a small sign points the way. A real estate agent bought the house, which is vacant except for the occasional tourist who paid a dollar to walk in the home to look at the huge boulder in the master bedroom.

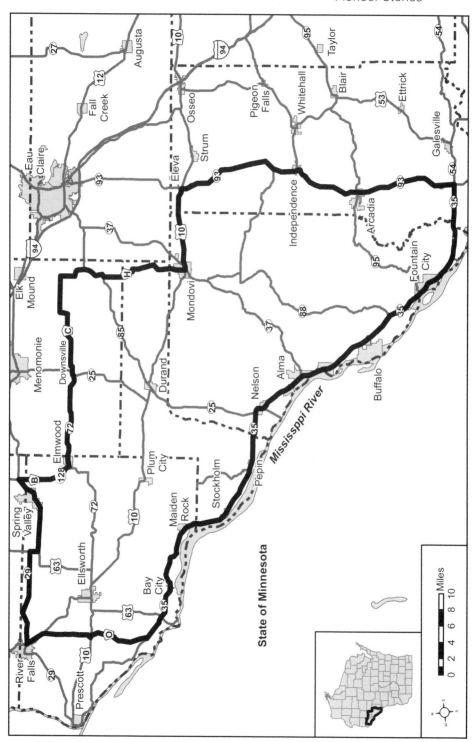

PIONEER STORIES 216 MILES		
Miles	**Destination**	**Total**
00	Fountain City	00
36	Pepin	36
22	Bay City	58
25	River Falls	83
18	Crystal Cave	101
54	Mondovi / U.S. 10	155
27	Independence	182
34	Fountain City	216

This area is one of the most striking along the entire length of the river, and we are going to enjoy it on the Great River Road—route 35. Two miles north of town is Merrick State Park, offering camping and recreation on the shores of the river. Just north of the park is Eagle Bluff, at 550 feet the highest point on the upper Mississippi. Fabulous views are afforded from atop this bedrock mount.

For the first roughly ten miles there is a broad plain between the road and the river, but the bluffs are tight against route 35 on the east side. Near the north end of this stretch we will pass by the town of Buffalo, beyond that the strip of land on which we are riding between the hills and the river becomes very narrow. Spectacular views of both are again the order of the day for mile after scenic mile.

There are of course many places along the river road to pull over at scenic overlooks, but if you want one that provides a marvelous view of a lock and dam system, you can't do better than in Alma. Buena Vista Park in Alma provides a bird's eye view of the river and the lock system. Go east on CR-E a few blocks to Buena Vista Drive, then left to the top of the hill in the park. It will be worth the short ride.

The tour continues for many marvelous miles with views that will never fail to amaze. Things that make a strong impression continue to induce the same powerful feelings for years to come. I can still clearly recall the first motorcycle trip I took on this road in the late 1970s. Riding an XS750 Yamaha (a very cool Triumph-like triple) with everything I needed for a week on the road securely lashed behind me with bungee cords, I had the trip of a lifetime. My head was swiveling left and right so much I should have developed a bad case of muscle cramps, but

*Stupendous views are the norm along the Mississippi River,
resulting in frequent stops.*

I just wanted to take in all the marvelous scenes of bluffs, forests and river. My young bones didn't complain about sleeping on the hard ground with just a cheap sleeping bag, as I immersed myself in the physical beauty of this marvelous region as fully as I could. I have never lost that same sense of awe whenever I am fortunate enough to ride or drive along the Mighty Mississippi. In fact, that trip and hundreds since serve to remind me of one of the fundamental differences between seeing the world around us from inside a car versus on a motorcycle. In a car, we are passive observers. On a motorcycle, we are active participants. We are a part of the action, not just passing through it.

Eventually we arrive in the small town of Pepin, perhaps still best known by most people as the birthplace of author Laura Ingalls Wilder. The countryside north of Pepin was the location for her early life as told in the *Big Woods* stories. There is a small museum in town right along route 35 if you don't want to ride out of town several miles to see the log cabin replica. A small railroad museum is adjacent to the Wilder museum, and there is a small park in front, providing a handy place to take a break from the road.

Pepin's small museum tells a large story about the region's frontier days.

North of Pepin I encourage riders not to be in too much of a rush, and take the time to stop at a couple of scenic overlooks and historical markers. The first overlook provides a marvelous view, as does the second, but that one is across from Lake City, MN, which spoils the view a bit. A historical marker 3 miles north of Pepin tells the story of Fort St. Antoine, built in 1686 by Nicholas Perrot to stake a claim for French sovereignty over this region. This was in response to British inroads along the Mississippi and upper Great Lakes areas. Other historical markers along route 35 north of Pepin tell the story of this region's long and fascinating history.

The riding is great for many miles. Upon arriving at Hager City and U.S. 63 the terrain changes and traffic picks up, so we are going to leave route 35 for improved motorcycling opportunities.

About three miles beyond route 63 you will find county road O. At this corner there is a high rock cliff, and atop the cliff is a high-flying American flag. Turn right onto CR-O, a designated scenic road, for miles of fabulous riding. This fun road closely follows the meanderings of the Trimbelle River through a heavily forested expanse. Enjoy the marvelous isolation and beauty of the area as you waltz through the curves. After several miles you will reach the crossroads village of Trimbelle at U.S. 10. Jog west just a block or two and proceed north on CR-O once again. The second half of CR-O is a bit more sedate than that south of U.S. 10, but it is a very nice road in its own right. Eventually 'O' will end at route 65, where a left turn toward River Falls is in order. In less than three miles route 65 will intersect with route 29, on the east side of River Falls. Turn right onto route 29, and leave the urban congestion of this small college town behind. We will be on route 29 about 19 very enjoyable miles. Though this isn't a hyper-caffeinated Type A road, it is nevertheless a perfectly enjoyable ride through scenic surroundings as it takes us to the town of Spring Valley and out next attraction. Spring Valley is a small town seemingly taken out of a picture book. It is a pleasant village in a very scenic setting, situated as it is in a river valley with wooded hills on either side. On the west edge of town you will see the sign for Crystal Cave, which claims to be Wisconsin's longest cave. This privately owned cavern is open for tours during the motorcycling season. If you enjoy exploring the underground, check them out at acoolcave.com or 800.236.CAVE.

Continue east on route 29 once you are finished doing whatever your heart desires in Spring Valley, and soon you will come to the 4-way stop at route 128. Turn right at this corner and begin another superb biking adventure. Route 128 is great. There is minimal competition for lane space, the road has many traits that will endear it to serious motorcyclists, and the landscape along the road is appealing. Moreover, it gets better the closer to the town of Elmwood that one gets. Elmwood is another small town off the beaten path that will take you back in time. While there, stop at Twiggy's Long Branch Bar for a burger if the time is right. We join up with route 72 in Elmwood and it becomes our riding partner for many enjoyable clicks east across the countryside to route 25. Turn left on 25 for a couple blocks, across the Red Cedar River, to County Road C and the village of Downsville. Turn right on 'C' through Downsville, then east close to fourteen miles as the road makes frequent curves and clearly marked jogs. The first portion of the trip on 'C' is very scenic and geologically interesting with bedrock walls frequent sights along the road, then it suddenly flattens out into lush farmlands for the last 4 miles. This obvious demarcation in the landscape just happens to mark the boundary between the western upland and central plain geologic regions.

A bit less than 14 miles east of Downsville CR-C intersects with CR-H—our next road. We'll be on 'H' for many miles, across the Chippewa River, and then a short stint partnering with route 85, then on its own again, this time more enjoyable than ever as it twists and turns all the way south to the town of Mondovi. The city of Mondovi sits in a very scenic and fertile area, thanks to the presence of the Buffalo River, and two creeks that converge with the river in town. When first

Exploring caves and caverns is a unique way to cool off on a hot summer day.

explored by prospective settlers the Buffalo River valley was known as Pancake Valley. These early explorers described the river valley as a very desirable place to settle, with abundant water and fertile lands for farming. The original settlers named the up and coming village Mondovi in 1858. Interestingly, the name was selected because it was the site of a 1796 battle in Italy at which Napoleon fought and prevailed against the Kingdom of Sardinia. My guess is that an early village founder had a family connection to that battle or to Sardinia itself.

At the 4-way stop sign in Mondovi turn left onto U.S. 10, taking it ten miles east to Eleva and state route 93. Highway Ten in this stretch is an okay road. It is mostly open countryside and traffic is quite light.

Route 93 will guide us south many miles; all the way to the town of Arcadia. This road is a relaxed ride with almost constant graceful curves along its entire distance. The land gets quite hilly for the first several miles as you ride south. As is common in this part of the state, the road is in a valley, following Chimney Rock

Creek and then Elk Creek, with hills in the near distance. South of the village of Independence, the road closely follows the Trempealeau River in a fairly broad river valley.

Our next stop is Arcadia. This small city is aptly named. The word not only refers to a region in Greece, but more fitting for our use is the definition of the word as being a place of rural peace and contentment. This handsome region certainly qualifies in that regard. Before leaving town, a person really should stop at Memorial Park and walk the Avenue of Heroes. This park honors America's fighting men and women, and the displays and statuary are what one would expect to find on the Mall in Washington D.C. Displays also commemorate the history of the region. It is an unforgettable experience to stroll through the park and you won't regret the time spent doing it. To get there go west on route 95 to Pearl Street and turn left / south. You will run right into the park after a few blocks.

Continuing south of Arcadia on route 93 is where good motorcycling gets even better. Just south of town the road climbs to over 1,200 feet, and then follows a ridgeline for a couple miles. Following this spectacular stretch of road it then makes a roller coaster run that will leave you grinning broadly. The scenery south of Arcadia is beautiful with magnificent vistas from atop the hills. As I said, the name Arcadia is very fitting.

As we approach route 35 things get straight and flatter for the last mile. At the intersection with routes 35 / 54 turn right, as this is our ticket back to Fountain City and the end of this splendid ride.

Helmet Hair Quiz Answer

Belleville—located in Dane County, south of Madison. The town has a UFO Days celebration every year.

Indianhead Country

Helmet Hair Quiz

Wisconsin's first newspaper, *The Intelligencer*, was begun in what city and in what year?

THE NORTHWEST PORTION of Wisconsin that follows the St. Croix River is called Indianhead Country because the border resembles the profile of an Indian chief, or so somebody once noted, and the name has since stuck. I kind of see the likeness so it makes sense to me.

Though by any definition this tour is in northern Wisconsin, this neck of the woods has a different look than areas to the east and north. It is less forested and has better soil for agriculture. In fact, the area straight north of Menomonie, our starting point, is predominantly farmlands. About half of the ride, in the north-

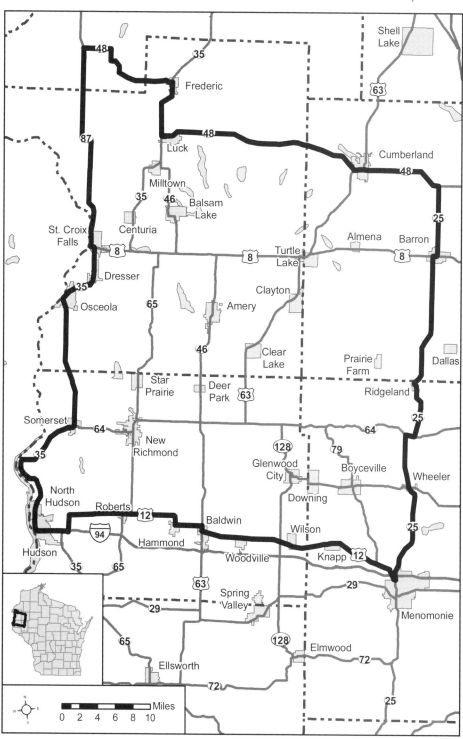

INDIANHEAD COUNTRY 204 MILES		
Miles	Destination	Total
00	Menomonie	00
39	Barron / U.S. 8	39
43	Luck / CR-N	82
40	St. Croix Falls	122
17	Somerset	139
16	Hudson	155
24	Baldwin	179
25	Menomonie	204

west portion, is in lake country and has all the charms that come with roads and landscape that share space with many lakes.

Our excursion takes us north on route 25 for many miles, in fact all the way north to route 48. Route 25 is pleasant and enjoyable, though somewhat subdued. It traverses a primarily agricultural region, but traffic isn't heavy and the road and surroundings are agreeable. Some stretches of 25 are more scenic and fun to ride because of hills and curves, and others are straighter and essentially flat.

At route 48 turn left and follow it into Cumberland, the island city. This locale grows a lot of specialty vegetables and a large Libby's plant processes and cans them for distant markets.

West of Cumberland route 48 enters lake country and the riding is quite enjoyable as we follow the twists and turns of the meandering pavement. Route 48 joins forces with highway 35 for several miles south of Frederic, and then works its way west again to SR 87. This stretch is very nice as the road winds among the many lakes. It is also a bit hillier and more wooded.

Route 87 south all the way to St. Croix Falls is quite nice. It is a pleasant mix of nicely rolling land and lakes, with enough forestland thrown in to keep it from being overwhelmingly farmland. The town of St. Croix Falls is a good place to park and stretch your legs, enjoying the scenic river. Crossing the bridge over to Minnesota to view the St. Croix Dalles will take just a couple of minutes, and I think the view is better from the west side of the river.

Upon leaving St. Croix Falls go east on U.S. 8 a very short distance to route 35, which will carry us south again.

The Cascade Falls are worth a visit, offering a chance to stretch your legs and enjoy this natural area.

In the town of Osceola you should park along the street next to Wilke Park and walk the 156 steps down to the valley bottom to view Cascade Falls and dawdle a bit. It is an easy walk and a nice diversion. Our road is a pleasing ride south through primarily agricultural lands, though the scenery is good and the ride relaxing and enjoyable.

Unfortunately, stretches of route 35 south of Somerset have been upgraded and it is no longer the enjoyable road I remember from many years ago when I rode it for the first time. The divided four-lane highway has neither the soul nor sex appeal of a wonderfully winding and undulating two-laner through an untarnished area.

Route 35 isn't completely tamed and there is no shortage of motorcycling enjoyment as we work our way south to Hudson. You may have noticed that in several of my rides I have cautioned against making the tour a large-group event. This particular ride is one that is custom made for larger groups. The landscape and road conditions are expansive for the most part, light traffic except near the I-94 expressway in the vicinity of Menonomie and Hudson, and not many stops make this a good tour for larger groups.

In Hudson a highly recommended stop is to go one block west to River Front Park. This is a nice place to view the St. Croix River and better yet, take a walk across the 1913 pedestrian bridge. It started life as a toll bridge, but of course the need for such a bridge was nullified after construction of the mega-bridges that span the river today.

Riverboats berth at the south end of the park providing an enjoyable river cruise if the notion should strike.

We're going to follow U.S. 12 east back to Menomonie. In the immediate Hudson vicinity this requires a short ride on I-94. Just follow the signs. Once on 12 east of Hudson the riding is surprisingly nice. Because of the nearby X-Way traffic is very light on the old road, and it passes through a lot of wooded lands with interspersed farms, all situated on a nicely rolling landscape.

Arrival at Menomonie ends this enjoyable and relaxing 204-mile long day ride. My regards to the Indian Chief.

Helmet Hair Quiz Answer
The Intelligencer was first printed in Green Bay in the year 1833.

Cruising the St. Croix River is an enjoyable and relaxing way to see this very scenic waterway.

Southeastern Odyssey

I AM A STRONG BELIEVER that a person can enjoy motorcycling in all regions of the state, not just the most rural or scenic. Each part of Wisconsin offers enjoyable motorcycling with all the ingredients a biker desires; great roads, scenery, attractions, good friends, and places to explore along the way. The largely urban southeast corner of Wisconsin is no exception.

Not only are there delightful country roads and surroundings to please even the most discriminating motorcyclist, there are also lighthouses, maritime museums, and other lakeshore attractions that one doesn't find in most of the country. Don't sell this corner of the state short, it offers fabulous motorcycling potential as these next three tours will confirm.

Wind Point Lighthouse

The Gold Coast

Helmet Hair Quiz

Name five famous people from the entertainment and arts sector that were born in Wisconsin.

OUR NEXT RIDE TAKES us through perhaps the most diverse part of Wisconsin—the southeastern corner. This 271-mile tour, which I recommend taking two days to complete because of the many sites to visit and things to do, takes us through two very different features of Wisconsin; the most urbanized region, and some of the most scenic landscapes in the state.

We begin this tour of southeastern Wisconsin in the progressive and cool city of Kenosha. With a population of about 100,000, it is the fourth largest city in Wisconsin. It is a community that is large enough to provide innovative services and institutions, while at the same time maintaining a small town atmosphere. I suggest spending some time here prior to setting off on the ride, to get to know this interesting town better. For starters, take a ride on an electric streetcar; there aren't many places where one can do that today. They serve the downtown and shoreline areas and while they perform a very necessary people mover function they are also the city's top tourist attraction according to some reports.

Kenosha's history goes back to the earliest days of the Wisconsin Territory, with the first settlement named Pike in 1836. Settlers derived this name from the Pottawatomie word *Gnozhe,* which roughly translated to 'place of the Pike'. Spawning fish in the river and lakeshore were an important source of food during the spring for local Indians. Because it was the most southerly port in Wisconsin the town was later renamed Southport—a name still used in portions of the city. In the 1850s residents changed the name once again to Kenosha, an anglicized version of the original Native American place name.

No exploration of Kenosha is complete without a trip to the waterfront, where you will find Harbor Park and Simmons Island. From route 32 head east on 57th Street, through the old downtown area, and out to Harbor Park. Old timers in Kenosha will remember when this area was an unsightly industrial brownfield site following the closure of American Motors (remember the Rambler?) and Chrysler

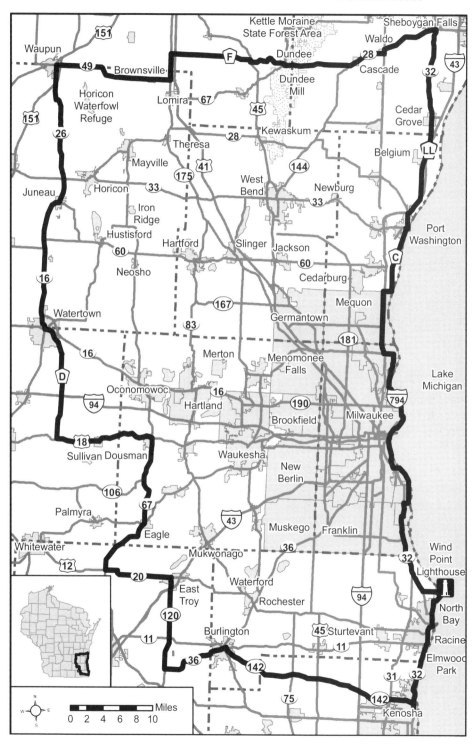

THE GOLD COAST 271 MILES		
Miles	**Destination**	**Total**
00	Kenosha	00
25	Burlington	25
19	East Troy	44
27	Dousman / U.S. 18	71
25	Watertown	96
33	Waupun	129
32	Dundee	161
31	Cedar Grove	192
33	Fox Point	225
32	Wind Point Lighthouse	257
14	Kenosha	271

factories. To say that the entire waterfront has enjoyed revitalization would be a fine example of understatement. The park and lakefront is a gem, attracting thousands to fish, walk its paths, picnic, and lounge near the fountain while the kids play in the child-friendly cascade, or just lay in the grass to read a book. Moreover, you will not only find the usual lakeshore attractions such as lighthouses, walking paths, and piers, but two highly recommend nearby museums. The Kenosha Public Museum includes a Wooly Mammoth skeleton that was unearthed in Kenosha in 1992. The new Civil War Museum is a one-of-a-kind facility exploring that pivotal event in our country's history, and its impact at both the local and national levels. This is a new facility and a portion is already open to the public. Both of these museums are located at the north side of Harbor Park. There is plenty of free parking in Harbor Park near the museums to be able to park the bike in one place and walk throughout the entire area.

<<<<◈>>>>

Following the lakeside street (6th Avenue) around to the north will take you to 50th Street and the bridge to Simmons Island. This is a hopping place in the summer! At the south end of the island are the old 1866 Southport Lighthouse and the adjacent keeper's house. The city of Kenosha now owns the facility, and the house is undergoing restoration to return it to its original condition. The tower is occasionally open for tours but the park and grounds are open at all times. Call the city at 262.654.5770 for tour schedules.

The Dinosaur Museum, located on Tenth Avenue, one block west of route 32, is a walk through a skeletal Jurassic Park, and admittance is free!

To begin our ride we are going to take route 32 north to Washington Street, heading west. A good gathering place for group rides is the Big Star Drive-In restaurant on Washington Street just west of SR 32. Washington

Christopher Columbus is depicted gazing toward new western horizons atop a fountain in Kenosha's Harbor Park.

Street becomes County Road S west of the city, morphing into state route 142 west of I-94. There is much development east of U.S. 31, evolving into more open space between 31 and I-94. West of I-94 our road becomes quite nice with farmland and wood lots replacing the view east of the expressway.

A gentle roll to the land and wide curves add some motorcycling zest to the experience. Starting at state route 75 you will ride for about four miles through the Bong State Recreation Area, a natural area that provides some variety to this part of the trip. This 4,515-acre parcel of open space was originally supposed to be a jet fighter base. The Area is named after Major Richard I. Bong, from Poplar, Wisconsin. Major Bong was America's leading air ace during World War II. The military base project was abandoned three days before the first concrete was to be poured for the runways. The state, and local citizens, had the foresight to protect this unique large open space located in heavily-developed southeast Wisconsin for future generations. The government bought the land in 1974 and it became a public recreation area. The property consists of rolling grassland, savanna, wetlands, and small isolated woodlands, and comprises Wisconsin's largest protected prairie. When seen from the air the area has an otherworldly look as the scars for the runway and other construction are still visible.

⤛⟨◆⟩⤜

We'll ride 142 all the way to Chocolate City USA—also known as Burlington. One note of caution; on route 142 east of Burlington there is a very large quarry. Use of this site by heavy trucks results in mud and stones often left on the road in that immediate vicinity, as well as trucks frequently pulling in and out of the quarry. Just be forewarned.

It is the presence of a Nestle Chocolate plant that gives Burlington its unique identity. Some of the candies you might enjoy, including delicious treats such as Crunch candy bars and Raisinets, and chocolate chips used in those cookies that most of us can't get enough of, are made in this town of 11,000. There is even a small chocolate museum on Chestnut Street in downtown Burlington, and each Memorial Day weekend the city hosts ChocolateFest; a celebration of their sweet claim to fame.

Foxville was the original name of the village in its earliest years, but soon after Wisconsin was admitted into the union the name was changed to Burlington, after Burlington, Vermont; reflecting the fact that many of the early residents came from New England. I have noticed that throughout the Midwest there are numerous cities and towns named after ones found in the eastern states, from which the earliest settlers came when lands west of the Appalachian and Alleghany Mountains opened up for settlement. It seems that even when folks leave their homes to begin a new life far away they want reminders of what they left behind. This phenomenon of course also explains the many European place names found throughout the U.S. and Canada.

Follow route 142 into Burlington, turning left on Jefferson Street to cross the Fox River (a different Fox River than the one that flows into Green Bay). At the bridge you'll see signs for south state route 36, which is what we want. Take Jefferson straight west until it intersects with route 36 (a small jog occurs just prior to reaching route 36).

Let the broad curves and gentle hills of 36 provide the entertainment as you ride about eight miles southwest to its juncture with route 120. West of the small town of Lyons is where route 36 is at its best because of more hills and better scenery.

Head north on 120, a road similar to route 36 as far as the motorcycling experience is concerned, on your way to the small town of East Troy—the next suggested stop. You will pass through the scenic Sugar Creek area and the Alpine Valley Resort, featuring golf in the warm months and downhill skiing when our

Trips on electrically powered rail cars operated by the East Troy Electric Railway carry passengers to a bygone era in beautifully refurbished coaches.

bikes are hibernating with their trickle charge lifelines attached. There is a stop sign at CR-D which delivers golfers and skiers to the respective pastimes, and then 120 continues north to I-43 where it officially ends.

North of the superslab route 120 turns into Church Street and take us right into downtown East Troy. The first portion of town you will come to is the downtown square, where various events are held and where people just hang out and enjoy the ambience of this small American Midwest town. The downtown business district is built on the outside of the commons square. On the northeast corner stands a historic three story stone building that today is the Cobblestone Inn. Just looking at this building, and its obvious age, you know it could tell fascinating stories if those stones could talk. What we do know provides enough information for a fabulous tale and a mystery.

The cobblestone building was built between 1846 and 1849 by one Samuel Bradley, to serve as a hotel for travelers on the trail between Milwaukee and Janesville. Astoundingly, Mr. Bradley, a stonemason, built the building primarily by himself, doing everything from collecting the thousands of stones and carrying them to the site, to making the mortar, and finally actually constructing the hotel with the help of another mason and a tender. It was considered the finest inn in southeast Wisconsin at the time, and was christened the Buena Vista House, after a recent victory by the U.S. Army in the Mexican War. It was in the Buena Vista

House that local people celebrated major events in their personal lives or in the affairs of the nation. Rumor even has it that Abraham Lincoln once stayed there.

According to the local chamber of commerce, the mystery arises when not long after they opened the inn, the Bradleys went to England for a trip—and never returned. Supposedly no word was ever received as to their fate or of what was to become of their beloved hotel. Friends kept the inn running for a while, but finally in 1868 it was abandoned. Ownership has changed hands many times over the years and the historic building has served many purposes; stagecoach stop, livery stable, restaurant, bowling alley and billiards hall, and even a Greyhound bus station. Fortunately, today it is once again in the business of providing food and respite for travelers and townspeople alike.

A 1931 article in the Janesville Daily Gazette tells a slightly differing account, stating that Bradley sold the building in 1849, and that it was sold again a year later. Perhaps the building and the dreams of Mr. Bradley were just too far ahead of their times.

<<<<◦>>>>

Just north of the Cobblestone Inn on Church Street is a fun attraction that is worthy of at least a few minutes of your time. Better yet, plan ahead and schedule a ride on the East Troy Electric Railroad as part of this tour. You surely won't be disappointed. The ETER uses electric trolleys on railroad tracks, just like hundreds of communities did a century ago. Their cars are the genuine thing, and have been refurbished to look as they did when they served travelers in cities such as Chicago, Milwaukee and Minneapolis. They glide silently down the track using power from overhead lines to propel them. They operate from mid-May to late October and offer a number of special rides to celebrate special events and holidays. Regularly scheduled dinner trains and wine tasting rides are also available for your enjoyment. Visiting the adjacent museum adds to the experience. Get more information at www.easttroyrr.org or call them at 262.642.3263.

Just south of the railroad museum is an old store filled with antiques. If you're in the mood for an old fashioned malted milk or ice cream cone, you are in luck because they would be happy to fix you up. If you're really hungry and would like some old fashioned burgers and fries, Gus's Drive In on the west edge of town will fill up your built-in fuel tank.

When you are ready to depart, simply continue north on Church Street a block, jog left one block, then go north again the short distance to state route 20. Turn west on route 20 and take it across eight miles of familiar southern Wisconsin farmland where stately farms testify to the fertility of the soil and work ethic of the owners, to route 67 where we turn north.

The village of Eagle is a favorite gathering place for motorcyclists enjoying scenic roads in nearby Kettle Moraine State Forest.

State route 67 is one of those roads that almost any Wisconsin motorcyclist from the southeastern part of the state will recognize by name. It is a road that hosts many rides, from individual bikers out for a bit of fun, to organized runs and rallies. The best part of 67 is north of route 20, which just happens to be where we begin.

Highway 67 will take us to the village of Eagle. Just south of Eagle you might be interested in exploring the Old World Wisconsin historic site. It is a living museum village with dozens of buildings that take visitors back to frontier days. You can watch people perform a variety of tasks and activities that daily life consisted of a hundred and fifty years ago, as well as explore the equipment and buildings that were a part of life for Wisconsin's early settlers. The park also hosts a number of special events ranging from baseball history days to Civil War enactments. As you are riding north on 67 you will first ride by the administrative offices of Old World Wisconsin, but the actual park is about a mile further up the road. Check them out at www.oldworldwisconsin.org.

The village of Eagle is a good place to arrange to be for lunch or dinner as there are two very enjoyable places to stop. The Knucklehead Pub & Grub and the Coyote Canyon Grille are just two doors apart, and both will make you feel right at home in your leathers and boots. Don't worry about wind-blown hair or the ever-popular helmet-head look, both are common sights in these two biker-friendly taverns. On Labor Day weekends the Knucklehead Pub sponsors KnuckleFest, a new annual three day bash of food, live bands, vendors, and lots of other things to see and do. The event is held at the Kettle Moraine Ranch on CR-S near Eagle. Check it out at knucklefest.com.

◄◄◄◙►►►

Route 67 north of Eagle is a designated scenic highway as it snakes its way through the hills and forests of the Kettle Moraine region. The Kettle Moraine district covers a large geographic expanse in southeastern Wisconsin, and the state manages several state forest units in the large piece of real estate between Eagle on the south and Kiel on the north side, that provide marvelous motorcycling and outdoor recreational opportunities.

The entire Kettle Moraine region of course has its roots in the last ice age. Two gigantic lobes of the glacier met here. The western lobe gave us Green Bay, Lake Winnebago and the wetlands of the Horicon Marsh area. The eastern lobe helped form Lake Michigan—no small feat! The places where these two ice sheets interacted (for lack of a better term) is today the Kettle Moraine region. Vast amounts of gravel and sand were deposited in a variety of geologic formations as the ice sheet melted back. Huge chunks of ice also broke off and were buried in the glacial drift. As these blocks of ice melted, they formed the many small kettle lakes found in the area. The entire moraine region is about three hundred feet higher than surrounding flat lands, with many of the hills surpassing 1,200 feet above sea level. The glacial drift atop the limestone bedrock is several hundred feet thick.

The fact that this area contains large blocks of scenic forestland rather than open farm fields is also a direct result of the glacier. Moraines are hills that are comprised largely of rock and gravel—not exactly the best soils that were being sought by the early settlers. Even in those instances where the poor quality land was cleared for farming its use in agriculture didn't last long and the property soon grew back to brush and forests. The state eventually purchased large blocks of this unwanted land (or in many instances land reverted to the state for failure to pay property taxes) to manage it for forestry, wildlife and outdoor recreation. The bottom line for motorcyclists is that the many hills and ponds result in roads that twist and turn, and rise and fall, as they negotiate the undulating landscape and skirt the many wetlands. So as you enjoy route 67 through the forest, remember to thank a glacier!

Route 67 will deliver us to U.S. 18, on which we turn west and ride this surprisingly nice biking road about twelve miles. I must confess that I am often pleasantly surprised when I travel a highway with federal jurisdiction that turns out to be a fun ride. I have a deeply ingrained condition that causes me to assume that roads always follow a certain motorcycling hierarchy, with county and state roads being the best biking routes, and federal highways always being the worst. I assume this because I subconsciously believe that U.S. routes are busy, flat, wide, filled with trucks, and boring. After all these decades, I am still nicely surprised when these assumptions are proved wrong.

One cautionary note about U.S. 18 occurs while in the town of Sullivan. A right turn is necessary in this small town to remain on 18. It is very easy to just keep going straight through town and a few miles later finding yourself in the village of Rome on county road F, scratching your head trying to figure out how in blazes you got there! So watch for the signs that call for a right turn in Sullivan.

County road D, just east of the village of Helenville, is our next riding objective. Follow CR-D north as it negotiates an appealing blend of farm and woodlands. "D" is an enjoyable ride as it lazily rolls along with gentle hills and curves, surrounded by the deep greens of summer. Just south of the city of Watertown CR-D will join with CR-E, and follow the Rock River into town from the south.

Watertown is a bustling city of 23,000. It was once (for a brief time) the second largest city in Wisconsin, with its roots going back to the mid-1830s. It is famous for being the place where the German concept of kindergarten was brought to the New World. This occurred in 1856. County Road E becomes South Concord Avenue in town. As you enter Watertown from the south you'll see signs for the Octagon House. This five-story residence was built in the 1850s and is quite remarkable to see—even just from the outside. It is a museum today run by the Watertown Historical Society and is open daily.

We want to go west a bit on route 19 then north on route 26 out of Watertown. As is the case all across Wisconsin, or at least so it seems, road construction can make getting from point A to point B difficult. Route 26 is being upgraded to four-lane divided highway status, and in time the construction will be completed and detours just a bad memory.

WisDOT is spending what must be a huge amount of money straightening and widening highways across the state. I have the feeling that every town of any size is going to have a beltway to divert traffic around, rather than continuing to go through, such towns. This is not a good thing, in my humble and perhaps even misguided opinion. Such construction has predictable, if unintentional, consequences. It invariably causes the degradation of some very cool and economically healthy downtowns, results in urban sprawl, replaces locally owned stores with big box behemoths, and of course converts valuable farmland into asphalt parking lots. Not to mention transforming hundreds of miles of fun two-lane biking roads into straight, flat, and wide super highways that have no soul or character.

The evocative End of the Trail *bronze sculpture is one of eight located in the small town of Waupun thanks to a generous benefactor.*

Head north on 16/26 out of Watertown and eventually route 16 will veer off to the west. We, however, continue straight north on route 26 to Juneau and Waupun. Route 26 traverses a vast low-lying area that is now a mix of wetlands, fertile farmland, woodlots and of course the 32,000-acre Horicon Marsh. As noted earlier, the marsh was created by the last glacier to scour this area, creating a vast low-lying plain that served as a waterfowl breeding ground following retreat of the glacier and before the first nomadic humans arrived about 12,000 years ago. A hundred years ago land speculators attempted to drain the swamp but those efforts proved futile. In the 1920s, conservationists, hunters and legislators recognized that the best use of this unique area was as a wildlife refuge and the endeavor to acquire land and restore the marsh began.

Migrating waterfowl don't care, but the marsh is actually divided into two properties—a 21,000-acre national refuge and an 11,000-acre state wildlife area. Watching the migration of birds in the spring and fall brings thousands of people to the area each year, making the refuge a major economic boost to the region. There are trails and special observation sites built around the marsh to allow people to see this marvelous wildlife drama played out each year without getting too close to interfere with the nesting birds.

Traveling north on route 26 from Juneau you will cross route 33, and two miles beyond that main intersection is County Road E. The Nitschke Mounds County Park is located on CR-E just a hundred yards or so east of route 26. This undeveloped park contains Native American effigy mounds, and is also adjacent to the Wild Goose State Trail. Unfortunately, if you are both a motorcyclist and a person interested in Native American mounds, there is extremely limited and unimproved parking available along the road, and what parking space is to be had is located some distance from the park and mounds.

If a person has never been to Horicon Marsh before, one thing that becomes obvious when traveling the nearby roads is that you cannot see much in the way of marsh wildlife or even the large wetland itself from the main roads. To accommodate those that want to see more than just adjacent farmlands a series of overlooks have been constructed. Also, a fifty-mile vehicular tour surrounds the marshlands, in addition to foot trails. Watch for the typical brown signs that identify the Horicon Parkway or parking areas and overlooks.

◄◄◄❖►►►

Continue north on route 26 all the way to downtown Waupun—the city of sculpture. Waupun has one man, sculptor Clarence Shaler, to thank for the eight magnificent sculptures located throughout the small town. The first, and perhaps most famous, was commissioned by Mr. Shaler in 1927 when he had sculptor James Earl Fraser create a large bronze version of a small sculpture Fraser did in 1894 called *End of the Trail*, depicting the plight of Indians who had been killed or forcibly moved off their ancestral lands. Shaler donated the bronze statue to the city of Waupun as a gift in 1929.

It is located at the mill pond in Shaler Park, on Madison Street north of highway 49. Shaler then sculpted seven more works in bronze for the city. One, called *The Pioneers,* is located in a small park on the west side of route 26 as you enter Waupun from the south. The remaining sculptures are located at various locations around town. The Waupun Chamber of Commerce (920.324.3491 / 16 South Mill Street) has a free map of the outdoor art in Waupun, which makes locating the various pieces much easier than trying to follow the signs or simply riding around blindly.

Another must-see site in Waupun in my opinion is The Citadel, aka The Waupun Correctional Institute. This massive and uniquely designed building will evoke various impressions in the viewer; everything from a massive Middle

Ages fort to late night showings of The Birdman of Alcatraz movie. This imposing structure is on Madison Street just south of Main Street.

Depending on your agenda and traveling style, the Waupun County Park just one mile northwest of Waupun off County Road–MM provides a quiet campground in a scenic wooded area on the Rock River.

When you're done exploring Waupun ride east on route 49. This road skirts the northern edge of the Horicon Marsh and there are a couple of roadside kiosks where you may wish to stop for further elucidation about this natural wonder. Midway across there is a historical marker on the north side of 49 that tells the story of how the land was reclaimed and the refuge created. There is also an interpretive and visitor center on route 49 at the northeast corner of the refuge that tells the natural history story of the marsh and the wildlife that dwell there.

East of the marsh route 49 is essentially flat and the land featureless except for the many wind turbines that dot the landscape in this region. It surprises me that there would be so many of these tall windmills so close to a major waterfowl migratory route, but apparently the birds are smart enough to avoid the massive spinning blades. The other noteworthy item to mention regarding route 49 from the marsh east to route 175 is that it's quite rough. Expansion bumps have erupted every ten yards or so that cause an annoying series of jolts. Hopefully this road will be resurfaced in the near future and this complaint can be retired.

Past Brownsville we turn north onto route 175, taking this flat and straight two-laner north just three miles to one of my favorite roads in this vicinity— county road F. We will ride CR-F for many miles, and it keeps getting better and better as we travel east. The first few miles are nice enough, with light traffic, smooth pavement and scenic well-maintained farmlands on either side of the road. The road makes a slight jog to the south at U.S. 45. Soon County Road F (which stands for fun!) enters the moraine and lakes area and hills, curves and forested lands become the norm. This stretch of road is an absolute delight to ride, like others in this unique and scenic geologic region.

In the heart of the Kettle Moraine State Forest, immediately east of the intersection with route 67, is the old Dundee Mill. This is a nice stop and a great picture. Like most places with so much history behind them, it's also a nice story. A mill was originally built on this site in 1855, using the power of moving water of the river to grind grain for local farmers. It burned down in 1925 and the present structure was built a year later. After eighty years, it was time for major renovation of the mill. A local committee was put together to oversee this work and when a major player in the project became critically ill the ABC television show Extreme Home Makeover got involved. The work crew from that television series came to Dundee primarily to rebuild the house of the community leader and volunteer, and while rebuilding his home they also completed work on the mill. The mill and small park surrounding it are now run by the Partners of the Dundee Mill. Each year they host various fun events (like pig wrestling) to raise money for operation and maintenance of the site.

Resume the tour by continuing east on CR-F. The enjoyable motorcycling continues even after leaving the boundaries of the state forest. County road-F travels across a background that includes many features that guarantee a fun ride; scenic surroundings, negligible traffic, and continued rolling land with enough sweepers to keep life fun. We will ride CR-F all the way east to its juncture with state route 28, just prior to Cascade. Route 28 itself is no slouch. Riding along on this road is a pleasant experience. It's not exactly an adrenaline rush but you'll surely enjoy the ride. Stay on route 28 until it intersects with state route 32 at Sheboygan Falls; turning south onto 32. Route 32 is surprisingly enjoyable all the way down to Cedar Grove. The road quite closely follows the Onion River between Sheboygan Falls and Cedar Grove, making for lots of subdued but enjoyable curves through a land of neat farms and woodlots.

At the main intersection in the town of Cedar Grove route 32 heads east, but we want to continue going straight south on Main Street, which quickly becomes County Road-LL. The land around us starts changing south of Cedar Grove. More suburbia becomes apparent as we closely parallel I-43. We motor along on CR-LL for twelve miles, until it rejoins route 32 on the north side of Port Washington. Turn left onto 32 and follow it through this historic and attractive lakeside city of about 13,000 fine citizens. Port Washington is one of those towns where the effort and time involved in doing some exploring pays off handsomely. There is much to see here, from the beautiful lighthouse at the end of the pier jutting into Lake Michigan, to the 1860's marine life saving station near the towering steeple of St. Mary's Church. The lakefront area and the historic downtown section are both areas where one can spend time sightseeing and appreciating the unique natural and manmade attractions that are found here. Therefore, as is often the counsel you will read in my motorcycling books—I encourage you to stop and see the world around you; don't just speed by in oblivious ignorance of all that is beautiful, unique, and admirable.

<<<<◉>>>>

We're going to leave Port Washington via County Road-C. Stay on route 32 to the downtown waterfront section where it will make a ninety-degree turn to the west (at the Holiday Inn). Just one block further west is the sign for CR-C, where a left turn is needed. CR-C makes a couple well-marked jogs in town and then heads south for eight miles through a pleasant countryside where wooded lands and farms line the road. Our road will make a turn to the right and go over the

I-43 expressway. Just west of the interstate is Port Washington Road, which is the one we use to continue our southward trip. Port Washington Road parallels the X-Way on the west side for six miles. (Route 32 joins the interstate for the stretch south of the city of Port Washington, thus we abandon it for local roads more suitable for motorcycling, avoiding high speed companionship with 18-wheelers). For the last mile, Port Washington Road merges with the highway. However, we exit after less than a mile along with route 32, heading east on 32 toward the lake in the town of Bayside, and then following route 32 south through the exclusive city of Fox Point. Riding through Fox Point on 32 is a chance to see how the other half lives. For several miles you will pass by mansions and estates set deep in wooded lots, with Lake Michigan on occasion visible behind them. This area has more trees than people and traffic is surprisingly light on the broad boulevard. I think that the lakeshore in this region definitely qualifies for the title of Wisconsin's gold coast.

Eventually 32 will pass through the suburbs of Whitefish Bay and Shorewood and as one travels south, the suburbs of Milwaukee take on a more typical appearance. Very near the northern city limits of Milwaukee is Kenwood Street and then Lincoln Memorial Drive leading east to the shoreline and Lake Park, and the large Veterans Park a bit further south. You definitely want to get off route 32 at this point and follow the shoreline road. Veterans Park is a large and highly popular place for beach goers and sun lovers, and the scenery here can be quite attractive, if you get my drift. This is certainly a good place to park the bike and take a walk to admire the lake and whatever other charming sights you might encounter.

Lincoln Memorial Drive hugs the shoreline for about three miles. At the south end of Veterans Park the drive seamlessly merges onto an in-town limited access highway (I-794) which carries you over the Milwaukee River and the heavily industrialized portion of town near the Port of Milwaukee. At the juncture of Lincoln Memorial Drive and I-794 you have the option of going west toward I-94 and I-43. If you want to visit the Harley-Davidson Museum then follow I-94 west to I-43 and go south, following the signs to the museum. If you just want to continue south on this tour then continue going straight south as you merge onto the superslab; no turns are necessary.

◄◄◄◄◉►►►►

Regardless of the brand of bike you ride, I highly encourage a trip to the Harley-Davidson Museum. The Motor Company spared no expense in creating this citadel of motorcycling history and it ought to be a stop for any motorcyclist

The new Harley-Davidson Museum is destined to become one of the country's premier motorcycling destinations.

who finds him or herself in the Milwaukee area. Tours of the Powertrain Factory are also available. The factory is located about ten miles west of the Museum on West Capitol Drive in suburban Wauwatosa. Call them at 1.877.883.1450 for more details.

If you are in Milwaukee in late August or early September be sure to check out the Milwaukee Rally. This is a large event that includes bikes shows, poker runs, various displays, tons of vendors, music and more. Check out their web site for more information: http://www.milwaukeerally.com/

Once past the port and industrial region you'll soon come to Oklahoma Street, where we exit 794 and follow it east to its end at the lakeshore, turning south on South Lake Drive in the town of St. Francis. After less than two miles Lake Drive joins route 32, which we once again ride south for many miles through the various southern suburbs. After several miles you will encounter major intersections for 'mile roads'—7 Mile Road south to 4 Mile Road. At 4 Mile Road, which is also County Road G going east, you want to turn east toward Wind Point and the very nice Wind Point Lighthouse. This is a Kodak Moment you don't want to pass up. The 112-foot tower and adjoining keepers house were built in 1880. Though the lighthouse itself is closed, the grounds are open to the public and provide a great place to admire the tower and the vast expanse of Lake Michigan. There is ample parking space next to the tower where you can safely park your bike for a stroll.

At the lighthouse the road continues south along the lakeshore and the Shoop Golf Course, then heads back west. A word of discretion here—the area near the lighthouse has a low speed limit and it is enforced, so even though the road may look enticing with its curves and relatively light traffic, keep your right wrist under control or it will likely cost you. After taking the loop south of the lighthouse and golf course you will be on 3 Mile Road. Take this just a few blocks and you will come to the intersection of Main Street / CR-G. Turn south and take this road one-and-a-half miles where we once again re-join route 32 in the northern portion of the city of Racine, locally referred to as the Belle City.

This city of 80,000 has a history that stretches back much further than most places in Wisconsin. The first Europeans to set foot on the soil here were a group of French explorers who sailed into the mouth of the Root River in 1699 to establish a post for trade with local Native Americans. Racine is the French word for root. The first permanent settlement here was established in 1834. Though Racine has a broad ethnic mix today, the city has the largest population of Danes outside of Denmark and Greenland. This helps explain the popularity of a Danish pastry called kringles, still authentically handmade in several local bakeries, including: O&H on Douglas Avenue; Larsen's on Washington Avenue; Racine Danish on Golf Avenue; Bendsten's on Washington Avenue; and Lehmann's on 16th Street. You unquestionably won't be disappointed by going a bit out of your way to sample one of these delicious treats while in town. The marina and pier head light are also nearby attractions that won't disappoint.

We remain on route 32 back to Kenosha to complete this marvelous 271-mile trip. And what a wonderful trip it has been. From vast expanses of forests viewed from atop a moraine to vistas of blue water stretching beyond the horizon; lighthouses to Indian mounds; one of the world's most famous waterfowl refuges to electric rail car rides; streetcars to roads custom made for motorcycling; a museum filled with over a century of motorcycle history to a water powered mill where history can also be seen up close and personal. A rider will learn much about their sport, their state, their history, and the marvelous natural world we live in by slowing down and taking this tour in two days, participating in the many opportunities for exploration and discovery that you will encounter. Enjoy the ride.

 Helmet Hair Quiz Answer

Actor, director and writer Orson Welles; architect Frank Lloyd Wright; artist Georgia O'Keefe; actor and director Gene Wilder; novelist and playwright Thornton Wilder; Liberace; escape artist Houdini (among others).

Racing in the Hills

Helmet Hair Quiz

What Wisconsin river is known as 'the crookedest river in the world'?

SOMETIMES ALL OF US want a ride that is a relaxing way to spend a few hours with friends or a riding partner. We don't want anything too taxing or long, or a route that is complicated with lots of turns or confusing directions to send us astray. We just want a ride that has nice roads, pleasing scenery, and perhaps a few things to see or do along the way. And for sure, we want an enjoyable place to stop for eats and conversation along the way, or better yet, perhaps a great spot to retrieve the fixings from the saddlebags and enjoy a picnic. Well, this 153-mile ride in eastern Wisconsin is just the thing for that kind of memorable day on the road.

I start this ride in Appleton on the north shore of Lake Winnebago, riding U.S. 10 east beyond the busyness of this area to a calmer more rural setting. U.S. 10 is one of the more historic of the country's federal highways. Though it is hard to imagine while riding the divided four lane mega-highway that is U.S. 10 today in the Appleton vicinity, the road had its humble beginnings in 1926 when the federal government finally got involved with highways in order to end the confusion brought on by the mish-mash of local roads. Prior to 1926 roads were a local affair. That was fine if one was only interested in getting produce from their farm to the nearest town. As the automobile became more popular and the concept of travel and tourism began to take hold, a road system designed for actual travel from one point to another became necessary. For a couple of decades local road boosters used a system of naming roads that went across a state, or across several states. Marking such roads was very much a hit and miss affair, however, and travelers often found themselves lost on a muddy trail with no idea where they were. There was also no central authority to set standards for road construction or how roads would be named. In fact, the private sector, with automobile and petroleum interests taking a lead, played the early lead in constructing and naming roads.

It finally became obvious that a better system was needed. A system that was uniform and enabled a driver to follow the correct road across state lines. The answer to the confusing network of local roads was a numbering system imposed

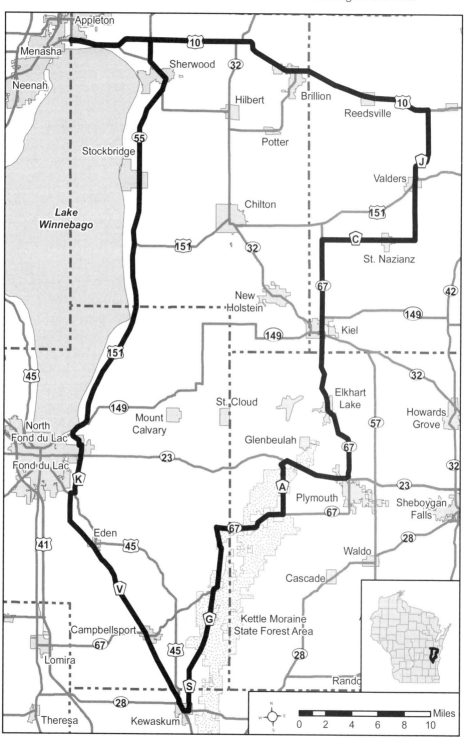

RACING IN THE HILLS 153 MILES		
Miles	**Destination**	**Total**
00	Appleton	00
30	Cato / CR-J	30
24	Kiel	54
17	Greenbush	71
23	Kewaskum	94
23	U.S. 151 / Lake Winnebago	117
36	Point of Beginning	153

by the federal government. The intent was to make long distance, especially interstate, travel easier. Oddly, even though U.S. 10 obviously ends with a zero, it was never a coast-to-coast road as this numbering system normally implies. (U.S. 20, 30, 40, 50 and so on all started out as true coast-to-coast roads) It originally went from Detroit to Seattle, crossing Lake Michigan on a ferry. In fact, U.S. 10 is one of only two federal roads that still include a ferry as part of its length. Today U.S. 10 is much shorter, running from Bay City, Michigan to Fargo, North Dakota. Expressways have replaced the decommissioned stretches.

We will ride U.S. 10 for a total of 23 miles east through a gently rolling landscape of farmland and the occasional small town. This was once the norm in travel—whether across the state or across the nation. It was on two-lane roads for the most part, which went through small town America. Today of course we have to go out of our way to see these same communities as expressways and four-lane bypasses whisk us around such towns and villages.

Eventually we arrive at the tiny village of Cato and county road-J. Turn right onto J and head south on this lightly traveled road through the nice countryside. The stretch at Clarks Mill is especially pretty as the roads dips through the Manitowoc River valley. We will be on CR-J for ten miles, beyond U.S. 151, through the village of Valders, and south to county road C. The change in the landscape becomes obvious as we get near CR-C. In fact, immediately upon turning right onto C we ride into some impressive glacial moraines. At the corner of county roads J and C is a large gravel mining operation, which is removing a large portion of the moraine you are riding on. It is a great place to see up close what moraines are made of, and to appreciate just how much sand and gravel, as well as large boulders, was left behind by the glaciers as they melted thousands of years ago.

County road C is an enjoyable ride west through this scenic hilly region. You will see few other vehicles, the blacktop is smooth, and the wooded hills and rolling farm fields blend together to form a scenic mosaic. CR-C takes us to state route 67, onto which we turn left to ride south into the busy small town of Kiel. Route 67 keeps us on the east side of this town of 3,500 perched on the banks of the Sheboygan River. Turn right onto route 32/57 if you want to visit downtown Kiel. South of Kiel route 67 gets more enjoyable and continues so as we work our way south.

Continue the ride down route 67 to Elkhart Lake and Road America, a destination for thousands of us each June to watch motorcycle racing at its best. And of course in the vicinity of Road America, just south of Elkhart Lake, you are likely to see lots of road racers or racing wannabes near this venerable race track. I have attended motorcycle races at a number of venues, and enjoy watching different modes of motorcycle racing competition. I have to say that my two favorite by far are road racing at tracks like Road America, and flat track racing, which is very popular across the Midwest. Road America has long been my favorite track to watch high performance road racing machines as they fly down the straights and slice through the curves at impossible speeds and lean angles. Add to this scene the background noise of screaming engines, the smells of exhaust and Castrol oil fumes mixed with the aroma of brats on the grill, and the outcome is the actualization of a racing fan's fondest dreams.

⊰⊰⊰◈⊱⊱⊱

On a recent trip to Elkhart Lake I saw a group of riders that helped reinforce the positive feelings I have regarding the future of our sport. Over a dozen women were riding in a group for what I assume was a gathering of friends doing what they loved to do—going for a ride on a beautiful summer day on a fun biking road. Women today, of course, have become very much a part of the motorcycling scene, and are no longer taking a back seat to anyone. The distaff side of biking is increasing in number and women are demanding the same level of attention and respect that male riders have received over the years. As new owners, they account for a significant part of the upsurge in motorcycle sales over the last decade, and they are as enthusiastic about their machines and what they represent as are male riders.

When many of us began riding the industry didn't cater to women, but fortunately that is no longer the case. From bikes manufactured with the female rider in mind, to functional riding gear designed just for women, the business side of motorcycling has gotten the message. There are also a growing number of support groups and organizations dedicated to the female rider so they can enjoy the same

Technicians make final adjustments to a race bike that will soon amaze and entertain spectators as its pilot circles the track at seemingly impossible speeds and angles.

social aspect of the sport as men have for decades. Regardless of what she's riding, I think it's just great when I see a woman's long hair flying in the wind behind her as she's roaring down the road on her bike.

Continuing south on route 67 takes you past the campground where thousands of us have camped over the years while attending events at Road America. A couple miles further south brings us to the north edge of Plymouth and route 23. Since 1985 the Dairyland Classic—billed as Wisconsin's premier flat track motorcycle race—has been held at the Sheboygan County Fair Park in Plymouth. It has traditionally been scheduled the same weekend in early June as the AMA Superbike races at Road America. With the smaller tracks and close seating typical of flat track courses, I have long thought that flat track racing is the most enjoyable and exciting motorcycle racing there is.

For this trip we are going to turn west onto state highway 23 for the short ride to Greenbush where some marvelous historic sites await our exploration. The Wisconsin Historical Society maintains a fascinating site that includes the Wade House stagecoach inn, a blacksmith shop, a water-powered sawmill, and a museum that features horse-drawn vehicles such as sleighs, buggies, and stagecoaches.

Sylvanus and Betty Wade started it all when in 1844 they built a cabin and adjacent tavern on a stagecoach trail between Sheboygan and Fond du Lac. Located at the midway point between the two large cities their tavern soon became a regular stop for stagecoaches traveling through the wilderness. As business thrived the accommodations grew to keep pace, and by 1850 the Wades built the stagecoach inn.

The Mullet River crossed the trail at this point providing water for their planned village and a source of power for a sawmill to turn the dense forest into lumber for building stores and homes. Ten years later a railroad was built between Sheboygan and Fond du Lac, running just north of Greenbush through the village of Glenbeulah. The rail line almost overnight became the primary source of travel between the cities and Wade's inn saw much less business. It survived another fifty years, however, and to make a long story short was ultimately restored and made part of this fascinating historic site.

This is a stop you don't want to miss. Be prepared to spend some time there to see it all. Check out their events schedule to plan your trip around a vintage baseball league game or to watch the Civil War encampment. History really does come alive here. Check them out at wisconsinhistory.org or call 920.526.3271 for more information about the Wade House historic site. The Wisconsin Historical Society are the same folks who protect and preserve other Wisconsin historic gems, such as Pendarvis, Stonefield, Circus World, the Madeline Island Museum, Old World Wisconsin, and more.

From Greenbush we are going to continue our ride down county road-A through the heart of the Kettle Moraine forest back south to route 67. We will then continue riding for many miles through the forests, fields and hills of this amazing region as we follow route 67 south. This is one of the more enjoyable lengths of motorcycling roads in the state with only a few straight stretches, and many blissful lengths of road where hills and curves reign supreme. Just prior to reaching the village of Dundee route 67 will skirt the edge of Long Lake for about three miles, adding another layer of charm and variety to an already marvelous route.

At the south end of Long Lake in the village of Dundee we want to turn right and follow route 67 for a very short distance and then turn south onto CR-G to continue our ride through the Kettle Moraine State Forest. I should make a disclaimer at this point that I am not responsible for the muscle strain and sore joints you may suffer as a result of waving to or otherwise recognizing the multitude of other bikers you will pass on the road south of Greenbush. Suffice it to say that unless you're out there in a thunderstorm or snow flurries you will see many fellow bikers enjoying the same roads and distinct geologic panorama.

The Ice Age Interpretive Center is located on CR-G just south of Dundee if you want to learn more about the fascinating natural history of this region and of the geologic forces that made it all happen.

Eventually CR-G leaves the boundary of the forest and suddenly the land reverts to flatter farms and fields. When the road turns straight south it seamlessly turns into CR-S, and a short distance later it becomes Riverview Drive as it shadows the Milwaukee River and delivers us to the town of Kewaskum. Formed in 1852, this small city is named in memory of Chief Kewaskum of the Pottawatomie Tribe.

Turn right onto route 28 and take it west the very short distance to U.S. 45. Go north on 45, past westbound 28, to CR-V, also known as the Old Fond du Lac Road. And in fact we're going ride this rural county road northwest in its former capacity as the main road to Fond du Lac, following it most of the way to U.S. 151. CR-V is another of those pleasant roads that criss-cross Wisconsin. Traffic is light, the scenery is pleasing if not dramatic, and the riding conditions are agreeable.

Just beyond the town of Eden you will see the very large Marblehead Quarry. Just north of the quarry is CR-K, onto which we want to turn right. Shortly after turning onto K it will jog east for less than a half-mile on U.S. 45 and then split off and head north again. CR-K will take us north all the way to U.S. 151, and the commencement of our trip north along the eastern shore of stunning Lake Winnebago.

The Door Peninsula, Green Bay (the bay, not the city), and Lake Winnebago are three physical features of Wisconsin that are immediately recognizable on a map. This is no ordinary lake. As you might guess, its origin was the last glacier that covered this area for thousands of years, grinding and digging as it crept southward and then retreating north after ice covered where we now ride for an unimaginable number of years. The presence of the Niagara Escarpment on the east side of the lake plays a role in creating the basin which ultimately helped form this mighty lake. At about ten miles wide and thirty miles long, it has almost 138,000 surface acres of water. With a maximum depth of twenty-one feet it is shallower than many might suppose. Even this depth was enhanced by two feet over its natural capacity when two dams and a series of locks were constructed long ago on the Fox River, which drains the lake northward to Green Bay. The lake is a part of the Fox & Wisconsin River water highway that was used by Native Americans and early explorers.

◄◄◄◄●►►►►

As you start the northward ride, notice the wind turbines to the east. The higher land east of the lake is a natural location for wind power as the prevailing westerlies are free to blow unobstructed across the low-lying lake and the flat lands to the west. These turbines represent a new paradigm. Because of this new technology, we are able to reduce our use of dirtier fossil fuels, but at a cost. Even clean energy has a price. There are those who would rather see the occasional smokestack than scores of huge wind turbines across the rural landscape; a landscape where trees and farm silos, and the occasional church steeple, were the only things that intruded on distant horizons. Perhaps some day we will pay no more attention to wind turbines with their mesmerizing blades slowly spinning in the wind than we do the cellular telephone towers that have sprouted on hilltops like so many gangly steel goliaths rising out of the earth.

Riding a motorcycle along the shoreline of a lake formed by the forces of nature thousands of years ago might seem a strange time to meditate on the changing face of technology, and of what constitutes good technology versus bad. Nevertheless, speaking as someone who simultaneously revels in the wonders of technology and modern gadgetry, while having a deep abiding respect for the natural world around me, I am often torn between the two. Perhaps never more so than while riding a modern technological wonder, my motorcycle, on a smooth road of asphalt coursing through a beautiful natural setting. It strikes me that it is just these sorts of conflicting principles that make our life interesting and challenging at the same time.

The universe of motorcycling opens up concepts and ideas that I suspect many non-enthusiasts don't connect with our sport. Notions such art versus science, form versus function, and ideas versus realism. I think most of us have considered these issues in our everyday lives, perhaps consciously with deep thought, or maybe just superficially as we wonder why things are what they are.

I often ponder thoughts relative to motorcycling as I cruise down scenic byways on days made for riding. Motorcycling in my opinion is an art, although we all appreciate that motorcycles themselves are science-based objects. These marvelous machines at their core are the product of engineering and metallurgy, not abstract drawings or hues of paint that have no meaning except in the minds and opinions of viewers. The concepts of form and function are both very pertinent when it comes to motorcycles.

I believe that the *act* of motorcycling, however, is in fact like abstract art. It is wholly in the mind-set of the participant as to what it means. I have tried with little success for nearly forty years to explain why I love motorcycling. However, that is like asking somebody why he or she likes a particular Monet or Picasso. They know why, and we motorcyclists know why we love to ride, but it is very hard to explain to another. In fact, explanations about art of any kind, including motorcycling, are valid only in one's own mind. Opinions about artistic concepts and qualities are not transferable values.

When asked for the umpteenth time why we enjoy motorcycling, most of us, in exasperation, end up simply saying something inane such as "If I have to explain you wouldn't understand." That familiar rejoinder, however, which I too have used many times, is transferring fault. In reality, it is we who are unable to explain our feelings more than it is listeners who are not capable of understanding. We are trying to explain a subjective emotion to people that are listening with objective ears expecting to hear an explanation that includes things like convenience, miles per gallon ratings, inexpensive transportation, and so on. To us those qualities are secondary—it's the joy, the art, of motorcycling that we motorcyclists are after, not quantifiable facts and figures.

In many places in the world motorcycles are not granted a metaphysical persona. To a farmer in Afghanistan, carrying his entire family on a motorcycle to a health clinic located fifty miles away, there is nothing romantic about them. For him riding motorcycles is cheap transportation—nothing more and nothing less. We are fortunate indeed to be able to elevate motorcycles and motorcycling to a higher plane, one that gives us great delight and satisfaction.

While the experience of riding motorcycles may be personal in nature and conjure up images of magic carpets transporting us to exotic places, the function of motorcycle operation is very much science and real world based. The laws of physics are hard at work, making a machine designed by engineers and manufactured with the help of advanced chemistry and metallurgy to stay upright in curves at high speeds, even though it may be leaning at a forty-five degree angle. The mass of those rapidly spinning wheels, centrifugal forces, gyroscopic effects, and other laws of nature all work together to enable us to turn the science of riding a motorcycle into the art of motorcycling. For that reality I'm everlastingly grateful.

But I digress. I often do while riding. I personally do not like to listen to a radio or an I-pod while riding. I prefer the sound of the road and the blank slate that my mind becomes, allowing me to fill it with thoughts and observations of the world around me.

Riding along the east shore of Lake Winnebago is a great place to let your mind wander. There is much less development and human pressures on this side of the lake than on the western shore.

Watching boats sail on the blue water and wondering who the occupants are and what kind of life they live; seeing the neat and tidy farmlands being lovingly nurtured by those who work the land and thinking back on my own farm boy youth; watching sea gulls flying low overhead and wondering why they seem to spend so much time and effort seemingly going nowhere; waving in unsaid recognition and appreciation to riders on the same road going in the direction from which I just came and wondering who they are and whether it would be enjoyable sharing a beer or coffee with them—these are the kind of things that keep my mind occupied as I ride. Perhaps I am easily amused, but I do think that we need much less artificial stimulation to keep our lives interesting than what we have been pressured to think we need by sellers of various electronic devices.

But don't daydream too much, because when route 151 turns off to the east we want to be sure to continue north on what becomes route 55. There are signs for some local and county parks that you might want to follow to spend some time on the water's edge where the immensity of this lake can best be appreciated. Calumet County Park, located on county road EE north of Stockbridge is an especially nice park on the lakeshore. The park preserves six Native American effigy mounds on top of the escarpment overlooking the lake.

One of the best natural areas along the lake is High Cliffs State Park at the northeast corner. Here the Niagaran cliffs are exposed near the shoreline, offering a dramatic sight. There are also Native American conical and effigy mounds on the top of the cliff. As with all state parks an entry permit is required.

Just north of the park and the town of Sherwood route 55 intersects with U.S. 10 and the way back to Appleton where we began the ride. Thus completes another wonderful tour of discovery. I think you will agree that it was a memorable ride.

 Helmet Hair Quiz Answer

The Kickapoo River.

Flat Tracking Fun

Helmet Hair Quiz

The largest Indian reservation in the state is nearly 235,000 acres in size. Which one is it?

As I HAVE NOTED BEFORE, I believe that virtually any locale can provide enjoyable motorcycling opportunities. When riding in an area that lacks the physical and scenic characteristics that make good riding great, the trip takes on more of a mental aspect as opposed to physical. By this, I mean that it is easy to enjoy a ride on route 35 through the Mississippi River bluffs, or across route 70 in the northern forests. The sheer beauty of the region or the great characteristics of a road that twists and turns and rises and falls over the land make for great riding regardless of whatever else may or may not be present.

In this part of the state the great beauty and technical riding roads are missing. However, that does not mean that one cannot enjoy a ride in the gently rolling farmlands and lake country west of the city of Oshkosh. We are still on a motorcycle riding free and happy; enjoying all the sensations that motorcycling provides. We are lucky to be alive and able to appreciate and participate in this great activity, no matter where the road may be.

I subscribe to the belief that one rides a motorcycle for the joy of riding; for the simple pleasure of being on your machine. If you can ride a beautiful roller-coaster byway surrounded by breathtaking mountain scenery that's great, but for the vast majority of us that's just not a daily reality. That does not mean that we can't enjoy all the benefits of motorcycling on a regular basis. We can! All we need to do is get on the bike and head for the open highway—where that road is doesn't matter. After all, it is the operating and riding of a motorcycle that is the essence of the experience. Any motorcyclist knows what I mean. It is the sound of the engine, the primal feeling you experience as you lean through and accelerate out of curves, the heightened invigoration and sensory awareness of the world around you that can be found only on a motorcycle.

Motorcycling opens up the world around us as nothing else can, providing opportunities to share the adventure with a close friend, a group of like-minded riders, or simply basking in the experience alone. In reality, the sensations are

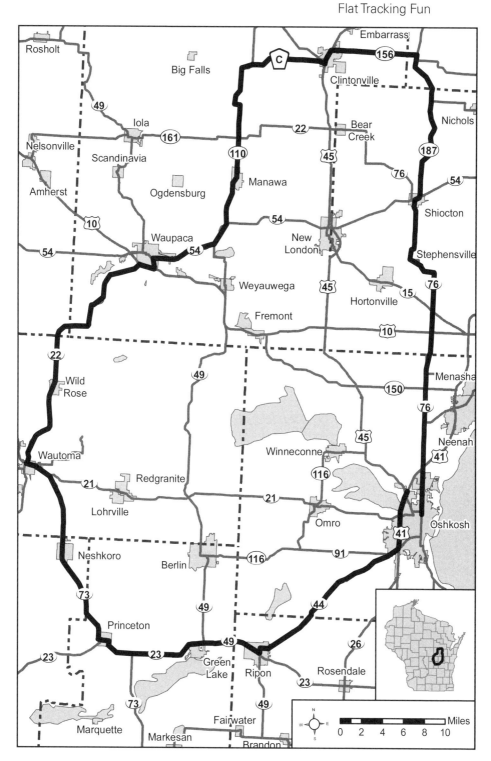

FLAT TRACKING FUN 172 MILES		
Miles	**Destination**	**Total**
00	Oshkosh	00
21	Ripon	21
26	Neshkoro	47
35	Waupaca	82
34	Clintonville	116
25	Shiocton	141
31	Oshkosh	172

essentially the same no matter the route or destination. Feel the air currents as they alternate between cool and warm, notice the lay of the land as you and your bike dip and turn and rise and fall with the earth as it was formed by nature, notice the smell of the countryside in spring, or the aroma of a summer evening—so thick you feel like you could bathe in it—or the wonderful but impossible to explain smell of fallen leaves in October. There aren't many things in life that cause ear-to-ear grins and the desire to just shout aloud as does riding a motorcycle down a country road on a beautiful day. Motorcycling is a wonderful way to restore a proper mental balance and outlook on life and the world. It is hard to be depressed or mentally drained while cruising down an open road on your horse of chrome and steel. A person does not have to be on one of America's fabled motorcycling roads to experience the best of biking—you just have to be on your motorcycle.

So while the physical characteristics of that part of Wisconsin west of Lake Winnebago may not be the most noteworthy, it too is a wonderful place to ride.

We start our ride in Oshkosh, a bustling city of about 63,000 people. Like many place names in Wisconsin the city's name has Native American origins; in this instance in honor of Chief Oshkosh of the Menominee tribe. The word means 'the claw' in the native tongue.

Oshkosh might be most famous for the Fly In Convention held here each year since 1969. The new name of the event is the Experimental Aircraft Association's AirVenture, and it is bigger and better than ever. It is held in late July each year. The EAA Airventure Museum chronicles the history of flight and has about 90

Camping while touring by motorcycle adds another layer to the experience and camping opportunities are abundant throughout the state.

rare or antique aircraft on display. Get more information on their web site or at 920.426.4800.

Closer to home for bikers is the Fox Valley Motorcycle Show. It is held the first Sunday in June and has become an annual event. Proceeds go to the Shriner's Children Hospital. For veterans, the Military Veterans Museum should be on your short list of places to visit. This organization is currently building a new and expanded facility that they are calling Fields of Honor. It should be a very high quality operation when completed. Check them out at mvmwisconsin.com or call them at 920.426.8615 for more information and progress update.

We are going to start the ride by heading south on U.S. 41 across the east end of Lake Butte des Morts. This impoundment was formed many years ago by an old dam, and is a broad but very shallow lake. Its name was derived from a hill on the north side of the lake that had been an Indian burial ground centuries ago.

Exit the highway at state route 44, near the Wittman Airport, and begin the ride across the fertile farmlands that make up this region. This is flat and fertile land, the result of it being old lake bottom in the post-glacial period. A few miles west of Oshkosh we enter what geologists call the Central Plain of Wisconsin.

Route 44 is enjoyable riding because it doesn't simply make a bee-line between Oshkosh and Ripon, rather it follows a carefree and indirect path. Route 44 will intersect with state route 23 in downtown Ripon, and twenty-three becomes our new riding host.

Ripon is a city of 7,000 whose most often cited claim to fame is as the birth-place of the Republican Party. The white schoolhouse where the first meeting was held still exists and is on the list of National Historic Places. The building is located at the corner of Blackburn and Blossom Streets, just a block south of the intersection of routes 44 and 23 in downtown. The city's name comes not from local Indians but rather from a town in England.

Depart Ripon on route 23, taking it west to Princeton. There are many lakes in this region, and Green Lake, midway between Ripon and Princeton, is one of the larger and at 237 feet deep it is the state's deepest inland lake. The village of Green Lake and the lake itself are popular tourist and recreational destinations. The lake is justifiably famous for its great fishing.

Continue west on 23 to Princeton, where we pick up route 73 and turn north. The land beyond Princeton begins to change around us, with more wooded lands and large expanses of wetlands managed for wildlife by the state. This entire region was once very swampy, and while much of the land was drained for the fertile soils underlying the swamp, a lot of wetland still survives throughout this district.

Route 73 takes us north through very nice countryside and the small town of Neshkoro and finally to Wautoma, where the locals like to say "the North begins". This is a region where outdoor recreation has long been a draw for locals and nonresidents alike. The many lakes in the area provide fishing and boating oppor-tunities and there is a long history of upland hunting in the woodlots and fields, as well as waterfowling opportunities in the area's swampy locales.

In Wautoma we leave route 73 and continue north on state highway 22, with Waupaca our next town of any size. Just prior to reaching U.S. 10 and Waupaca you will pass the village of King, located on the shore of Otter Lake. A left turn onto CR-QQ will almost immediately take you to the Wisconsin Veterans Home, origi-nally known as the Grand Army Home, established in 1887 for Civil War veterans. A small park there is a nice place to reflect on the role of the military and veterans, and their contributions to our way of life. A veterans cemetery is also at this facility.

With a name like Waupaca there would be a high likelihood that it has a historic Native American origin and apparently this assumption would be cor-rect. The prevailing theory is that the city is named after a Pottawatomie chief who defended early white settlers from angry Indians who opposed their coming into traditional Indian lands to settle and clear the land. Legend has it that the chief successfully argued against an Indian attack on early settlers, thus saving their lives and allowing the young community to take root. A historic marker to the chief can be found along route 110 northeast of town. Like the land to the immediate south, this region also has many lakes and is a favorite for outdoor enthusiasts.

Route 22 follows the U.S. 10 divided highway a mile to the east and then continues north again. It will join with route 110, which becomes our choice after route 22 departs north of the village of Manawa.

Eight miles north of the point where route 22 turns east CR-C intersects with route 110. Our ride takes us east on 'C' to the city of Clintonville. County road C will join U.S. 45 for a very short ride east, then a left turn onto route 22 (Main Street)

This monument to World War I dough-boys graces the ground of the Wisconsin Veterans Home, originally built for Civil War veterans, in the hamlet of King.

north through this busy city of 5,000 people built on the banks of the Pigeon River. We intersect with route 156 on the north edge of town, where a right turn is in order.

We will ride through the farmlands surrounding route 156 for eight miles to route 187 and a right turn to begin the southerly leg of the trip back toward Oshkosh. On route 156 we will pass the Embarrass River and the Wolf River before reaching route 187. Both of these streams have extensive wooded flood plains that add some forested land to an otherwise predominantly farmland region.

Route 187 is a decent road with quite a few curves that closely follows the Wolf River south to the town of Shiocton, where we pick up route 76 to continue our southward ride.

Route 76 carries us through a series of jogs at Stephensville, after which it straightens out and heads due south through the farmland on the west shore of Lake Winnebago back to Oshkosh.

I think you will agree that though our ride of 172 miles didn't take us down any roads that will be the topic of motorcycle blogs or magazine articles, it was a fun day under the sun on two wheels. What more could you want?

Helmet Hair Quiz Answer

The Menominee Reservation, located east of Wausau.

Northern Delights

T HE MEANING BEHIND this title, which is a cheesy play on the term 'northern lights' (please pardon both puns) is obvious. Northern Wisconsin offers delightful motorcycling; enough said. Let's ride.

To the Top of Wisconsin

Helmet Hair Quiz

What prime minister of a foreign nation grew up in Milwaukee?

I WON'T BE SO TRITE as to call this ride the high point of the book, but suffice it to say it is a very enjoyable ride on some great roads, through splendid scenery. In addition, it will in fact take a person as high in altitude as one can get in Wisconsin without leaving the ground. This tour carries us across a part of Wisconsin that lies within the Northern Highland geologic area. As the term suggests, the entire region is higher than surrounding areas as the result of ancient geologic conditions. Add to this uplifted bedrock the hundreds of feet of glacial drift left behind in the form of moraines, and you have some very impressive hills. Timm's Hill, in Price County, is the highest point in Wisconsin; the result of a glacial moraine deposited atop an elevated base of bedrock. We will explore the hills and forests in this beautiful region the best way possible—on motorcycles, riding on some of the most scenic and enjoyable roads in the state.

We begin the tour in Wausau, county seat of Marathon County. This city owes its existence, and in fact its very name, to the Wisconsin River. Not surprisingly, the town's beginnings were in the lumbering industry, given the presence of vast forests and unlimited waterpower provided by the river. There isn't complete agreement as to the origins of the city's name, though most seem to concur that it is derived from a Chippewa word that means "far away place"—referring to the location where the tribe made annual hunting expeditions. Other linguists argue that the place name came from Indian words meaning "noise like thunder," referring to the waterfalls in the river at this location. The French named these falls Big Bull Falls, allegedly because the noise reminded them of the bellowing of a bull, though even that isn't one hundred percent certain. However, none of this is important from our perspective. What is important is that we are going to begin our ride in historic downtown Wausau, at the Falls Bridge and adjacent park.

The city has done a very nice job preserving the waterfront in this vicinity, with riverside parkland and trails connecting the shoreline and islands. It is a great place to loiter and do some exploration on foot along this historic river locale.

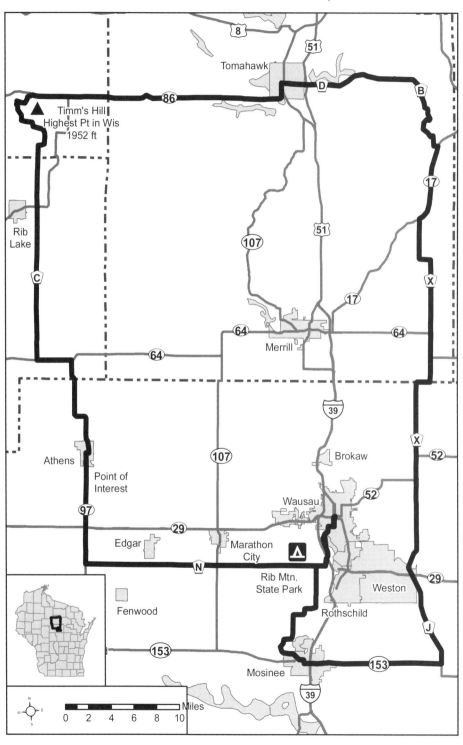

TO THE TOP OF WISCONSIN 191 MILES		
Miles	**Destination**	**Total**
00	Wausau / Falls Bridge	00
26	Route 97	26
45	Timm's Hill	71
25	Tomahawk	96
26	County Road—X	122
40	State Route 153	162
29	Wausau / POB	191

We leave town on the west side of the river, going south on 3rd Avenue from route 52 for less than a mile, turning right on Thomas Street. Take Thomas Street the short distance to 11th Avenue / county road N, following it across Lake Wausau, past the busy intersection with U.S. 51, to where it finally swings straight west on the south side of Rib Mountain State Park. CR-N is also known as Rib Mountain Drive and South Mountain Road in this stretch. Call the road what you may, it delivers us to the edge of this beautiful state park where you might wish to do some exploring.

Rib Mountain is unique in a couple of ways. It is the location in the state that has the most difference in altitude between a high point and adjacent flat lands. At 1,924 feet above sea level Rib Mountain isn't the highest point in Wisconsin, but the difference in altitude between the top of the hill and the base is a very impressive 670 feet. With this height difference, the view from the top is outstanding, and to make it even more impressive there is a 60-foot observation tower to further enhance the expansive vistas available at the top of the mountain. Several decades ago, prior to accurate measurements, Rib Mountain did hold the title of Wisconsin's highest peak, with an estimated height of 1,940 feet.

In this locale we have to briefly discuss an exception to the geologic rule I mentioned above. Though Marathon County is in the Northern Highlands, it is also part of the driftless or unglaciated region, having been spared the effects of the last ice age that scoured the rest of the Great Lakes region.

Rib Mountain, aka Granite Peak, is comprised of erosion-resistant quartzite that is well over a billion years old. It represents some of the oldest rock on earth.

The spectacular rock landscape wasn't impacted by the forces of ice, making the site unique not only visually but scientifically as well.

Our ride takes us west on CR-N for 21-miles through a very pleasant mix of farm and woodlands. This part of Wisconsin has one other unique feature, and that is the production of ginseng. Ninety five percent of the country's supply of this highly sought after food and beverage supplement is grown in this region. Eventually we stop at the intersection with route 97, where we turn north toward the village of Athens.

If you are interested in unique oddities, we will pass very close to one as we proceed north. Just shy of 7 miles north of CR-N on route 97 (2 miles south of Athens) will bring us to the spot where the 45th parallel crosses our path. This of course places us halfway between the North Pole and the equator. If you were to go four miles east of this point you will be at the intersection of the 90th meridian of longitude and the 45th degree of latitude—in other words, you will be in the exact center of the northwestern quadrant of the earth. There are only four such places on the planet, and two are under the ocean. The fourth is in China.

Our ride has us continuing north on route 97 about nine miles beyond Athens to route 64. A left turn onto 64 will deliver us to county road C, three miles to the west. On this road our fun really begins. For about eighteen miles CR-C is mostly straight but very enjoyable as it traverses an increasingly forested and hilly terrain. North of route 102 things really pick up. The best is saved for the last, however, and north of Spirit Lake the road becomes fantastic as it climbs and twists and turns in a rapid sequence of curves and hills, all in a heavily forested landscape.

Eventually you will come to a stop sign at CR-RR, a rustic road and our pathway to Timm's Hill. Shortly after you turn onto RR watch for a driveway with a green gate on your left. Unfortunately, the entry road into Timm's Hill county park is not well marked, so watch closely for the drive and iron gate and post once on RR. This one-way paved trail will deliver you to a parking area, from which a walking trail can be taken to the top of the hill. Once at the top of this forested hill you will have to climb the approximately 40-foot wooden observation tower to get a view. The trees block any view from the ground, even though at that point you are higher than anybody else in the state. Next to the observation tower is a metal fire tower that is higher than the public viewing tower. Fire spotters have to climb a metal ladder attached to the outside frame of the fire tower. Not my idea of fun! There are restrooms and a few picnic tables at the parking area, making this a good place to take a break from your travels.

Upon leaving Timm's Hill continue east on the narrow one-way road. Eventually it will take you out to state route 86, on which we ride east about twenty-two

The viewing tower on Timm's Hill rises above the tree tops to provide marvelous views from Wisconsin's highest point.

miles to the town of Tomahawk. This long stretch of state roadway is very pleasant, with meager traffic, respectable scenery, and an overall enjoyable ambience. We will follow route 86 as it crosses the Wisconsin River and turns toward the town of Tomahawk. Tomahawk is a resort town, with an economy largely based on tourism. Like many towns in northern Wisconsin it got a rather late start in life, being formed in 1891 as a company town for the lumbering business. The forest industry is still critical to this part of the state, but it is balanced with tourist dollars and small businesses, making for a solid economic base.

Of note for bikers is the annual Muscular Dystrophy Association ride held each September. This very large four-day event attracts about 40,000 riders, and although Harley-Davidson is a major sponsor of MDA rides, it is open to everyone. There are many events associated with this rally, including music, dancing, abundant food, and much more. Check out the Tomahawk Fall Ride for MDA for more information.

Follow route 86 as it turns east through town and ride it to U.S. 51, going straight across the expressway. Route 86 ends at the highway but county road D begins at that point without so much as a need to slow down. We will ride CR-D nine miles through a marvelous world of towering trees and beautiful scenery. At a wide spot in the road called Harrison you will come to a stop sign. At this point CR-D makes a ninety-degree turn north, but we want to continue going straight ahead on what is now CR-B. If CR-D was nice, 'B' is fabulous. The forests continue, but we now enter a beautiful area of lakes and hills called the Harrison Hills, much of which is over 1,800 feet in elevation. CR-B is an absolute blast to ride with tight curves accompanying the roller coaster hills. My only cautionary note about this stretch, as well as in the Timm's Hill area, is that parts of this tour are not compatible for large group rides. In fact, I recommend keeping groups to 6 or 8 at the largest in order to most fully enjoy the roads the way they're meant to be ridden.

County road-B will eventually deliver us to route 17. Turn right on SR 17, following it 6.5 miles to county road-X, turning left onto 'X'. This is one more road that will make me sound repetitive—it's great riding, has light traffic, and the scenery is very pleasant—though more open than the land east of Tomahawk. A couple miles south of route 17 'X' goes through a ninety-degree bend on the top of a hill, offering fabulous views to the east. CR-X carries us many miles south and is well marked along its entire length. This is one of those great rural roads where a person can relax and savor the here and now—no need for speed or to hurry to the next destination—just enjoy the ride. For a short distance it follows route 64, then continuing south again as 64 returns to its east and west travels. At the Marathon County line CR-X makes a short jog and resumes south as CR-J—nothing required on your part, just follow the pavement southward.

We will follow CR-J even more miles as it dissects the countryside east of Wausau and Weston. CR-J is one of those pleasant surprises that we sometimes find by serendipity. It might be assumed that what appears to be a fairly main road close to the Wausau / Weston urban area would be filled with traffic and lined with sprawl. That's not the case. This road is lined on either side with a mix of forest and fields, with the emphasis on trees. After going under the route 29 highway, the landscape gets even more wooded, all the way south to state route 153.

Our path has us turning right onto route 153, taking it west through farm and forest once again toward the increasingly developed area near airport and the 51/39 expressway in Mosinee. Just west of I-39 route 153 will cross the Wisconsin River, and very shortly after the river CR-B will angle to the right front—that's the road we want. We will be on CR-B for two miles and then it intersects with CR-KK. Turn right onto KK and follow it as it jogs for several miles northward, until it eventually arrives at CR-N at Rib Mountain State Park. Turn right on N, taking it back into Wausau and the end of this high-flying ride.

Helmet Hair Quiz Answer

Israeli Prime Minister Golda Meir. She lived in Milwaukee from 1906, when her family fled a Russian pogrom, to 1921 when she and her husband moved to Palestine. She became Israeli PM in 1969.

In Chicago's Shadow

Helmet Hair Quiz

What major river outside of the Lake Superior basin in Wisconsin flows to the north—a rare occurrence in the U.S.?

THIS RIDE WILL OPEN up the northeastern portion of the state for exploration, and we will learn some interesting things along the way. We begin in Marinette, a city at the mouth of the Menominee River in the northern portion of Green Bay. Given its location on a river that drains a large heavily forested region, it is logical that Marinette had its genesis and boom days during the heyday of the logging era of the late 19th century. A logging museum in downtown, on Stephenson Island, tells the story of that era. Check them out at marinettecountyhistory.org/.

Start our exploration by riding west on route 64 to the 4-way stop sign on the west edge of town. This places us at route 180, which we take to the north, following the Menominee River for many miles. This river forms the boundary between Michigan and Wisconsin, and is a beautiful river in a very scenic area. Several of the more remote stretches of the Menominee have some of the fastest white water rapids in either state, rated for experts only.

Until the 1840s it was assumed that the boundary line in this region was formed by two rivers rising from the same small inland lake; the Menominee River draining south to Lake Michigan, and the Montreal River flowing north to Lake Superior. A later survey found this was not the case, and this caused confusion for many decades until it was finally settled less than one hundred years ago. For years, decision makers in Washington thought the Lake Superior region was wilderness of little value for settlement because of poor soil quality and a short growing season. It took the discovery of iron ore and copper and the realization that a treasure trove of lumber needed to build the cities of a rapidly growing nation existed in this wilderness, to convince people that this isolated region had great economic potential. Determining exact borders suddenly became very important. In 1908 the state of Michigan drafted a new constitution, in which they claimed that the original border established by Congress in 1838 should stand, not the boundary as surveyed in 1848. This legal question was ultimately settled

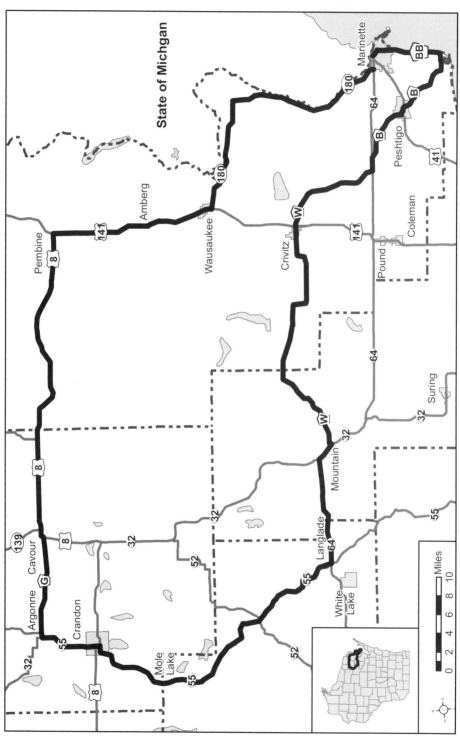

CHICAGO'S SHADOW 215 MILES		
Miles	**Destination**	**Total**
00	Marinette	00
31	Wausaukee	31
70	Crandon	101
36	Langlade / Route 64	137
42	Crivitz / U.S 141	179
21	Peshtigo Fire Museum	200
15	Marinette	215

by the U.S. Supreme Court in 1923. The court ruled that sixty years of possession of the contested land by Wisconsin made Michigan's claim moot, and this frontier border was finally clarified.

Route 180 is a fairly tame road with no extreme characteristics, and these qualities make for enjoyable motorcycling. It goes through a mostly wooded and flat landscape, with smooth easy curves being the norm for its entire length. The only traffic encountered will be local users, with nearby U.S. 41 and 141 handling the brunt of any commercial and tourist traffic in this locale. Eventually 180 swings to the west and joins with U.S. 141 at the town of Wausaukee. Our journey takes us north on 141 to U.S. 8. One forty one is a main highway for this region but it is a nice biking road just the same. The land gets a bit more rolling as we get further inland and away from the flat lake plain. Dave's Falls County Park, located just south of Amberg where the Pike River crosses the road, is a nice roadside stop. The park is named in remembrance of a logger, yes, with the name of Dave, who was killed here many years ago while trying to clear a logjam in the nearby falls. A relatively short and easy walk, with built in steps, takes viewers down the hillside to see these picturesque cascades. North of the village of Amberg 141 becomes quite flat and straight, though the land along the road remains mostly forested.

At the village of Pembine turn west onto U.S. 8, which will be our guide for 34 miles across a rugged, wooded and rocky land that continues to this day to resist man's attempts at taming it. Nature prevails here and I find that reality to be a large part of this area's charms. The countryside isn't extraordinary in any way except for its vast scale. The land is mostly flat to rolling, but the earth is rocky and trees and wildlife are still its main crops.

Motorcyclists gather for one of the many charitable fundraising events held each year in Wisconsin.

After near 34 miles on U.S. 8 you will pass the route 139 intersection and cross the Peshtigo River. At this point route 8 swings straights south. Almost immediately after making the southerly turn you will see county road G heading to your right. G is our road, and we'll ride it eleven miles further west to route 32 / 55 and the village of Argonne. I might add that the CN railroad parallels route 8 and CR-G all the way from Pembine to Argonne.

Ride 32/55 south to the village of Crandon, located on the north shore of Lake Metonga. Crandon is the county seat for Forest County, but it is better known by bikers and other gearheads as the home of the Crandon International Off Road Raceway. This famous site has been in operation for four decades, and of interest to motorcyclists is the fact that after being absent for several years, motocross has returned to CIORR.

At Crandon routes 8 and 32 head east, but we stay on state route 55 for beaucoup miles of entirely delightful riding between Crandon and Langlade. For the first several miles route 55 dodges between a number of lakes, then it picks up the Wolf River, which it shadows for many more miles with the usual meanderings of a streamside road; overall making for fabulous riding through a rolling land blanketed with mature forests.

There are two historic markers of interest in this stretch. The first is at Mole Lake and it describes an 1806 battle between the Sioux and Chippewa over rights to historically important wild rice beds in the area. The Chippewa had harvested the wild rice each fall for many generations. A ferocious battle was fought when the Sioux came into the area from the west to take over this vital food source, resulting in at least 500 combatant deaths. The Indians from both tribes were buried in a mass grave near the marker. This spot of course has special significance to Native Americans, but it is also a reminder to the rest of us that people lived their lives here, and history was being made, long before the first white settler built a cabin in these woods. The Mole Lake Indian Reservation and nearby Rice Lake are modern reminders of this region's history.

Several miles south of Mole Lake, just south of the village of Pickerel, is another interesting historic marker. Located in a nice roadside park, this sign marks the location of the old Military Road carved through the harsh wilderness between Fort Howard (Green Bay) and Fort Wilkins, located at the tip of Michigan's Keweenaw Peninsula. Though authorized by President Lincoln in 1863, the road wasn't finished for several years. In the end it served as the means of travel for explorers and settlers more than it did for its originally intended military purposes. There are places in northern Wisconsin and the western Upper Peninsula of Michigan where the name Military Road is still attached to intermittent stretches of roadway.

South of the intersection with route 52 our road goes through a nice hilly region in an area called Ninemile Hills. The great riding continues all the way to route 64 and Langlade, alternating between flat lands near swamps and lakes, or rolling and rocky forested lands. At all times in this area the road is greatly influenced by the nearby Wolf River, matching it curve for curve.

At Langlade turn east on route 64. Just north of this corner is another interesting roadside marker that tells the story of the man who is often referred to as the father of Wisconsin. His is a fascinating story, so I will print the entire wording of the historic marker erected in his memory:

> *The Village of Langlade and Langlade County were named for Charles Michel de Langlade, who has been called the "Father of Wisconsin." Born at the trading post of Mackinac in 1729, de Langlade's character, military ability, and influence left a commanding impression on Wisconsin's early history. He was among the first permanent settlers to locate on the present site of Green Bay about 1745. During the French and Indian War, de Langlade led Wisconsin Indians against Fort Duquesne, and from there to Fort Cumberland, where Braddock was in command, and where George Washington*

served as a young lieutenant. In 1759, De Langlade fought under General Montcalm in the Battle of Quebec, which ended the French Empire in North America. After active service with the British in the Revolutionary War, de Langlade returned to Green Bay. He died there in 1800.

I think that qualifies as having lived a full and interesting life!

⋘◈⋙

Route 64 is straighter than 55 but that trait doesn't seriously detract from its motorcycling credentials. It is a very enjoyable road through the Chequamegon Nicolet National Forest. After roughly twelve miles it joins company with route 32 and heads southeast toward the village of Mountain. In this small town turn left onto county road W, and be prepared for many more delightful miles on twisting and rolling asphalt through the forest. The road curves around the many lakes in this area, as it traverses a land of rock and trees. There are some rock outcroppings in this stretch that are so unique that geologists and geology students come from far and wide to study them in order to better understand the last couple billion years of earth's geologic history. Our ride will be both technically enjoyable and scenic all the way east to the town of Crivitz. Once we leave the national forest behind the land gradually opens up and even eventually turns into farmlands, where the road straightens and, regrettably, takes on a more civilized demeanor.

Continue east on CR-W to Crivitz and across U.S. 141. The Gateway Bar & Grill, at CR-W and route 141 in Crivitz is a good place to enjoy a hearty meal if the time is right. Beyond town CR-W makes a southeasterly turn and eventually it will join with route 64 again. We are going to be on this state road for just over a mile at which point we turn right onto county road D, which takes us southeast a few more miles to the town of Peshtigo, and what I think is the most important and poignant stop of the day.

In Peshtigo you will come to a stop sign at Oconto Street. Turn left there, taking it east a short distance to the Peshtigo Fire Museum. (You will have seen signs for this museum for the last several miles, just follow them to the site).

The Fire Museum and adjacent cemetery vividly tell the story of one of Wisconsin's darkest days. On October 8, 1871, the worst forest fire in America's history burned across northeastern Wisconsin and the western UP. The final figure will never be known but somewhere between 1,200 and 2,400 men, women and children were killed that fateful day, most of them in this very locale.

Because this was also the same day of the famous Chicago fire, the Peshtigo forest fire has never received the level of attention and its proper place in our col-

*This poignant sculpture rests between the fire museum
and adjacent cemetery in Peshtigo.*

lective national historic consciousness that it deserves. Many people have never heard of it.

The period of roughly 1870 to 1910 was one that saw massive forest fires burn across great swaths of the Great Lakes states. As farmers cleared land for farming, and as millions of acres were transformed from virgin forests to piles of slash and brush, fires, both deliberate and accidental, burned rampant. With no way to contain them, some burned for days across great distances, wiping out everything in their paths.

Many of the victims of the Peshtigo fire were never identified and are buried in a mass grave in the cemetery adjacent to the museum.

From the museum, go east just a block to route 41, taking it east across the Peshtigo River. Once across the bridge you will see the sign for county road B (aka Front Street in town). Turn right onto B, taking it a mile then turning onto county road BB when B turns straight east. CR-BB will follow the Peshtigo River toward its rendezvous with Lake Michigan.

CR-BB will eventually swing east and then north along the shoreline. At the south Marinette city limits it becomes Shore Drive. Follow this road north into town, turning left when it 'Ts', with the St. Thomas of Aquinas Academy across the intersection. This street will take us to downtown Marinette and deliver us back to U.S. 41, and the end of yet one more great motorcycle ride that has the added benefit of leaving us smarter and more aware at the end of the ride than we perhaps were at the start. I call that a great day on a motorcycle; and that's saying a lot!

 Helmet Hair Quiz Answer

The Fox River.

A Clearly Superior Ride

Helmet Hair Quiz

Prior to statehood, Wisconsin was part of what five U.S. Territories?

PACK YOUR BAGS for a two-day trip through what many Wisconsinites call God's Country. The northwest corner of Wisconsin is a rugged and beautiful region where a motorcyclist can lose him or herself, basking in the beauty and relaxing in the leisurely pace that makes this region different from places that seem to take themselves too seriously. This district really does have it all; wilderness, scenic beauty, fascinating history, great roads, and friendly people.

While you may think that a ride of this length is a good one-day ride, plan for two if possible. The schedule assumes time spent exploring the various attractions along the way. It would be a shame to simply ride the roads and not delve into the many stories and natural and manmade sites awaiting our arrival.

The adventure starts in the city of Superior, the most urbanized part of this tour and this corner of the state. I recommend two stops in Superior before leaving on the ride. They are both on the waterfront. First, a stop to visit the Richard Bong World War 2 Heritage Center is an interesting immersion in the history of this fascinating aviator and of the war. Major Bong was and is still America's premier flying ace. He shot down at least forty Japanese planes during the war, winning the Medal of Honor for his incredible bravery and skills. Tragically, he died at the end of the war while serving as a test pilot in California. Bong was from nearby Poplar, and is a true American hero.

Nearby is the *S. S. Meteor*, the last surviving ship of the whaleback design. The *Meteor* was manufactured in Superior in 1896 and was eventually brought back home after its retirement. Touring the ship and museum are great ways to better understand the maritime heritage of the Great Lakes. A stop at the Old Firehouse and Police Museum is interesting if you'd like to see a 1906 steam pumper and other antique fire fighting equipment. The museum is in an old fire station. Call them at 715.398.7558 if you would like more information.

Start the ride by heading east on U.S. 53 / 2 to just beyond the city limits where we meet state route 13. Point the bike east on route 13, following it all the way

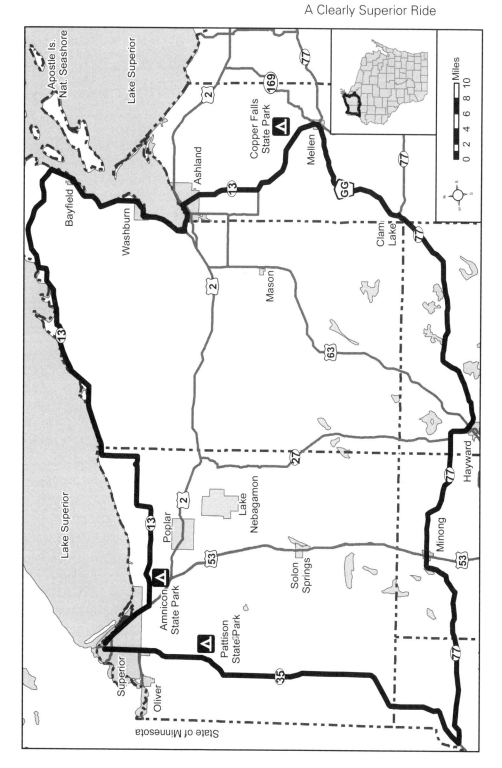

Miles	Destination	Total
00	Superior, WI	00
44	Port Wing	44
36	Bayfield	80
22	Ashland	102
25	Mellen	127
20	Clam Lake	147
33	Hayward	180
21	Minong / U.S. 53	201
27	State Route 35	228
54	Superior	282

A SUPERIOR RIDE 282 MILES

through the Bayfield Peninsula and ultimately to Ashland. This loop is a hundred enjoyable miles, so unwind and savor the ride and the scenery. A cautionary note here; route 13 is very close to Lake Superior. Experienced riders know that while the temperature might be a balmy eighty degrees inland, there very well could be cold fog and drizzle near the lake. Be prepared with proper cool weather clothing and rain gear, just in case. Maybe it is just my bad luck, but I have encountered cold, foggy, and wet weather along the Lake Superior shoreline probably as often as not.

On the west shore of Chequamegon Bay is the popular tourist destination town of Bayfield. You will want to park your bike here and walk around town and the waterfront. It is an interesting and enjoyable place to explore, and if you happen to be there during one of the many events the town hosts the fun meter points even higher. In Bayfield you can take a narrated cruise through the Apostle Islands National Lakeshore on a large cruise ship (highly recommended, plan on at least a half-day), take a sailing excursion in the bay or through the Apostle Islands archipelago, visit a local maritime museum, or simply walk, talk and gawk. The Chicago Tribune once called Bayfield the best small town in the Midwest, and it is easy to see why.

In the late 1800s, brownstone, a highly popular building material at the time, was mined on several of the Apostle Islands, especially on Basswood Island. Cities across the country utilized this attractive and distinctive brown sandstone to

Scenic waterfalls tumble from adjacent highlands to join the cold waters of Lake Superior. Majestic cascades can be found throughout the Lake Superior basin.

make striking buildings ranging from courthouses to row houses—especially in the east and Midwest. Many brownstone buildings in Chicago had their origins in Apostle Island quarries. One of the more extraordinary brownstone buildings in Wisconsin (and there are many) is the Grant County courthouse in Lancaster.

Riding south on route 13 is great fun, with the road near the water for the most part. Thirteen will eventually take us to U.S.2 and the Ashland area. At U.S. 2 I recommend making a right turn and going the very short distance to the Northern Great Lakes Visitor Center. This marvelous facility is operated in partnership with several governmental and private organizations. It offers many exhibits and programs highlighting the natural and cultural history of the Lake Superior region.

Ashland is our next destination. There are several things worthy of your time in this port city. Entering town from the west the most striking shoreline feature is the massive ore dock; so massive in fact that they are the largest docks of their type in the world! Chequamegon Bay stretches to the north from Ashland. This Ojibwa word is frequently used throughout northern Wisconsin by many places and organizations. It originally specifically referred to this Lake Superior bay, however, and it means 'place of shallow water' in the native tongue. It marked the location where Indians gathered to harvest fish in the shallows. The eastern and southern sections of the bay are shallow for significant distances out, creating excellent fish habitat and spawning areas, as well as making it easier to harvest those fish at certain times of the year.

Many commercial buildings in Ashland along Main Street and Chapple Street have large murals painted on their otherwise unappealing blank walls, depicting a variety of historic or cultural scenes. The 4th of July is always a good time to get away, and if you are in Ashland over this holiday be sure to check out the Bay Area Rod and Custom Car Show.

◄◄◄◄◗►►►►

Our ride through the north woods continues south on route 13 roughly 24 miles to the village of Mellen. But what a wonderful twenty four miles it is! Let's see; it has smooth pavement, great scenery, the road has the kind of characteristics bikers desire, and there are marvelous sights to see along the way. This sounds like world-class motorcycling to me!

For the first couple of miles the land is fairly flat and open, as one would expect being on the lake plain and near town. Then things improve rapidly. Forests become the predominant landscape feature, and starting with the scenic gorges of the Bad River, the land itself takes on much more character with hills and impressive rock outcroppings becoming the norm.

But these are not the adolescent sandstone or limestone formations of southern Wisconsin. No sir, these rocks are the granddaddy of all rocks, consisting of some of the most ancient rock on earth at well over a billion years old. We are riding on the Canadian Shield, also called the Precambrian Shield. This rock foundation is actually the roots of ancient mountains and volcanoes that were eroded down over hundreds of millions of years by wind, water and ice, finally scraped bare by the series of glaciers that crept south over the last two million years. This land is still rebounding from the weight of the most recent mile-thick ice, resulting in some of the most dramatic waterfalls and whitewater gorges in this part of the country as rivers continue to carve down into the ancient bedrock.

Elk once again live wild and free in northern Wisconsin, restoring an important part of the state's natural ecosystem.

Just north of Mellen you will see signs for Copper Falls State Park. I certainly recommend a side trip to the park to view the waterfalls and whitewater cascading through rock gorges up to one-hundred feet high.

As wonderful as the trip has been thus far, I think the best part is just beginning. In Mellen turn right onto county road GG, aka Markle Memorial Drive. This road, which I lack adequate superlatives to describe, carves through twenty miles of national forest land. It is very lightly traveled smooth asphalt through some of the nicest scenery around, with many curves and other traits bikers want. In short, this sunlight-dappled road was custom made for some of the best motorcycling you will find anywhere.

Eventually we arrive at Clam Lake and state route 77. After a right turn our fun continues unabated. Route 77 is one of the best roads in the state in my opinion, and we will be on one of the finest stretches of this superb byway. The 29-mile section of route 77 from Hayward east to Glidden and route 13 is designated as the Great Divide Scenic Highway. This road travels on and near a barely

A variety of bragging-size fish thrive at the Fishing Hall of Fame in Hayward.

perceptible ridge that marks the divide between the Lake Superior and Missis-sippi River watersheds.

Very soon after starting west on 77 you will start seeing signs warning of the presence of Elk. If the lights are flashing then you had best slow down because that means that an animal wearing a radio collar is near the road. In fact, even though route 77 has all the makings of a great biking route, I recommend a more leisurely pace through here. The scenery is too nice to ignore, and there are enough large wild animals present in the form of bears, wolves, deer, elk, coyotes, and so on that you need to ride in recognition of the fact you are on their home turf now. Hitting any one of these furry folk could screw up your day fast.

After 33 miles of wonderful riding on route 77 we arrive in the fun tourist town of Hayward. I will get right to the point regarding this town's most famous attraction and say that yes, you should visit the fishing museum, officially known as the National Fresh Water Fishing Hall of Fame. Having your picture taken in the jaws of the 140-foot long and 40-foot high giant Musky is worth the price of admission, though there is much more to see than just this iconic structure. The museum has many fascinating displays of interest if you have even a rudimentary level of curiosity in fish or fishing.

Hayward is also the site of the Lumberjack World Championships, where the best lumberjacks on the planet come to compete. Fittingly, it is also the home of America's only licensed chainsaw carving school—the Wisconsin School of Chainsaw Carving.

The CruzIn Car Show is a fun time if you are here in mid-June.

⋘◆⋙

We continue our ride west on route 77 beyond Hayward. This road lays on the northern edge of a region of lakes that results in a landscape comprised of water as much as of land. The riding across this stretch is great, with the land along the road taking on a hillier and more rugged aspect west of Minong and U.S. 53. Chill out and take pleasure in another premier motorcycling road.

Ultimately we arrive at route 35 and head north across the St. Croix River valley and back toward the city of Superior. Route 35 is a bit tamer than what we have become used to on this ride but it is by no means shabby. The riding is relaxing and enjoyable mile after scenic mile. Just south of Superior we encounter Pattison State Park where the beauty of waterfalls and rock gorges are once again ours to enjoy. Viewing Big Manitou Falls and a hike through Rocky Gorge are enough to make nature lovers out of even the most skeptical couch potato. At 165-feet, the Big Manitou Falls are the highest in Wisconsin.

I have only hit the major attractions on this ride. Along the way you will see many other enticing places that call for a stop and exploration. You will want fully charged batteries and plenty of memory space available in your camera because opportunities for stunning pictures will be plentiful.

As you can see, this ride offers up many clearly superior opportunities for activities beyond simply riding a motorcycle. I hope you take advantage of as many as time allows, and that you plan ahead to ensure that enough time is allotted.

Helmet Hair Quiz Answer

The Northwest Territory (1787—1800), the Indiana Territory (1800—1809), the Illinois Territory (1809—1818) the Michigan Territory (1818—1836) and the Wisconsin Territory from 1836—1848, when it became a state.

The Real McCoy

Helmet Hair Quiz
Where is the only remaining ferry on the state's highway system?

THERE IS MUCH GEOGRAPHIC and cultural diversity in Wisconsin and this tour will prove that fact. Additionally, the starting point, Sparta, supports another observation that I have made over the years—the number of noteworthy men and women who come from the small towns and farms of America. From my observations, I believe that if a compilation were made of America's best, bravest, and wisest, a disproportionate number would have been born in small towns or on farms. I think this is one of our country's enduring strengths—that hard work, ambition, dedication to principles, and intelligence are more important than one's social birth class.

The starting point of this tour just further proves my hypothesis. Two men of great stature are from the Sparta area—General Robert McCoy and astronaut Deke Slayton.

General McCoy came from a military family and had an ancestor who fought in the American War of Independence. McCoy grew up in Sparta. He fought in the Spanish-American War, Mexican Border skirmishes, and World War I in France, where he distinguished himself with honor. He was also very instrumental in convincing the military to establish a nearby military base, which of course took on his name.

Donald "Deke" Slayton was a local farm boy who became a World War II fighter pilot, and ultimately one of the original seven Mercury astronauts in 1959. His most famous space accomplishment occurred in 1975 with the historic docking of spacecraft from the U.S. and Soviet Union—the first time ever for this very technically complicated, and politically significant, undertaking.

The city of Sparta is known as the bicycling capital of America. Two popular bicycling trails intersect here, and the state's first rails to trails bike path was formed here. They have a bicycle museum should you wish to check it out.

We start our ride east on state route 21. A couple miles to the east check out the very large concrete wildlife on display in the little town of Angelo. Route 21

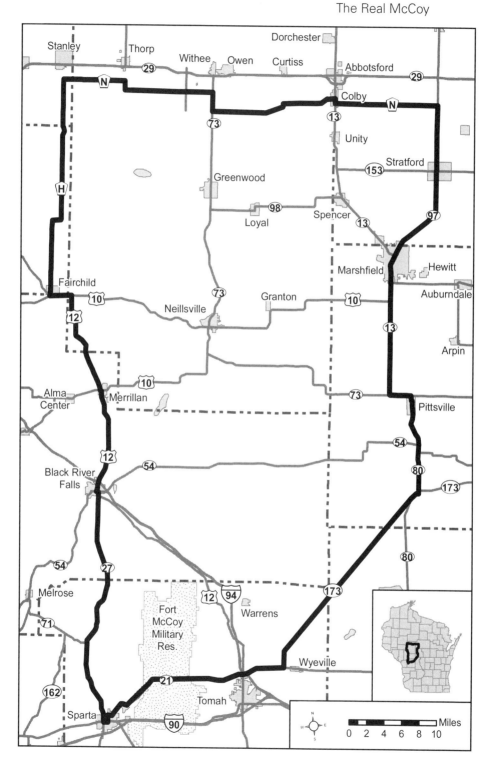

	FORT MCCOY 217 MILES	
Miles	**Destination**	**Total**
00	Sparta	00
19	Tomah	19
39	Pittsville	58
19	Marshfield / Route 97	77
18	County Road N	95
46	County Road H	141
25	Fairchild	166
26	Black River Falls	192
25	Sparta	217

is flat and unexciting through this area, which is precisely why Fort McCoy exists in this location. It was thought that these flat sand plains would be perfect for training the newly mechanized army of a century ago. Fort McCoy sits on 60,000 acres and is the only U.S. Army installation in Wisconsin with facilities focused on providing what the Army calls total force training.

The base has provided on-site support and facilities for the training of over 100,000 personnel from all services per year over the past decade. The fort is one of 15 bases that the Army calls Power-Projection Platforms, which have the mission of supporting the mobilization of reserve units. Fort McCoy also hosts the Wisconsin State Patrol's training academy.

⏴⏴⏴◆⏵⏵⏵

Eventually 21 will take us past Tomah and I-94 to state route 173. By the way, from I-94 to the next gas station is 35 miles, so if your tank is nearly empty fill up now rather than take a chance.

This region is the cranberry capital of Wisconsin, and when traveling north on route 173 it is easy to understand why; it is flat, low and wet! At the barely discernable village of Valley Junction route 173 makes a beeline northeast across a landscape that looks like a subarctic tundra plain. It is of course flat, and to a large extent vegetation is wetland brush and small trees. The area on the south side of 173 is mostly a state owned wildlife area, while to the north is where you will find most of the cranberry marshes. Riding on this road is very different from what we are accustomed. It is flat and straight, but also very intriguing. Traffic is light and the road is wide open. It makes for a different kind of ride, but an enjoyable outing just the same, where one can bask in the solitude and openness that surrounds you.

As we ride certain roads, memories of earlier rides can't help but creep into our mind, and this road has a deeply ingrained memory that I still occasional tell folks about, while shaking my head in disbelief. I was caught in a sudden and very severe thunderstorm, with high wind, hail, torrential rain, and lightning that lit the black afternoon sky in a pyrotechnic show the likes of which I have rarely seen. The crosswind was so fierce and the rain so heavy I could no longer keep the bike on the road so I parked on the shoulder, as no shelter of any kind was within several miles in any direction. It soon became obvious that I would be better off taking cover in a small stand of mature trees a hundred feet off the road than standing in the open with lightning flashing all around.

Leaving my helmet on for rain protection, I walked into the woodlot and stared in alarmed amazement at the unbelievable display of nature's most power-ful forces being demonstrated in front of me. Suddenly I felt a major blow to my head, which for a fraction of a second had all kinds of thoughts running through my mind. A maniac in the woods in the storm with a baseball bat? A Frankenstein type character roaming the woods preying on lost travelers? What in the world could be going on, my mind flashed, as I stumbled and nearly fell. It turned out that a long branch, about four inches in diameter, had fallen from the top of one of the trees under which I was standing. I shudder to think what would have hap-pened had I not had my helmet on. At the same time, I still cannot believe that the entire scenario and this particular event had even occurred on a day that just a couple hours earlier was a beautiful summer afternoon that looked like a perfect opportunity for a ride. Ride prepared for the unexpected is the lesson that was reinforced yet one more time.

<<<<●>>>>

It is twenty-two miles as straight as an arrow from Valley Junction to route 80, where we leave route 173 and turn north toward Deckerville. Route 80 will even-tually 'T' at route 13, where we turn left and follow it north to the bustling city of Marshfield. The land around us changes dramatically once north of Deckerville, turning from swamp and brush to high and fertile farmland. There isn't a lot of special significance to see along here and the road is fairly blah, so just relax and enjoy the ride. About two miles south of U.S. 10 notice the car perched atop the 40-foot farm silo on your left—you don't see that every day!

*Fort McCoy in western Wisconsin has become an integral part
of the military's defense preparedness system.*

In Marshfield we leave route 13 and pick up route 97 to continue northward. Route 13 north of Marshfield is quite heavily developed and busy, which seems odd given the location and the chiefly agricultural nature of this area.

Check the schedule for the Marshfield Super Speedway, a half-mile paved oval located three miles west of Marshfield on county road H. They have a motorcycle racing division as well as various classes of stock cars. Half-mile ovals guarantee high speeds and the ultimate in racing excitement.

Along route 97 the land is primarily farm country but higher in elevation and more rolling than to the south. After passing through the small town of Stratford we'll ride north seven more miles to county road N, where a left turn starts us on the westward loop.

CR-N makes a northerly jog in the village of Colby and then proceeds west again, with a few more well marked jogs ahead of us. We will ride across this scenic farm road for forty-seven miles before turning again. The path is mostly straight but makes up for this with its delightfully rolling nature and the beautiful and bountiful farmlands through which we are traveling.

After nearly 47 miles CR-N curves north as CR-Nn, and county road Mm goes straight west. We want to make a careful turn at this curve onto Mm, taking it one mile to CR-H, where we turn left and start riding south.

We will enjoy the wonderful charms of CR-H for twenty-five miles, all the way south to the town of Fairchild and U.S. 12. Though mostly straight, CR-H is fabulous riding, and the further south one rides, the better it gets. We leave the farmland behind after 3 or 4 miles and from that point south we enter a heavily forested region where delightful motorcycling is the order of the day. The road is in good condition and traffic is sparse in this scenic out of the way countryside.

In Fairchild CR-H becomes Center Street and intersects with U.S. 12 / route 27, which we ride south and southeast all the way to Black River Falls. For the most part highway officials haven't "improved" U.S. 12 in this region (though I think they're working their way here) and it is still a very nice biking road with lots of curves, hills and pleasing scenery. Five miles north of Black River Falls is NCN North Campground, the location of the annual Black River Rumble motorcycle rally (adults only!) Call them at 1.888.345.2267.

Just south of Black River Falls routes 12 and 27 diverge and we stay on state route 27.

This road will take us all the way south to Sparta, and it provides marvelous riding. The road gets better the further south one rides, with an especially nice stretch north of Sparta where the road follows the curving valley formed by a series of small streams. There are high hills on either side of the winding asphalt, making for a scenic riding smorgasbord that will delight the senses. All good things unfortunately must come to an end, including this tour. Route 27 will eventually deposit us back in Sparta after a very enjoyable ride through a part of the state that provides a level of diversity not found in most places.

Helmet Hair Quiz Answer

The COLSAC III free ferry crosses the Wisconsin River as part of state route 113. The ferry is based in Merrimac. COLSAC is an acronym for Columbia and Sauk Counties—which border on the river.

Hodags and Saloons

Helmet Hair Quiz

How many miles of roads are there in Wisconsin?

THIS TOUR TAKES US THROUGH the magical land that is northeastern Wisconsin. It is an immense place of lakes and forests, ancient rock hills and river valleys, waterfalls and wildlife. It is a bountiful and beautiful land laced with roads made to order for motorcycling. In short, we are now in motorcycling paradise.

The ride begins in the active small city of Rhinelander, county seat of Oneida County and home of 8,000 good folks. The town, like almost all towns in northern Wisconsin, started out as a lumbering center in the late 1800s. Unlike many of its peers, Rhinelander did not fade away after the virgin timber disappeared from the surrounding countryside. City leaders fought hard to diversify the economy—an effort still made in many 'rust belt' communities to this day as underlying economic conditions continue to change. They were successful and today the city has a strong commercial and small industry base as well as being in the heart of a major recreational area, which prompts tourists to come here and part with their dollars.

The Rhinelander Logging Museum Complex, located in Pioneer Park on Business U.S. 8 (Oneida Avenue in downtown), is an enjoyable stop to explore before beginning the ride. It features an 1870s logging camp, railroad museum, old school, and much more. Admission is free with donations at the discretion of the visitor. Located near the intersection of U.S. 8 and route 47 is a company that offers riverboat cruises down the Wisconsin River aboard *The Wilderness Queen* riverboat. They offer a wide variety of types and lengths of round-trip cruises south to the Hat Rapids Dam. I have never taken this particular cruise, but it is very tempting. A boat ride down this wilderness stretch of river would be a wonderful way to spend a few hours.

You can't go far in Rhinelander without seeing or hearing references to Hodags. This mythical creature has become part of the culture of local residents. The story of how this phenomenon began is an interesting one that I think makes a good tale that should be told. It began in the lumberjack culture, where men

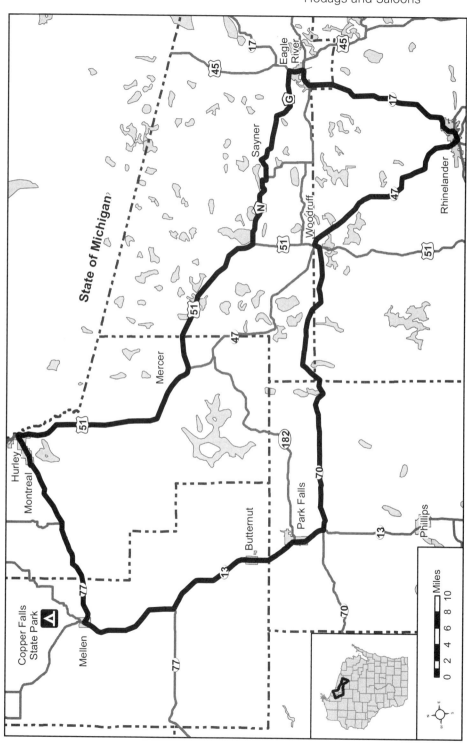

Miles	Destination	Total
HODAGS & SALOONS **221 MILES**		
00	Rhinelander	00
24	Eagle River	24
26	U.S. 51	50
20	Manitowish	70
26	Hurley	96
26	Mellen	122
32	Park Falls	154
43	Woodruff	197
24	Rhinelander	221

whiled away their few hours of rest telling fantastic stories and tales much the way Boy Scouts continue to do in their overnight camping expeditions. This story was created by local jester and practical jokester Eugene Shepard in the early 1890s. It grew larger as time went by, attracting more believers with each passing month. A book written many years ago tells the story best so I thought I would include an excerpt here.

"In the autumn of 1896, Shepard and a group of lumberjacks surprised a Hodag in its den and asphyxiated the monster with a heavy dose of chloroform. Shepard then transported the Hodag to the Rhinelander fairgrounds and confined it to a pit resembling its den "in order that the animal would not discover the deception being practiced upon him." Days before the opening of Oneida County's first fair, Shepard announced that he would proudly exhibit his recently captured beast.

"The Hodag, displayed near the entrance gate of the fair proved the event's main attraction. On Monday and Tuesday, the first two days of the fair, "the tent was filled with a crowd of curious people throughout the day." On Wednesday, "a large number of spectators gave up their dimes to see this strange animal and hear its history as told by Eugene Shepard himself." Entering a dimly lit tent, and separated from the beast by a curtain and a

good distance, the fair-goers witnessed the beast move and growl. Very few left the fair grounds not believing in the authenticity of Shepard's Hodag. From this introduction the Hodag and its boastful owner toured county fairs and even the Wisconsin State Fair in Madison. Furthermore, Shepard displayed his monstrosity in a shed at his Rhinelander home for all to view. In this capacity the Hodag attracted thousands of curious spectators and brought a disproportionate amount of attention to a small frontier community in the uppermost regions of the Wisconsin River Valley.

"Eventually the Hodag was discovered to be an elaborate hoax, its body, a carved stump covered with an ox hide; its horns and spikes derived from oxen and cattle; its movement controlled by wires; and its growl supplied by Shepard's sons hidden in the monster's lair. This discovery, however, took nothing away from the Hodag's popularity. People from across the state and region continued to travel up the Wisconsin to Rhinelander to view Shepard's concoction. Although the original creature was destroyed by a fire near the turn of the century, the Hodag continued to gain popularity. By the 1920s, an extremely popular postcard portraying the Hodag's capture circulated throughout the region. Soon Rhinelander became known as the Hodag city, and its inhabitants proudly touted its unique identity and the piece of local color on which it was based." [1]

So there you go; the Hodag seems to have evolved from a money-making myth to a genuine cultural icon that isn't fading away any time soon.

Embark on this marvelous ride in downtown Rhinelander proceeding north on route 17. This road will take us mile after sinuous mile through forests and alongside tree-rimmed pristine lakes. Though this road crosses an area that is relatively flat, it is nonetheless quite high in elevation—averaging near 1,600 feet. This region isn't without its own variety of development and commerce. Gifts left behind by the last ice age in the form of gravel are extracted in two large gravel pits along the road, and quarries and forestry products continue to be economically important to this part of the state. Farmers try to scratch out a living in scattered pockets along the way but poor soil conditions and short growing seasons pose serious challenges.

Eventually route 17 joins with state route 70, going east two miles to the City of Eagle River. Route 17 continues north from town in company with route

[1] *Long Live The Hodag! The Life and Legacy of Eugene Simeon Shepard: 1854-1923* by Kurt D. Kortenhof (ISBN: 0-9653745-0-5).

32 and U.S. 45. After route 17 / 32 / 45 turns north in town, travel two miles at which point county road G will be seen heading west. This is our road across the countryside for many more scenic and enjoyable biking miles. This area continues to be mostly flat with many lakes and swamps, which G skirts around in a manner appreciated by motorcyclists. Eventually CR-G will 'T' at CR-N, where we turn left and follow N into the village of Sayner where it makes a half-mile jog to the north, then heading west once again to U.S. 51. Much of our travels on county roads G and N will be through the Northern Highland American Legion State Forest. The land gets a bit more rolling as we ride west, but lakes and forests still reign supreme, with dramatic hills and striking rock escarpments yet to come.

Route 51 north will be our riding partner for dozens of wonderful miles of more lakes and forestlands, with the occasional mix of farms and recreational properties.

◄◄◄◄◉►►►►

At the village of Mercer the land begins to change noticeably along the road, with hills and rock outcroppings becoming more obvious, adding a different and more rugged texture to the scenery. The town of Mercer proclaims itself as the Loon Capital of Wisconsin. As if to prove this point, a huge concrete loon rests in front of the Chamber of Commerce building. Mercer is in the heart of forests, lakes and wild land. There are over 200 lakes within a twenty-mile radius. That is a lot of fishing opportunity and potential to lose oneself in this beautiful land! The Antler's Pub on Lakeview Street in Mercer is a friendly place to enjoy a good meal and company.

A few miles north of Mercer route 51 turns straight north, and near this point you will also see a continental divide sign. North of this sign water flows to Lake Superior and south of it water flows south and southwest to the Mississippi River. When viewed on a map depicting watersheds the Lake Superior basin is actually surprisingly small. More area in northern Wisconsin is in the Mississippi watershed than Lake Superior's.

Just north of the divide sign Pine Lake will appear on the east side of the road. This lake is the headwater of the Montreal River, which flows north and soon becomes the common border between Wisconsin and Michigan. U.S. 51 parallels the river about a mile to the west all the way north into the town of Hurley in Iron County. Note the impressive Vietnam Veterans park on 51 just south of Hurley—it's hard to miss the chopper and tank.

The small city of Hurley is large on history. It dates back to the lumbering period and received a major shot in the arm when rich veins of iron ore were dis-

The haunting call of the loon can still be heard across much of northern Wisconsin, one more reason to consider camping while touring by motorcycle.

covered nearby. The iron ore in the western UP and northeastern Wisconsin, in the Gogebic and Penokee ranges, was amazingly concentrated, being between 60 to 68 percent pure iron. Like western gold rushes, millionaires were literally made overnight in the mid-1880s.

It was long known that iron ore, along with copper, was in this region. Early surveyors noted decades earlier that the presence of ore was causing their compasses to be erratic. Indians had mined and traded the copper for centuries before the first whites arrived. But the discovery of rich veins of iron ore in easily mined locations changed everything overnight. An 1886 article in the Chicago Tribune speaks of how the area was transformed from trackless unexplored wilderness to a region of booming towns within one year. Hurley prospered more than most towns and gained a reputation as a wild and roaring frontier city that it still exploits to this day. At one point the region had hundreds of saloons, most of which were in Hurley. Its red light districts and lawless ways were known far and wide, and many miners and lumberjacks lost their week's wages during wild Saturday nights in Hurley or other boom towns. For Hurley this *modus operandi* lasted all the way through the 1930s. It really was a roaring town during the Roaring Twenties!

Today it is a very nice city of about two thousand citizens, nestled on the banks of the Montreal River, across from Ironwood, Michigan, a larger adjacent city to the east. This region is a beautiful history-filled locale that deserves some investigation.

We'll do some of that exploring as we turn west on state route 77. This road began life as a muddy trail over which tons of ore in heavy carts were pulled by horses. Today the same path takes us through the heart of the Gogebic Range on smooth asphalt. Just west of Hurley is the village of Montreal, which was a major iron and copper mining center. A century ago the village was a company town, with the Montreal Mining Company providing prefab houses for its workers. That part of town is listed as a national historic site. A sign on the east side of the village notes the site of the world's deepest iron mine. If you look carefully, large slag piles made up of tailings from the several mines that once operated here are seen along the road.

We will enjoy the amazing biking charms of route 77 westward all the way to the town of Mellen and the juncture with route 13. Route 77 is another of my favorite roads. It is truly a very cool stretch of pavement that will have you grinning ear to ear. It runs through the heart of the Gogebic Range and many rugged hills line the north side of the road, and as we progress west route 77 runs in a sort of shallow valley between two ranges of hills. Just east of Mellen if you look to your left you can see two impressive hills—Eagles Peak and Mt. Whittlesey, which stands 1,872 feet above sea level.

From Mellen we follow route 77 / 13 south many miles. The view from the seat doesn't change as we proceed south. The landscape is gorgeous and the riding is great mile after mile. Just north of a wide spot in the road called Glidden route 77 parts ways and heads west. At this juncture the large and scenic Great Divide Wayside Park is on the west side of the road.

We continue south on route 13 over hill and through dale to the town of Park Falls, over the Flambeau River, and eventually to state route 70. Turn east onto 70 and the good times continue unabated. Route 70 twists and turns through a region that becomes increasingly hilly, and as we progress east the number of lakes increases to the point where it seems that the world around us is equally divided between liquid and solid. For a several mile stretch 70 cuts across the southern portion of the Lac Du Flambeau Indian Reservation. Eventually we reach U.S. highway 51, on which we turn left and go into the town of Woodruff. On the north edge of Woodruff turn right onto state route 47 and continue the southward ride back toward Rhinelander. Route 47 is more of the superb sameness as the earlier portions of this tour—great views and great riding; all in all just a grand place to be a motorcyclist.

About midway between Woodruff and Rhinelander the Wisconsin River joins company on our left side and we chase it downstream to Rhinelander. Watch your rear view mirrors in this stretch; there just might be a Hodag hot on your trail.

It's an enjoyable and scenic ride all the way to U.S. 8 and Rhinelander, and the end of yet another marvelous motorcycle ride through this great state.

Helmet Hair Quiz Answer

108,000 miles of roads criss-cross the state per the Wisconsin Department of Transportation.

Many Wisconsin motorcyclists and veterans make the annual Rolling Thunder pilgrimage to Washington D.C. each Memorial Day to remember the nation's prisoners of war and missing in action.

Remembering the Chippewa

Helmet Hair Quiz

How many dairy cows call Wisconsin home?

WE BEGIN THIS FUN DAY ride in the town of Chippewa Falls, located in Chippewa County, and situated on the Chippewa River. I think it is fair to say that the Chippewa Indians have had an influence in this state's history! Another institution that has certainly set deep roots in this city is the Jacob Leinenkugel Brewing Company. Started by Jacob Leinenkugel in 1867 to serve the exploding population of thirsty lumberjacks in northern Wisconsin, the beer has taken on an almost cult following among its loyal devotees. Five generations of Leinenkugel have overseen the brewery and its future looks bright indeed. Tours of the brewery are available by calling 1.888.LEINIES. Tours are free but advance reservations are recommended.

Start by riding north on route 178. In short time the road begins running very close to the Chippewa River, and it will hug its shore for most of the distance to the town of Cornell. Route 178 is very nice. It is mostly forested along the river with lots of twists and turns that unfold in front of you. My favorite ride on this road was very early one summer morning; it was just me and a few fishermen floating on the river, with haunting morning mists rising off the water.

About five miles south of Cornell you'll see the Cobban Bridge spanning the river. An historical marker highlights this bridge because it is the oldest of its type in the state. What is interesting is that the bridge was initially built in 1908 further up the river. It was dismantled when a dam was built at that location. Locals moved the parts and pieces and in 1918 it was rebuilt in this current location. The bridge is called a two-span Pennsylvania overhead truss bridge, in case the question is ever raised during conversation with friends.

In Cornell route 178 seamlessly joins with east bound route 64, which carries us across the river and eastward through a land about equally divided between forest and field, with more farmland showing up as we ride east. Though mostly straight it is a real nice ride and the surroundings are pleasant. Beware though, there are many Amish in this area and they use route 64 often. Eventually we

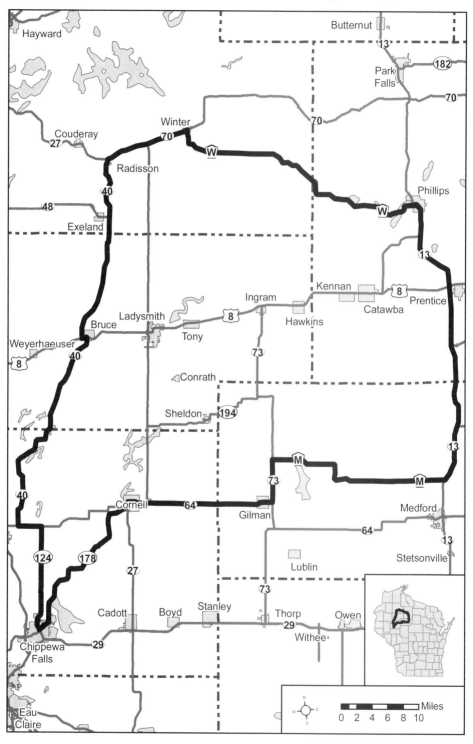

REMEMBERING THE CHIPPEWA 223 MILES		
Miles	Destination	Total
00	Chippewa Falls	00
24	Cornell	24
19	Gilman / Route 73	43
30	State route 13	73
37	Phillips / CR-W	110
36	Winter / Route 70	146
35	Bruce	181
42	Chippewa Falls	223

arrive at Gilman on the Yellow River. Gilman has a small park on the river (look for the army tank) that has a swinging suspension bridge over the water. It's kind of famous for this bridge, though some folks must have complained because the Boy Scouts have built a firmly planted wood structure nearby.

Just east of Gilman we turn north onto route 73 and ride this road for five miles to county road M, where the real fun begins!

We will ride CR-M east for twenty-five great miles. It is a lightly traveled road, about half of which is through hilly national forest lands. East of the national forest the road straightens out but the surroundings don't change much. Just east of the forest boundary watch for a most unusual attraction on the right side of the road. I can best describe it as a monument to chain saws. The landowner has taken dozens of chain saws and inserted them in tall tree trunks in his front yard adjacent to the road. It is hard to describe but makes for quite an interesting sight. I noticed a for sale sign there recently so perhaps this attraction won't survive the change of ownership.

County road M will deliver us to state highway 13 where we make a left turn. Thirteen is our road for many miles northward, all the way to the town of Phillips. In between here and there is an enjoyable two-lane road with gentle horizontal and vertical curves, in a mostly wooded setting. Route 13 won't cause an adrenaline rush, but it is an entertaining road that provides many miles of relaxing and fun motorcycling.

The area south of Phillips sits upon a high plain and we will ride past the state's highest point near the village of Ogema, just south of highway U.S. 8.

An intriguing collection of over 200 folk art figures made of concrete, colored glass, and various bits of scrap metal adorn the grounds of Fred Smith's Concrete Park. It is a site that must be seen to be fully appreciated.

Eventually route 13 will drop us at the doorstep of the town of Phillips—an 'up north' town if ever there was one. It is an outdoor recreation center situated on two lakes and surrounded by miles of forestland. Like many northern lumbering communities, Phillips had to endure a trial by fire. In the summer of 1894, after an extended drought, fire swept across the cutover forestlands, burning much of the town. Thirteen people were killed. Allegedly a drunk man started the fire after a fight with his wife.

Coming into Phillips from the south takes you past Fred Smith's Concrete Park. I highly suggest stopping at this unique park and walking amongst the fascinating collection of some 200 concrete sculptures. Admission is free and the park is open year-round during daylight hours. It is very cool!

<<<<◉>>>>

At the north edge of town, across from a small city park on the lake, you will see signs for county road W. Turn left onto W and prepare for over 35 miles of fabulous riding. County road W provides great fun as it twists and turns between lakes and rises and falls over hills through a beautiful forested countryside. The asphalt is smooth and traffic is very light. It is a wonderful ride all the way to the village of Winter and state route 70. Watch for deer as the trees are quite close to the road shoulder.

In Winter (the village, not the season) we turn left onto route 70 and ride this typical northern Wisconsin road eleven miles west to Radisson. A few miles west of Winter we join company with the Chippewa River, crossing the river about midway, and then closely following the river valley into Radisson. It is a nice ride, and as noted above, typical for this region.

The Chippewa River makes a southerly turn at Radisson and we follow the river south on route 40. We will enjoy the company of route 40 for many miles, in fact all the way south to state route 64. Riding along 40 provides a good open-air classroom for Wisconsin's varied geology and land cover. Near Radisson forestry is still the main crop, and the fields are rocky and of poor soil quality. As we move south the soil quality improves and land becomes more level and fertile, with forests being replaced with field crops.

But the road itself remains enjoyable, and even though the surface is level there is a constant supply of sweeping curves to keep things interesting and enjoyable.

At U.S. 8 we enter the village of Bruce. I want to digress here to talk a bit about lodging in small northern towns. If a traveler looks for chain motels in many of these small villages he or she will likely come up empty. However, there are alternatives in almost every rural community, and these are the small hotels that still exist in many of the downtown sections. These hotels are a throwback to a century or more ago, and I encourage you to give them a try. Most will have a room available at short notice and the rooms are usually charming and very different from the cookie-cutter accommodations found at the chains. Yes, sometimes you may share a common bathroom, or walk on a wood floor that is well over a century old and that creaks underfoot, and the room might have fewer amenities than modern chains. However, if you get pleasure from being able to sit down with the owner and have a conversation about whatever topic you wish, or like to sit on the front porch after a day's ride and watch life in small town America, these places are great.

In Bruce, the MacArthur Hotel is a perfect example. It has been owned by the same family for over a century, and they offer a friendly place to stay for the night in a manner that you will want to tell friends about and will remember far longer than a typical night spent at a chain motel.

Continue riding south on route 40 and just south of highway 8 we encounter a ten mile stretch where lakes again are the main geographic feature. The pavement nicely winds among the lakes and is great fun.

This monument to chainsaws on county road M north of Medford reflects north-
ern Wisconsin's rural culture and logging history, and stands in grand testimony
to imagination and effort.

At the south end of the lake region is the Chippewa Moraine Ice Age State
Recreation Area, and then south of that the land changes suddenly from 'up north'
to farm country. At route 64 point the bike east, riding three flat arrow-like miles
to route 124, where a right turn will point us toward Chippewa Falls. The last few
miles on 124 are pleasant if unexciting riding through open farmlands. Shortly
the Chippewa Falls city limits sign will welcome us back to our starting point and
the end of yet another splendid exploration of the Badger State.

Helmet Hair Quiz Answer
1.37 million!

The diverse geography of the Great Lakes region provides a mix of dramatic scenery, including maritime scenes not normally found in the middle of a continent.

Great Lakes / Great Rides

Taking trips entirely around the Lakes has long been an objective of many travelers in the Great Lakes basin. Any book about Wisconsin motorcycling opportunities would not be complete without coverage of these opportunities given its location between Lakes Michigan and Superior.

Because I believe that the whole purpose of a Great Lakes circle tour is to see the lakes as much as possible, you will note that some of my roads differ from the official routes, which are based completely on state and federal or provincial highways. After all, shouldn't a rider stay as close to the water as possible and not ride several miles inland just to stay on a major state or federal highway? I believe so, and that is why I try to find just those waterside roads rather than simply follow the official routes.

Scenes of majestic beauty are commonplace throughout the Great Lakes Region.

The Lake Michigan Circle Tour

Helmet Hair Quiz

Which Wisconsin county has more miles of shoreline, more lighthouses, and more state parks than any other county in the United States?

OF ALL THE GREAT LAKES, Lake Michigan is unique because it is the only one situated completely within the U.S. It is of course the largest lake in the country and the lake basin is home to over 11 million people. It is also unique due to the vast difference between the sparsely populated northern region and the heavily industrialized and populated southern portion. The greater Chicago urban area makes a trip around Lake Michigan a difficult proposition. One must either skirt around Chicago and therefore not ever see the water, or go through many miles of heavy urban congestion in order to stay near the water.

However, there is another option that is available—take a ferry across the lake. This alternative adds a special flavor to the trip, as well as allowing one to avoid that portion of the lake from Milwaukee south through Chicago, and Gary, Indiana. There are two ferry options. The first is to take the *S.S. Badger* from Manitowoc to Ludington, MI. The Badger has been around many decades. It is a very large boat and offers more of a relaxed cruise feel to the crossing. Call 888.337.7948 or surf over to ssbadger.com for schedules and reservations. Be advised that you need your own tie downs for this ferry.

The second ferry is the *Lake Express,* which sails between Milwaukee and Muskegon. This service started operations in 2004 and takes a different approach to crossing the lake. It is a high speed but smaller vessel, just under two hundred feet in length. Call 866.914.1010 or go to lake-express.com for reservations or sailing times. Port information for the two ferries is listed in the sidebar on page 171.

Let's start this adventure in Milwaukee. This tour and the accompanying mileage data will assume a Milwaukee to Muskegon crossing—not because of any recommendation of one ferry over the other, but simply because this will provide the greatest amount of road information. If you take the Ludington ferry then the road description south of Manitowoc and Ludington is irrelevant. Since I talk

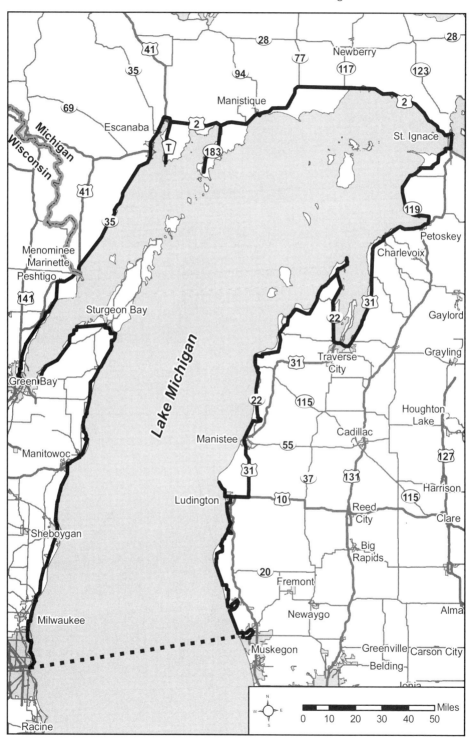

LAKE MICHIGAN CIRCLE TOUR 918 MILES		
Miles	**Destination**	**Total**
00	Milwaukee	00
00	Muskegon, MI (ferry)	00
93	Ludington State Park	93
71	Frankfort	164
69	Leelanau Point Lighthouse	233
86	Charlevoix	319
70	Mackinac Bridge	389
92	Manistique	481
41	Fairport	522
61	Peninsula Point Lighthouse / Stonington	583
90	Marinette, WI	673
54	Green Bay	727
68	Algoma	795
123	Milwaukee	918

about Milwaukee in other tours in this book, let's just get on the ferry and head east across the vast expanse of freshwater that lays before us and go to Muskegon.

<<<<◆>>>>

The city of Muskegon is a fairly large old industrial town which in recent years has taken great pains to change its image as old chemical and manufacturing plants have closed, or been replaced with new and cleaner and more attractive operations. If you have interest in World War II fighting ships then a stop at the Great Lakes Naval Memorial & Museum is a must. It is the home to *USS Silversides*, a WWII Pacific Theater submarine. A tour onboard the submarine is a fascinating and humbling experience. The museum also is home to the *USCGC McClane*, a Coast Guard cutter built in 1927. There is a large selection of various naval paraphernalia as well. The museum is located at the west end of Muskegon Lake at the channel. The museum is only accessible from the south shore of the lake, not too far west of the ferry docks.

To start heading north we first have to skirt around the east shore of Muskegon Lake, then swing back west on the north shore. When leaving the ferry dock turn right if you want to go to the museum and ships, otherwise turn left onto Lakeshore Drive. This will shortly turn into Shoreline Drive. In turn, Shoreline Drive will take us to business 31. Turn left onto business 31 and take it a short distance to state route 120. One twenty will cross the Muskegon River and we quickly turn left onto Lake Avenue. After a few blocks the road jogs north two blocks to Rudiman Drive, which travels west along the north shore. Rudiman Drive eventually morphs into Memorial Drive, which we take the rest of the way to the shore of Lake Michigan. Memorial Drive terminates within the boundaries of Muskegon State Park and at this point you turn north on Scenic Drive, which runs along the Lake Michigan coast for roughly the next eight miles.

SS Badger

Manitowoc—Take W-42 south to 10th Street, a one-way street going south. Follow 10th Street south to Madison Street, then east a short distance to the docks.

Ludington—Take US-10 west to downtown Ludington, on east side of downtown James Street will take you south to the port.

Lake Express

Milwaukee—Located at the Port of Milwaukee, on South Lincoln Street south of Veterans Park. Get off at exit 3 of the I-794 expressway, or follow Lincoln Memorial Drive south along the shoreline.

Muskegon—Located on the south shore of Muskegon Lake, at 1920 Lakeshore Drive, at the Great Lakes Marina.

This is a very nice stretch of road and one of the first things that a visitor from Wisconsin will notice about the opposite shore of Lake Michigan is that it is very sandy. So sandy, in fact, that some of the largest sand dunes to be found anywhere in the world are along Lake Michigan's east shore. These unique dunes make for a very scenic and interesting tableau. Many of these rare dunes and their associated special dune ecology are protected in state parks that line Lake Michigan's shore in Michigan.

Lake Michigan's east coast is also lined with what are technically called drowned river mouths. These are lakes that formed when a river has been "impounded" by the sand dunes at the shoreline, creating a lake with a narrow opening or channel at the point it empties into Lake Michigan. Many of these drowned river mouth lakes don't have bridges across them at their channels resulting in the need to skirt around them by going inland. This was not only the case with Muskegon Lake, but with White Lake, located eight miles north, and several others up the line.

*The Great Lakes Naval Memorial and Museum in Muskegon offers
a rare, up-close inspection of a World War II submarine.*

Scenic Drive becomes Shore Drive as it skirts White Lake on the south shore.
Cross the White River on BR-31 then make a west turn again right after the bridge
on Old Channel Trail which follows the north shore of White Lake and will deliver
you back to the Lake Michigan shore. The shoreline road makes an east, and then
a west, jog as it continues north into Oceana County, becoming 48th Avenue.
At this point you're about a mile inland, but one-and-a-half miles into Oceana
County a left turn puts you back on Scenic Drive and more coastline travel. No
turns are involved, but Scenic Drive becomes 16th Avenue on its way north. At
Buchanan Road our road takes a half-mile jog east then continues north until it
Ts at Silver Lake Road—also called Lighthouse Road heading west to the Lake
Michigan shore. I recommend taking this short ride out to Lake Michigan to see
Little Sable Point Lighthouse. This very scenic light reaches over one-hundred feet
high and makes a gorgeous picture as it stands alone surrounded by sand dunes
on one side and the blue water of Lake Michigan on the other.

Heading east on Silver Lake Road will take you to Silver Lake State Park and
the famous Silver Lake sand dunes. This park has a wonderful beach of unlimited
sand, and several dune buggy concessionaires will take you for very enjoyable

rides on the dunes in their specially modified buggies. The Silver Lake area is a very popular summer vacation destination. You will either love it or want to leave it as quickly as possible. It is a beehive of activity.

We have to skirt around Silver Lake to its east shore, then head north again, first on Shore Drive for a short distance then onto Ridge Road. Ridge Road closely follows the Lake Michigan shore heading north. The circumnavigation process has to be repeated again several miles up the road to get around Pentwater Lake. This time BR-31 will be the road we take back west once beyond Pentwater Lake. As BR-31 makes its way back east toward the expressway you'll see Lakeshore Road heading north on a narrow strip of land squeezed between Bass Lake on the east and Lake Michigan on the west. Take Lakeshore Road north about eight miles to Iris Road which we must take east to get around Pere Marquette Lake—yet one more drowned river mouth—this time for the Pere Marquette River.

Before turning east on Iris Road, I recommend you head north a short distance to White Pine Village—a reconstructed community of over twenty-five old buildings that recreate Ludington's past. It's a "living" interpretive village museum that has thousands of fascinating displays and artifacts. A bit further north on this road is a memorial to Father Pere Marquette.

About halfway between Bass Lake and Pere Marquette Lake you'll pass the giant Consumers Energy Company pumped storage facility perched on the hillside to the east. This is an electrical power generating plant where water from Lake Michigan is pumped uphill to the lake-sized pond during low energy demand periods, and then released through tubes that feed waterpower to generators to create electricity during high-energy demand periods.

Upon reaching Old US-31, follow it north two miles to the intersection with US-10. I recommend taking US-10 west at this point to downtown Ludington and Lake Michigan, and then turning north on M-116. M-116 is a dead end road that takes you out to Ludington State Park. The Park itself isn't the destination here as much as the ride along the lakeshore out to the park. It is a fabulous ride through the sand dunes and with parking allowed along almost all of its length, the road provides a great place to stop and enjoy the shoreline and scenery.

After you have explored Ludington and the beauty along M-116, head east nine miles on U.S. 10 to the town of Scottville and U.S. 31. Go north on 31 and it will deliver you to the city of Manistee. This city is squeezed between Manistee Lake and Lake Michigan. On Manistee Lake is an attraction that many folks will enjoy visiting. It is a national historic landmark as well. I am referring to the *City of Milwaukee* Great Lakes rail ferry. It was built in Manitowoc in 1923, and is the last remaining Lake Michigan railroad ferryboat. Its permanent mooring facility is along U.S. 31 at the northwest corner of Lake Manistee. Boat tours are available during the motorcycling season, with a full tour taking one hour.

◄◄◄◆►►►

About one mile north of town you will see M-110 going straight north along the shoreline. Follow 110 along this very pretty stretch and it will eventually swing easterly to get around Portage Lake. In so doing it will connect with M-22, a wonderfully scenic road that will be our riding companion for many miles, taking us to the tip of the Leelanau Peninsula and to Traverse City before we finally leave it behind.

M-22 between Portage Lake and Traverse City is a wonderful mix of hills, curves, farms and forests, and perhaps most of all, great scenery. This is perhaps the premier motorcycling road in northwest Lower Michigan. Folks come from far away to ride from Manistee north to the Leelanau Peninsula, with its scenic hills, vineyards, and orchards.

Lake Michigan creates its own microclimate, and on the east side, with the prevailing westerlies, that means perfect conditions for growing fruit and for making wine. Winter and spring temperatures are moderated by the lake, while summer temperatures avoid the searing heat found further away from the water. The absence of late frosts near the water usually means a good harvest, though late freezes do sometimes wreak havoc.

North of Frankfort the road skirts the west edge of beautiful Crystal Lake and then swings north past Platte Lake. At Platte Lake we enter the Sleeping Bear Dunes National Lakeshore, a very large expanse of forested sand dunes that must be seen up close to be appreciated. One way to do this is to ride out to the trailhead for the Empire Bluffs in the village of Empire. Watch for the signs beginning just south of the village at Wilco Road. The bluffs are 400-foot high dunes that overlook Lake Michigan and offer a stunning vista of forested hills and endless deep blue water. Appropriately enough route 22 in this region also goes by the name Scenic Drive.

Stop at the Lakeshore headquarters at the intersection of M-22 and M-72 in Empire to learn more about this marvelous geologic wonder. While at the M-22 / M-72 intersection, also head west on what will be Front Street for three blocks, then north a couple of blocks to the parking lot on Empire Beach. At the north end of this park you'll find the Manning Memorial Light. This is Michigan's newest lighthouse, built in 1991 in honor of a local citizen.

Just north of Empire route 109 splits off of M-22, going straight north while twenty-two heads east. I encourage you to go north on 109 to Pierce Stocking Drive—a one way narrow asphalt road that loops for several miles through the forested dunes. It is a wonderful ride that offers a parking lot on top of a high dune

Construction of the Mackinac Bridge in 1957 accomplished the dreams of early explorers and modern transportation officials by linking Michigan's two peninsulas.

TRAVEL MICHIGAN

overlooking the lake and hundreds of acres of shifting sand hills. The Drive loops back to route 109. From there you can either go back south to M-22 and continue north, or continue north on M-109, which goes through the park and swings back east to connect with M-22 once again. You can't make a wrong decision here, and they both ultimately take you to M-22 northbound.

As you follow M-22 north into the Leelanau Peninsula you'll pass through friendly small towns like Leland and Northport where you should park your bike and explore them on foot. Leland is an old commercial fishing village that has preserved the channel with old buildings and docks now used for B&Bs and restaurants as well as fishing boats.

You will pass lighthouses and wineries, grand overlooks and historic sites, and all the time riding with an appreciative smile and uttering the occasional WOW! to yourself or your partner. The Leelanau is a unique part of the state of Michigan. Its high hills and microclimate provide a perfect combination for orchards and vineyards, and there is an abundance of each.

In Northport, follow the signs and county road 629 north to the tip of the peninsula where you will find the stately Grand Traverse Lighthouse in Leelanau State Park. Follow the same route back to Northport and once again onto M-22, which takes you south along the east side of the Leelanau Peninsula, and along the west coast of Grand Traverse Bay. Being on the leeward side of the peninsula the scenery is quite different here than on the windward west side where towering sand dunes rule. Here the shoreline is flat and rocky with glacial hills and ridges paralleling the shoreline just a bit inland. South of Suttons Bay the waterfront development pressure that is targeting this part of the state becomes more obvious.

A half-mile north of M-72, just prior to entering Traverse City, you will see a business called Traverse Tall Ship Company on the water's edge. They have a large sailing vessel, the tall ship *Manitou,* on which one can take sails ranging from two hours to four days, on Grand Traverse Bay and beyond. The *Manitou* is one of the largest sailing vessels on the Great Lakes. Sailing on this ship is an amazing experience as one relaxes while watching the crew work the sails, enjoying the scenery, and soaking in the sound the wind and waves as the ship slices through the water. Call (800) 678-0383 for more information.

All good things must end, including M-22. When it does you're left eastbound on M-72 for a short distance and then US-31, which runs east and west through the bustling city of Traverse City along the south shore of Grand Traverse Bay. Unless you truly enjoy riding your bike in very heavy traffic, jostling through crowds, and waiting in lines for basic services, plan to avoid Traverse City in early July when they celebrate the nationally famous Cherry Festival. Many thousands of people jam the streets for this event and while it is an enjoyable time to party, the crowds can be nerve-racking if you weren't expecting them. A person should also plan to make advance reservations if an overnight stay in Traverse City on a summer weekend is in your plans.

Follow US-31 through town and take it up the east side of Grand Traverse Bay. Like M-22, US-31 will transport us through great countryside and lakeshore for many miles. The upcoming area—Elk Rapids, Charlevoix, Petoskey, and Harbor Springs—is an upscale area. These resort towns have served many generations of families. It is a land of well-kept houses, flower-lined streets, and lots of history. You might call it Michigan's Gold Coast. It is also Ernest Hemingway's childhood stomping grounds. Young Ernest made many trips here with his family, vacationing on Walloon Lake near Petoskey. There is a small Hemmingway museum display at the Little Traverse History Museum Center—located in an old railroad depot in Petoskey on the waterfront.

We will stay on US-31 all the way to the east side of Petoskey where a north/left turn onto M-119 takes us to the next very nice part of this journey. M-119 isn't a great motorcycle road for the first few miles. First, you have to get through the upscale town of Harbor Springs—another town where you may want to park and walk around. Whereas several of the "old money" towns in this part of the state have lost some of their charm due to sprawling development and invasion of big box stores, Harbor Springs still retains a sense of tradition and old families with their genteel ways and finances to afford the lifestyle.

Once beyond Harbor Springs M-119 gets progressively better, until it turns into the "Tunnel of Trees", as it is called. M-119 is the only state highway in Michigan where special rules apply. There is no shoulder and the trees are literally right on the edge of the pavement. There is also a severe shortage of any straight sections. Many of the curves are tight, so even though it is very tempting to go fast, try to show some semblance of restraint and keep your speeds reasonable for the road you are on. M-119 runs along the crest of a high bluff overlooking Lake Michigan. Unfortunately, the land all along it is private, with many drives heading down the bluff to palatial second homes. M-119 is a blast to ride, to put it succinctly, but don't throw all caution to the wind or you may have to pay the piper, as it is also unforgiving.

The state highway ends in the village of Cross Village, and here you should pull in at Legs Inn, even if you aren't hungry. This restaurant is famous for its hearty Polish cuisine, ambience, and scenery. Its location on a high hill overlooking the lake is but one of its charms. The stone building itself is unique, its internal decorations are special, and the food is unforgettable. It is a highly recommend stop to at least take a look. If you are lucky, you might arrive in Cross Village when it's time for lunch or dinner.

The lakeshore route continues north from Cross Village several more miles. Continue following Lakeview Drive north along the coast until it finally gives up at the southern boundary of Wilderness State Park (a good place to camp) and curves inland heading east. Follow the easterly pavement and it becomes County Road 81, and after going east for several miles turns and goes straight north to the shoreline and Wilderness Park Drive. Turn right on Wilderness Park Drive and follow it into Mackinaw City and the Mackinac Bridge. Turn left if you wish to go to Wilderness State Park.

Common questions are: Why is the word mackinac spelled two ways? What or who the heck is a mackinac anyway?

Well as is common in this region the word has its origins in Native American language. Mackinac is a French derivation of michilimackinac which itself is a shortened version of the Ojibwa word "missilimaahkinaank" which means "at the territory of the mishinimaki"—which was an Indian tribe that lived in the straits area long ago. The correct spelling is Mackinac, but the British anglicized it to Mackinaw when they conquered the area during the French and Indian War.

Mackinaw City is a great place to park yet again and walk. You will not be the only biker there. It is a favorite gathering place for motorcyclists, and you will see quite a selection of machines parked in the lot that runs the length of downtown. Relax, eat some homemade fudge, and watch the other people who are watching you, with everyone trying to figure out which T-shirt or tourist knick-knacks to waste their money on. Fort Michilimackinac and the old Mackinac Point Light are favorite sites to explore. Old Mackinac Point Light in particular is a great spot to sit in the shade near this marvelous old structure and watch the activity on the Straits and be amazed at the size and beauty of The Bridge. A ferry ride out to Mackinac Island is always a fun way to spend the day if time allows. Mackinac Island is steeped in history and it is one of the few places left in North America where motorized vehicles are forbidden. Horse-drawn buggies, bicycles, or shoe leather are the transportation choices available to residents and visitors alike. The island was initially declared a national park in 1875, and later became Michigan's first state park. Eighty per cent of the land is public, but there is a year round population that lives there as well. Numerous attractions await visitors, including historic forts, Arch Rock and skull cave, stores and shops offering a wide variety of crafts, memorabilia and food, the Grand Hotel—one of the most famous in the world, and much more. Renting bicycles to take an eight mile ride around the perimeter of the island on M-185 is a fun and invigorating experience. The ride will take you to many places of interest, including old battle sites and geologic attractions. The entire trip is on the coastline, so the water and marvelous views are never far away. (Yes, there is a state highway here even though no motorized vehicles are allowed, only bicycles or horses.) Plan on a large part of the day to be spent on an island excursion, however, as this side trip is not one that a person can do in anything less than that.

◄◄◄◄◉►►►►

After downing your last bite of fudge and buying a box for the road, it is time to head north across the Mighty Mac. If you have never been across this roadway suspended from two towering pillars you are in for a real treat. I have ridden over the bridge dozens of times on a bike and it is still a thrill each time. The view from the top of this five-mile long engineering marvel is just incredible. Water horizons stretch forever to the east and west, freighters are making their way through the center channel of the straits, and smaller boats leave their white wakes in the dark blue water nearly two hundred feet below you. To the east ferries going to and from Mackinac Island produce magnificent rooster tails of water as they speed across the strait—each ferry company trying to be faster or flashier than their competition. Riding on the inside lane of the suspension portion of the bridge, where an iron grid rather than concrete forms the roadway, is an extra source of excitement as you look down through the grid and see the water below you. If this isn't your idea of fun, the outside lanes in each direction are paved and very solid.

Once in St. Ignace (one of the oldest cities in the country, with a mission first established here in 1671) head west on US-2 and relax. This popular lakeshore route will carry us across the north shore of Lake Michigan, with many opportunities to pull off to soak in the view or just take a break. Several restaurants offer authentic Upper Peninsula food in the form of fresh fish or a Cornish pasty when it is time for lunch or dinner. Signs for various attractions are all along the route so you can pick and choose just how much you want to do. Just west of Manistique you will find M-149 and signs pointing north for a short detour to the Palms Book State Park and Michigan's largest spring, called Kitch-iti-kipi—The Big Spring. The spring is 200 feet across and forty feet deep. Ten thousand gallons a minute pour from underground fissures. The water is sparkling clear and a glass-bottom boat allows a unique perspective on this natural wonder.

A little further west is state route 183, a newly paved road that heads south onto the Garden Peninsula. This peninsula was formed by the same geologic feature that is responsible for Wisconsin's Door Peninsula—the Niagara Escarpment. In fact looking at a map will show that the two peninsulas nearly meet, and islands associated with them congregate midway at the state line. The Garden Peninsula is a unique area, given its limestone bedrock, forest cover and interspersed farmlands. A century ago the town of Fayette was a major iron smelting company town. Everything needed for smelting iron was nearby—the raw iron ore, limestone, and a plentiful supply of wood for charcoal. Today Fayette is a historic state park that features the reconstructed iron smelter village. White limestone cliffs line the shoreline adjacent to the park. The park is an out of the ordinary place to visit and you surely will not be disappointed. Continuing south from Fayette State Park takes one to the land's end and the tiny town of Fairport. There isn't much to see here, but it is a unique area, and the road literally ends at the dock from which commercial fishing boats ply their trade.

From the Garden Peninsula we continue west on U.S. 2 again. Next stop— county road T and the Stonington Peninsula, with the focus of this side trip being the 1866 Peninsula Point Lighthouse. The last mile or so is on gravel but it is certainly not a problem for most folks to navigate. The lighthouse is open to the public for climbing if desired.

After leaving Stonington Peninsula and the lighthouse, a short trip further west on U.S. 2 through Rapid River and Gladstone brings us to the largest city in this area—Escanaba. The town of Escanaba is located on the west shore of Little Bay De Noc (as opposed to Big Bay De Noc, which is east of the Stonington Peninsula). Escanaba is a good-sized city with lots of services, including motorcycle repair shops and dealers. Escanaba hosts a large antique car show called Krusin' Klassics the first weekend of June each year. This large event includes cruises, car shows, tractor pulls, food, dancing, and in general a good time for young and old. To get a feel for the culture of the upper Great Lakes region one only has to watch Jeff Daniels' *Escanaba in da Moonlight,* a hilarious movie about deer hunting traditions and the interactions of family and friends in an Upper Peninsula deer camp come the opening day of deer season.

The origin of the name Bay De Noc is another of those place name questions that frequently arises. Well, again, you can thank the Indians and the French. The Nokay (spelled Noquet in French) were a small Algonquin tribe that lived in the area of Green Bay north to the vicinity of what is now Escanaba. The French called the two bays on either side of the Stonington Peninsula the bays of the Noquet, or Bays De Noc for short.

With that piece of arcane knowledge under your belt to sustain you as you finish the last of your Mackinaw City fudge, our journey now turns southward along the west shore of Lake Michigan—specifically Green Bay which extends from near Escanaba south to the home of the Packers.

We leave US-2 in Escanaba as it continues its westward journey to the State of Washington, and we head south on M-35 to Menominee. M-35 is about as close to the water's edge all the way between Escanaba and Menominee as you can get without getting wet.

I know you're thinking about how a city gets the name Menonimee, so I'm going to tell you. You guessed it— Native American language. There is a tribe, still very active and healthy, in the Green Bay area called the Menominee (note the spelling difference between this version and Menomonie, Wisconsin—a difference that I'm not sure why exists). According to a 2004 publication by the Milwaukee Public Museum, the Menominee called themselves Mamacoqtaw—meaning The People. Other tribes referred to them as Menomini—a derivation of the Algonquin word for wild rice— that was a staple of the diet for Indians in that region. Prior to settlement, the mouth of the Menominee River was a large marsh where wild rice was abundant.

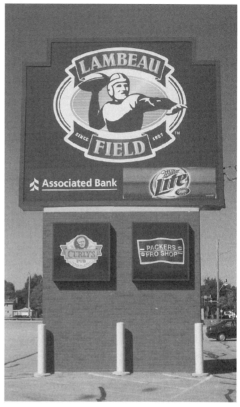

No self-respecting cheesehead could go to Green Bay without paying homage at the home of the Pack.

Lakeside travel gets a little dicier back in Wisconsin because there isn't one road such as US-2 that provides a water side route. A person either takes one of the major roads and stays away from the water, or whenever possible take the many county roads that do provide a pleasurable ride near the water, away from the crowds and major highways.

US-41 joins M-35 just north of Menominee and you cross the Menominee River on US-41 into Marinette. In Marinette stay on US-41 as it heads out of town taking you to the town of Peshtigo. I write about Peshtigo's fire history in another chapter, so I won't repeat myself here, except to say that if this is the only time you will find yourself in Peshtigo, by all means visit the fire museum at 400 Oconto Avenue.

On the west side of Peshtigo County Road Y splits off US-41. Follow "Y" as it heads south, then southwesterly along the lakeshore. Immediately after turning onto CR-Y from route 41 the surroundings change for the better. Though there is a dearth of curves, the forest is thick and lush all along this road, and traffic almost disappears on this new and wonderfully smooth asphalt. Because we are on the lake plain the ground below us doesn't vary from the horizontal, but the riding is still agreeable.

Just prior to the Oconto River it curves inland a bit and in the village of Oconto the lakeshore road swings south again as County Road S. CR-S is very similar to CR-Y before it—new smooth pavement, heavy forest cover along the road, and light traffic. It continues south for a number of miles and at the village of Little Suamico the pavement's name changes to CR-J. It perhaps sounds confusing, but it isn't as the roadway is easy to follow even with the occasional change in its name as different towns are traversed. County road J is being essentially rebuilt from the ground up, which of course will mean years of great riding on the silky smooth asphalt.

In Saumico Township, at the Barkhausen Game Preserve, CR-J ends and we turn right onto Lineville Road, taking it a couple blocks over to U.S. 141 and heading south on this divided highway.

◄◄◄◀◉▶►►►

We'll tag along on U.S. 141 through Green Bay and just east of the Fox River bridge our ride takes us east on state route 54 / 57. Route 54 eventually branches off and we remain on route 57 as it makes its way northeast across the lower portion of the Door Peninsula to Sturgeon Bay. At the tiny village of Namur we want to go north on CR-N, taking it north along the west side of the peninsula to CR-C, which we then take east into Sturgeon Bay. We explore the northern portion of Door County in detail in the Door Peninsula ride, so we won't retrace those same miles on this tour. Instead, take route 42 across town, turning right on CR-U on the east side of Sturgeon Bay. Follow "U" south to Lake Drive, riding this road east to Lake Michigan Drive, which we will follow south along the water for several miles at which point it rejoins CR-U and continues as a waterfront road. Keep the goal of the Great Lakes circle tours in mind—riding as closely as possible to the water is key, not taking major roads several miles inland.

CR-U ends at CR-S, which is ridden south into Algoma and there we once again get on route 42 on which we ride all the way to Kewaunee. Just south of Kewaunee Lakeshore Road splits off 42, following the shoreline for a few miles, before once again joining with route 42 and continuing south for two miles, only to have Lakeshore Road split off once again, rejoining 42 in Two Rivers. Route 42 takes us to Manitowoc. The Wisconsin Maritime Museum is a suggested stop while in Manitowoc. Tour the USS COBIA, a World War II submarine and see many displays and artifacts depicting the Great Lakes maritime history. Call them at 920.684.0218 or Google them for much more information. The museum and sub are on the river in downtown Manitowoc.

When you have done everything you wish to do in Manitowoc, turn south from route 42 onto 10th Street, and follow it south where it eventually becomes CR-LS. As you travel further southward CR-LS' pavement becomes Lakeshore Road, and then 15th Street in the city of Sheboygan, and joins route 28.

If you happen to be in Sheboygan in mid-June check out a new annual motorcycle event called the Roar on Sheboygan's Shore. This growing two-day event includes live music, lots of vendors, bike shows and much more.

Taking 28 southward out of Sheboygan you'll come to a point where it veers straight west and CR-OK keeps going south ahead of you—take this county road. CR-OK will eventually become the Sauk Trail, which we will continue to follow south—this time on the inland side of the I-43 expressway. Eventually Sauk Trail becomes CR-LI and goes south many miles to Port Washington, where it joins route 32 for a short distance. Heading south out of Port Washington turn south on Wisconsin Street and follow it south as it turns into County Road C and then Lakeshore Road and once again it is called CR-C (just follow the pavement, it's much more obvious than it sounds). County Road C does eventually turn westward and just after crossing over I-43 you want to leave it behind once and for all by turning south on Port Washington Road, which runs parallel to the expressway on the west side. Take Port Washington Road south to where it joins route 32, then taking 32 south along the shoreline. You will finally see Lincoln Memorial Drive angle off route 32 and follow the lakeshore. Take LMD south as it winds through Lake Park and then Veterans Park, finally ending in Milwaukee at the I-794 expressway, and the end of our ride.

By the way—if you don't mind expressways you of course can pick up the I-43 Xway just west of Manitowoc and take it south to Milwaukee for the last leg of this trip, rather than the shoreline routes described above.

This trip is a bit over 900 miles, depending on how many of the recommended side trips one takes. I recommend at least three days for this trip. As usual, there is just too much to see and do along the way to hurry it.

Helmet Hair Quiz Answer

Door County (250 miles of shoreline, 10 lighthouses, and 5 state parks).

The Lake Superior Circle Tour

Helmet Hair Quiz

What was explorer Jean Nicolet looking for when he discovered Wisconsin in 1634?

ALL OF THE GREAT LAKES circle tours are unique and make fabulous trips, but I've always thought that the trip around Lake Superior was the crown jewel. It is probably because I would rather be in the middle of Lake Superior Provincial Park in Ontario surrounded by cliffs and forests than in any large city in the world that prejudices my thinking. The Lake Superior trip is just stupendous. No matter where you are on the trip—Michigan, Minnesota, Wisconsin or Ontario—you're never far from magnificent vistas, waterfalls, historic lighthouses, islands, small towns with their wonderful stories to tell, majestic overlooks, and always that view of the lake itself with its watery horizon stretching seemingly forever into the distance. Adjectives fall short when it comes to describing this area. Superlatives like tremendous and spectacular are overused today and thus watered down. The Lake Superior region is one place where they really are applicable.

The Chippewa Indians called this inland freshwater sea Gitche Gumee, which Longfellow made famous in his epic poem Hiawatha.

By the shores of Gitche Gumee,
By the shining Big-Sea-Water,
Stood the wigwam of Nokomis,
Daughter of the Moon, Nokomis.
Dark behind it rose the forest,
Rose the black and gloomy pine-trees,
Rose the firs with cones upon them;
Bright before it beat the water,
Beat the clear and sunny water,
Beat the shining Big-Sea-Water.

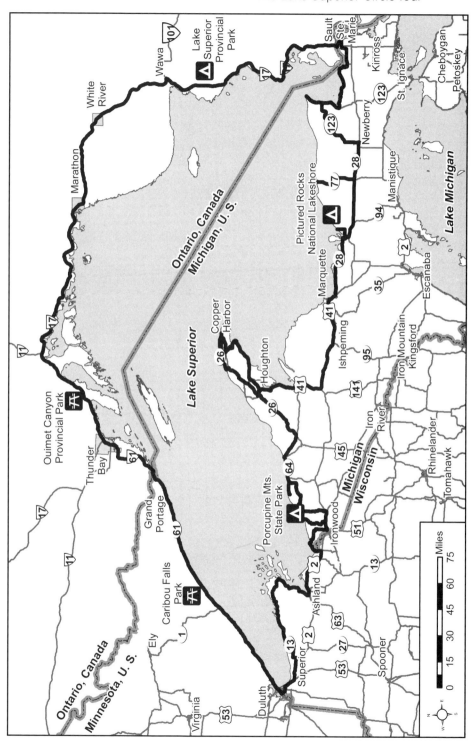

LAKE SUPERIOR CIRCLE TOUR 1483 MILES		
Miles	**Destination**	**Total**
00	Superior, WI	00
81	Bayfield	81
23	Ashland	104
53	Ironwood, MI	157
21	Black River Harbor	178
70	Porcupine Mountains / Lake of the Clouds	248
74	Houghton	322
61	Copper Harbor	383
20	Route 26 / Brockway Mountain Drive Loop	403
51	Hancock	454
99	Marquette	553
43	Munising	596
176	Whitefish Point	772
76	Sault Sainte Marie	848
143	Wawa, Ontario	991
302	Thunder Bay	1293
190	Duluth, MN	1483

In 1632 French explorer Samuel de Champlain named the lake *Grand Lac*, and forty years later French maps show the name *Lac Superior de Tracy*, in honor of the Marquis de Tracy. Eventually the name of Superior stuck. Today this fitting moniker is usually interpreted to mean that the lake is the largest, deepest, and most impressive, but it originally meant that it is the furthest "upstream" in the Great Lakes system.

Knowing that you are riding through a territory populated with wolves, moose, bears and woodland caribou adds to the flavor of the trip. This is still mostly wild lands not conquered by man's hand. The roads are on par with the fabulous scenery through which they run. Sometimes the pavement will have you on the water's edge and at other times you'll find yourself riding an asphalt roller

Bayfield is the home port for many sail boats used to explore the waters and islands of western Lake Superior.

coaster in the wilderness as the road rises and falls over forested hills made of ancient bedrock. This is truly a dream-come-true trip for any motorcyclist!

For those who perhaps are unfamiliar with the Lake Superior region I want to warn of the realities of riding in this region. First, the weather near this coldwater inland sea can change rapidly, and even in the summer the temperature frequently drops into the forties. This isn't meant to discourage anyone, but be prepared with cold and wet weather riding gear in the event it is needed. I have been caught in some sudden cold spells and thick fog and drizzle adjacent to the lake when the temperature went from eighty degrees to a very cool and damp fifty degrees in short notice. If you camp in one of the many parks adjacent to the lake chances are you will need a sleeping bag designed for cool weather.

Secondly, make sure your machine is in good working order and that you keep the gas tank topped off. I'm not trying to imply that the area is roadless wilderness, but there are long stretches where a person does not want to run out of gas or have a mechanical problem due to lack of maintenance. Motorcycle dealers and repair shops are few and far between.

Finally, watch out for wildlife. It's a thrill to see them in the woods or swamps near the road, but you certainly wouldn't want to hit one of the large critters that inhabit the region. Please note that the distances provided in the mileage table include various described side trips; they are not necessarily all point-to-point distances.

⋘◈⋙

I start this marvelous trip in the aptly named city of Superior, which seems like a very logical place to begin a trip around the lake of the same name. Today Superior is a bustling city of about 28,000 hardy souls, and its roots go back to 1854. It is the county seat of Douglas County (named in honor of Stephen Douglas, a powerful U.S. Senator during the 1850s and most remembered for the famous Lincoln / Douglas debates of 1858).

Superior is a port city and Great Lakes maritime history runs deep. The city was a major ship building location, and you can still see the fruits of that technology by visiting the *S.S. Meteor,* berthed just offshore on Barkers Island. Launched in 1896, the *Meteor* is the last surviving ship built in the "whaleback" style. This architecture allowed carrying more cargo in shallower water than conventional keel designs. The *Meteor* is now part of a larger maritime museum that also features a history of local ship building and Great Lakes shipwrecks, among other things. Another nearby museum is the Richard Bong World War II Heritage Center. Wisconsin native and Medal of Honor winner Major Richard Bong is featured in this museum, as well as other WW2 combatants and their stories.

Upon leaving Superior follow U.S. 2 / 53 east, (it's a limited access divided highway at this point) and just beyond the city limits exit the highway and head east on Wisconsin Route 13. This very nice biking road will carry you out to the Bayfield Peninsula and the city of Bayfield. This quaint town is the gateway to the Apostle Islands National Lakeshore, a beautiful archipelago of twenty-two islands, rock formations and a great collection of historic lighthouses. Boat tours through the islands are very popular, as are hiking trails on the islands themselves. I discuss this region in more detail in another tour so I won't repeat myself.

Route 13 runs south on the west shore of Chequamegon Bay and rejoins US-2 just west of Ashland, WI. Get back on US-2 and ride east through Ashland. Notice the huge dock facilities, which tell of the long and proud history of this important international port city.

Almost exactly twenty-five miles east of Ashland turn left onto Wisconsin Route 122. This great stretch of road goes north to the lake then east along the lake several miles, turning into CR-505 when you enter Michigan. Continue on CR-505 as the pavement meanders east and then southerly. CR-505 ultimately heads straight south to the town of Ironwood, MI and U.S. 2 once again.

Five-and-a-half miles from this intersection, in the town of Bessemer you'll see Moore Street at the stoplight (aka CR-513, which becomes Black River Drive). Turn left and take this road up to the Black River Harbor on Lake Superior. Even though it requires that you double back on the same road to get back on US-2, you won't mind having to ride this road twice! The Black River Drive is a beautiful fifteen-mile stretch of winding road along the Black River, replete with waterfalls, hills, curves, forests and wildlife. Eagle sightings are common in this area and five waterfalls in the Black River gorge are accessible from the road, though the walks vary in length. You will also pass the Copper Peak Ski Flying Hill—the world's tallest ski jump. The view from atop the 18-story observation deck is unlike any other in the Midwest.

After completing the Black River Drive diversion take it south to US-2 and head east again a few miles to Wakefield where US-2 intersects with M-28. Turn north on M-28 for about a mile and you will intersect with CR-519—the road you want. Take 519 north to the South Boundary Road of the Porcupine Mountains Wilderness State Park, referred to by most folks as "The Porkies." Follow this great stretch of road as it meanders through the south portion of this nearly 60,000-acre pristine wilderness park, ultimately turning north and ending at M-107. This entire stretch is through an area of fabulous scenery and great motorcycling. It's the kind of road that makes a person want to turn around and make the run again just for the sheer delight of it all.

Turn west on M-107 and climb it to the overlook at the Lake of the Clouds—a must-see on this trip and well worth the cost of a daily state park permit. The park's visitor center is also at the park's northeast entry on route 107 and this is a great place to learn a bit more about the history and geology of this unique area. The region got its name long ago when the Ojibwa Indians observed that one of the high hills in the park resembled the back of a crouching porcupine when viewed from a distance on the waters of Lake Superior. There are many hiking trails in the park—some short and some long wilderness trails. Bears are very common in this area so if you camp or hike follow the advice of the park rangers and take appropriate precautions regarding food storage.

Once finished in the park head east on M-107 to Silver City where the road joins M-64, which will take you to the town of Ontonagon. Follow M-38 (The Ontonagon—Greenland Road) out of Ontonagon all the way past the small town of Greenland, where you will turn east onto M-26 which you will take up to the Keweenaw Peninsula.

In Greenland, on M-38 you will see the Adventure Mine—an early copper mine that operated from 1850—1920. Daily-guided tours into the mine are offered. It is a very informative and interesting diversion.

Continue on M-26 all the way to Houghton, cross the Portage Canal Bridge, and turn right again on M-26 in the town of Hancock. The Keweenaw Peninsula is a place that deserves a day or two all to itself. There are several great routes on the peninsula so if possible abandon any strict time and distance schedule you may have created, and don't be in a hurry. This tour describes the various circle tours that the Keweenaw offers. You can either just take US-41 up to Copper Harbor and head back south—missing much of what the Keweenaw has to offer—or you can take the several small tours that I spell out here in order to see the peninsula the way it should be seen and experienced.

If you're in a hurry and must do the peninsula in one round trip then take US-41 to the end at Copper Harbor and head south on Brockway Mountain Drive out of town. Brockway Mountain Drive is a must-do. The Drive ends at M-26 at its south end and 26 then joins U.S.-41 making the loop very easy to do.

However, I highly recommend that you don't just do the US-41 / Brockway Mt. Drive loop. You will miss out on so much!

Instead, when you enter the peninsula at Hancock, follow M-26 as it goes easterly, then north, to the town of Lake Linden. In the small town of Lake Linden you will see Bootjack Road going east off M-26. Take this road a short distance and you will see Traprock Valley Road going to the north. (The very names of these roads evoke adventure!) Take Traprock Valley Road a little less than two miles to Gay Road where you will turn right and follow it all the way to the water where it will swing to the north and hug the west coast of Keweenaw Bay along the east side of the peninsula. The village of Gay is the destination of many riders who venture into this region simply to have their picture taken in front of the Gay Bar. The village derived its name from Mr. Joseph E. Gay, a mining company executive who ran the milling operation here a century ago. The remnant of the huge mill on the shoreline exists in the form of the massive 265-foot concrete smoke stack that dominates the skyline.

Follow this scenic road along the water's edge almost twenty miles to the small crossroads town of Lac La Belle. Turning left on Lac La Belle Road will take you to U.S.-41 near the town of Delaware, and the Delaware Copper mine site. This underground mine was in operation from 1847—1887 and guided or self-guided tours of the mine are available. The mine is a very interesting place to visit. In addition to the well lit mine tunnels they also have a display of antique machinery and engines. The mine is located on US-41 and is open 7 days per week from June—October.

When you're done touring the mine head north on 41 to Copper Harbor. Whether you are on a Gold Wing, full dress Harley or a crotch rocket, you will find yourself leaning forward and playing road racer on this renowned motorcycling road.

Copper Harbor is Michigan's northernmost city. In Copper Harbor I recommend a stop at the Harbor Haus restaurant on Brockway Avenue for a great lunch or dinner with an outstanding view of the lake. They also run a great bed & breakfast if spending a night here fits into your schedule. A boat tour of the islands in the bay and to the Copper Harbor lighthouse is a great way to really appreciate this unique area and see the 1800s lighthouse up close.

Fort Wilkins State Park is literally at the end of the road just outside of Copper Harbor and is a very interesting stop. The fort was built in 1844 and manned by army troops to keep the peace between settlers and Indians. You can imagine that the soldiers stationed there must have felt that they were truly at the end of the world, especially in the long cold winters. In the 1850s a military road connecting Fort Howard in Green Bay with Fort Wilkins was constructed. This road was improved during the Civil War in order to ensure a supply of copper from the Lake Superior region. U.S. 45 in the Watersmeet area in Gogebic County is on the same alignment as this old military road and in fact the name Old Military Road is still used in some stretches.

The need for Fort Wilkins quickly faded and it was abandoned in 1870. As a state park the fort has been reconstructed and has very interesting displays of military and frontier life during the 1800s in the Lake Superior wilderness. Depression-era programs to get people working (WPA, in particular) were largely responsible for the restoration of this fort. The park offers camping if the day is near its end.

<<<<<<●>>>>>

When you are done enjoying all that the Copper Harbor area has to offer there are two loops that a biker should take out of town—requiring doubling back—but what a reward there will be for this effort. Leave town on south M-26 (though you will actually be heading west, not south) about eight miles to the junction with Brockway Mountain Drive. Ride back to Copper Harbor on BMD. You will not find a better road for many miles around. Turn around and head right back on Brockway Mountain Drive, as it's a delightfully new and different perspective from the opposite direction. If you are still looking for a place to spend the night, staying at the Keweenaw Mountain Lodge (906-289-4403) on US-41 will be an experience you'll never forget. The Lodge is a fascinating building, built during the worst of the Depression when the local mines had shut down and unemployment in the region was severe. Like the Fort Wilkins reconstruction, construction of this lodge was actually a federal WPA project, not a private enterprise. Today in addition to the lodge, there is a beautiful golf course for those skilled enough to play on the hilly and very stony terrain.

TRAVEL MICHIGAN

First opened in 1855, the locks at Sault Ste. Marie allow 10,000 vessels, including ocean-going freighters, to make the passage from Lake Superior to the lower lakes and the St. Lawrence Seaway each year.

Once back to M-26 you can then follow this road along the Lake Superior coast through the quaint lakeside villages of Eagle Harbor and Eagle River, before finally rejoining US-41 and reluctantly heading south out of the Keweenaw. There are many wonderful things to see in Copper Harbor, Eagle River and Eagle Harbor so don't be in too much of a hurry. The lighthouse and associated museums in Eagle Harbor is an especially good stop.

◄◄◄◄◉▶▶▶▶

Sooner or later you will have to leave the Keweenaw, and when you must take US-41 south through the villages of Baraga and L'Anse. About 3.3 miles southeast of L'Anse on US-41 Old 41 veers off. Old 41 is a much more interesting and enjoyable riding road, so I recommend taking the Old 41 loop. It rejoins the new highway just north of the town of Alberta, and then Old 41 splits off again a mile later just south of town, this time for quite a bit longer stretch.

It is no accident that Old 41 goes through the Village of Alberta. This village has a very interesting history. It was a company town built out of the wilderness by Henry Ford and Ford Motor Company in 1935. Ford at one time had huge holdings in Michigan's Upper Peninsula—in the range of 500,000 acres. Ford wanted a dependable supply of the right kind of wood products guaranteed for his automobiles, which in the 1920s and 1930s had a large number of wood components. Ford built several large sawmills in the UP, and in fact, in the town of Kingsford at one time 8,000 people worked in his various plants and mills.

Ford wanted his workers to live near the land and to work on the land. As a former farm boy, Henry Ford never lost his love of the land and his belief that working the land was one of man's highest callings. Alberta was built out of the forests with comfortable homes for the workers and a state-of-the-art sawmill.

In the 1950s when wood was no longer utilized in cars or trucks, Ford Motor Company donated the town and 2,000 acres of surrounding land to Michigan Technological University for use as a forestry research and education center. There is a museum in Alberta that tells the story of Alberta and Henry Ford.

After splitting off the new highway just south of Alberta, Old 41 eventually rejoins the new highway in the burg of Tioga. This is moose country so if you're alert you may see one of these massive members of the Cervidae family in a nearby swamp with its head submerged eating aquatic vegetation.

Head east on US-41 all the way through and just past Marquette. In Marquette you can tour the beautiful and historic county courthouse, made famous in the 1958 movie and book *Anatomy of a Murder*. The Marquette Maritime Museum and Harbor Lighthouse is another stop you should make while in this enjoyable city. (300 Lakeshore Blvd. (906) 226-2006). But for the lack of tides and saltwater, Marquette could easily be mistaken for a coastal town on Maine's rocky coast.

Where M-28 and US- 41 split east of Marquette you want to stay on M-28 as it hugs the shoreline east all the way to Munising. There are so many things to see and do in this area it is difficult to list them all. Watch for road signs about waterfalls, scenic overlooks, lighthouses, and other attractions. In Munising, boat trips to the spectacular Pictured Rocks formations on Lake Superior make a very enjoyable half-day diversion.

In Munising you will see signs for the route to Miners Castle. This rock formation is about ten miles northeast of town perched high above the water on the cliffs. Follow county road H58 east from downtown, then turn north on H13. The views at Miners Castle are very impressive and worth the ride.

When you are satisfied you've seen and done everything you want to do in the Munising area, head east again on state route 28. The state is currently paving a gravel road that connects Munising with the town of Grand Marais, located on Lake Superior at the east end of the Pictured Rocks Lakeshore. In a few years that will be another option for enjoyable motorcycling in this region. At the present M-28 east of Munising cuts inland as there are no paved roads in the vicinity of the lakeshore.

Eleven miles southeast of Munising on 28 is the small town of Shingleton. Immediately east of this crossroad village you enter the legendary "Seney stretch"—a portion of route 28 that is perfectly straight and flat for twenty-five miles. It isn't as boring as one might think, however, as the road goes through a wild area of forests, lakes and streams, including a long stretch bordering the large Seney National Wildlife Refuge.

At the east end of this straightaway is Seney. In its lumbering heyday Seney was famous for its bars and wild frontier town reputation. However, a forest fire a century ago wiped it off the map. Today it is a small town that serves as base for outdoor activities such as canoeing, hunting, and snowmobiling.

Like the Petoskey area in northwestern Lower Michigan, this part of the UP is also Ernest Hemingway Country, of which he writes following his World War I experiences. One of my favorite short stories in his Nick Adams series, *Big Two-Hearted River,* was based here. It is a story of Hemingway's fictional self returning from World War I to a world, and a man, forever changed. He steps off the train in Seney to find the town gone—all familiar landmarks burned by a forest fire that swept across the region. The river, and the trout which he had pursued in earlier more innocent days survived, however. And that was all that mattered.

Realistically this area is actually much more scenic today than in Hemingway's day. He saw a land made barren by indiscriminate logging, followed by the ravages of forest fires that burned the slash and logging residue. Today the land has been healed and the forests reborn.

The Nick Adams Stories is one of those books, like Aldo Leopold's *Sand County Almanac,* that I take off the shelf to re-read every few years. Some books just speak to you in a loud and clear voice.

At Seney route 77 will take you north again to the town of Grand Marais on the lake. This is another worthwhile side trip. M-77 takes you to the eastern gateway of the Pictured Rocks National Lakeshore, where a surprise in the form of huge sand dunes awaits you just west of Grand Marais. The west portion of the Pictured Rocks features magnificent waterside rock cliffs, while at the east end a huge sand dune lines the shore. There is a short paved road going from the town of Grand Marais west to the dunes and the park's visitor's center.

Unless you want to ride on gravel and sand to the east of Grand Marais you will have to take M-77 back to Seney and M-28 and once again ride east to the junction of state route 123 where we head north into Newberry (designated by the state legislature as the Moose Capital of Michigan) and beyond. M-123 is a delightful road to ride. The main attraction between Newberry and Paradise are the Tahquamenon Falls. The Tahquamenon River gained its name from Native Americans. It means "dark waters," a name derived from the river's dark copper-colored waters, which is caused by high levels of tannic acid as a result of flowing through the coniferous forests of the area.

The Upper Falls of the Tahquamenon is a very impressive sight as the 200-foot wide river plunges fifty feet over a cliff. The well-marked entrance to the state park where the falls are located is on M-123. The Lower Falls are tumbling rapids as opposed to more traditional cascading waterfalls, and as such make for a less impressive sight.

◄◄◄◆►►►

If someone tells you that you can go to both Hell and Paradise in Michigan they're not pulling your leg. The village of Hell is in southeastern Michigan and Paradise is on the Superior coast where route 123 hits Whitefish Bay. From Paradise we ultimately need to follow M-123 south, but first another side trip, this time north to Whitefish Point, is in order. Going north out of Paradise on Whitefish Point Road will take you to the Point, with its shipwreck museum (including the two-hundred pound brass bell from the *Edmund Fitzgerald*), the Audubon Bird Observatory, and lighthouse. It is well worth making the approximately twenty miles round trip to the Point and back. In the spring and fall this is a favorite spot for birders due to a wide variety of birds migrating across Lake Superior at this narrow point.

Leaving Paradise on M-123 will take you south along the shore of Whitefish Bay. Almost ten miles south of Paradise you will see a paved road going east—take it. This is a shoreline road that hugs the coastline, rather than going inland as the designated Circle Tour route recommends. This road, the Curley Lewis Highway, later becomes Lakeshore Road, (also designated as the Whitefish Bay Scenic Byway). It takes you past Iroquois Point lighthouse, an old Indian Mission, and the Bay Mills Indian Reservation with its very large gambling casino. Iroquois Point was the site of a major battle between Native American tribes in 1662. The invading Iroquois were defeated in a surprise attack by outnumbered local Chippewa Indians. The two surviving Iroquois warriors were sent back east to warn other Iroquois bands to stay out of the upper lakes area. This battle was instrumental in opening up the upper Great Lakes region for further exploration by eliminating the Iroquois threat that up to that time had significantly hindered movement by Europeans and Natives alike.

Lakeshore Drive will ultimately turn into 6 Mile Road just southwest of Sault Ste. Marie, and the last few uneventful miles will get you just beyond the I-75 expressway to Old Mackinaw Trail where a left turn takes you north three miles to 3 Mile Road. Turn east onto 3 Mile Road and ride it to the island studded St. Marys River. When you hit the water, turn left and follow the pavement into Sault

Ste. Marie. This city is one of the oldest in the nation, dating back to the 17th century. It derived its name from early French explorers marking the location as the falls, or rapids, of the St. Marys River. In its original condition, there were major rapids in the river as Lake Superior fell twenty-one feet to the level of Lakes Huron and Michigan through this narrow channel. Lake level control structures and the massive locks have forever altered the natural state of the river, but the force of the rapids can still be seen as one crosses the International Bridge to Canada.

If I had to make just one suggestion about a must-see site here, it is the Soo Locks. These impressive structures are of fundamental importance to shipping on Lake Superior. A person can actually take a tour boat ride through the locks, but I think it is just as impressive to simply sit in the adjacent bleachers and watch a massive freighter make its way through the lock system.

I wouldn't be in too much of a hurry to leave the Soo, as it is an enjoyable place to explore, especially along the waterfront. It is also one of the oldest communities in North America, far older than many of the eastern cities that we consider our most historic places. As a sign of this history, consider that in 1671 a representative of King Louis the XIV of France gathered the leaders of fourteen Indian Nations in the Great Lakes and upper Mississippi River region to the Sault to publicly proclaim that the land was being claimed for King Louie.

⋘◉⋙

When you are ready to head north, follow the signs for the International Bridge into Sault Ste. Marie, Ontario. For a long time routine trips into Canada and back into the States were a breeze—a friendly border guard asked a few pertinent questions and you were on your way. Unless there was something about what you said or how you answered the questions the whole process seldom took more than a couple minutes. While the border between the U.S. and Canada is still very open and hundreds of thousands of people routinely cross it each day for business, travel, or recreation, things have noticeably changed since the foul acts of 9/11.

Be prepared to answer several questions about your travels and quite likely even have a cursory search made of your belongings—especially when crossing back into the U.S. Years ago I didn't even bother shutting off the engine or taking off my helmet when crossing the border; today I do both as soon as I pull up to the inspection gate. By the time this is printed passport requirements may well have become the law for cross-border travel. At a minimum you'll need your drivers license and proof of citizenship, such as a birth certificate. Don't try to carry a concealed weapon into Canada. Even if you are fully licensed to carry a handgun in the states, it is a major hassle, and if caught with a weapon your trip will definitely take a wrong turn. Border security has become a very important part of our national security so don't view travels across the Canadian border quite the same as we were fortunate enough to have done for generations.

Because you will be in Canada for about 400 miles, a stop at the Ontario Travel Information Centre just beyond the bridge to pick up some brochures and maps and exchange some currency is recommended. Though most things cost more in Canada, the exchange rate for the U.S. dollar is normally in our favor. If you spend more than $50 in Ontario save your receipts because upon leaving the country you may be eligible for a refund of some or all of the Goods and Services portion of sales taxes that you pay in-country. It gets a bit complicated, but it is worth saving receipts especially if you have motel, restaurant, gasoline, and other routine expenses that are bolstered by the purchase of items such as clothing or equipment.

Some legal issues to keep in mind when riding in Ontario are that helmets are required, radar detectors are illegal, right turns on red lights are legal after a full stop, and remember that speed limits are posted in kilometers per hour. In general, speed limits are a bit lower in Ontario than in most of the U.S.

Sault Ste. Marie, Ontario is a fairly large city that in many ways is the capital of northern Ontario. There are many things to do and see here, ranging from the Canadian Bushplane Heritage Centre to the Agawa Canyon tour train. The Agawa Canyon train offers a 228-mile day trip into the heart of northern Ontario's wilderness. It's a trip you won't soon forget.

It is extremely easy making the Ontario portion of the loop—just get on and stay on the Trans-Canada Highway / Route 17, from the Canadian Soo all the way to Thunder Bay. In Sault Ste. Marie, Ontario you will be on 17B when you get off the bridge. This road changes names as it goes through town, but it's always 17B. (Bay Street, Queen Street, Church Street, Pim Street, and finally, Great Northern Highway) Once you reach the northern city limits and Route 17/ Great Northern Highway, you don't have to think about directions for the next three hundred miles.

As you head north along the east shore of the lake the surroundings and the road gradually improve for the better. After about a half-hour you'll start enjoying what the trip is all about—great scenery and great riding. Between the Soo and the town of Wawa there are so many things to see that one just has to be willing to stop occasionally and smell the flowers—or watch the moose. You will see signs for attractions such as waterfalls, scenic overlooks, lighthouses, historical markers and more. To really savor the flavor of this area take the time to make side trips to the many things to see along the way. The stretch from Batchawana Bay Provincial Park north to the town of Wawa is just one scenic delight after another. In fact, this is true for the entire trip! Lake Superior can be said to be lacking in only two things—warm water and sandy beaches.

South of Wawa in Lake Superior Provincial Park an enjoyable trip through the park should include walking to the Agawa Rock Indian Pictographs. These ancient drawings on the shore of the lake are reached by a trail that is fascinating in its own right. You walk in a deep cleft between two rock walls, which are actually massive boulders and uplifted rock that has split forming a narrow "tunnel" to walk through. I have spent many enjoyable days camping and hiking in Lake Superior Provincial Park over the years and I have yet to explore 10% of it. If you are dressed and equipped properly, there is just no better way to see and experience this park than on a motorcycle.

◄◄◄◄◉►►►►

North of the park follow the signs (if you don't mind riding on a hard-surface gravel road for about a mile) to the Magpie River High Falls. These beautiful falls are 75 feet high and also very wide. Access to the base of the falls offers a splendid vantage point for viewing the cascading water as it tumbles down the not-quite vertical cliff face.

The city of Wawa (Ojibwa for Land of the Wild Goose) is a good place to stop and refuel both yourself and your bike. You will know you're there when you see the famous Wawa Goose. If you haven't seen it yet, you will know it when you do.

Route 17 curves inland for a stretch north of Wawa around Pukaskwa National Park, a huge wilderness park on the lake. The next town you'll come to is White River. If you're into canoeing, fishing, wilderness hiking or hunting then this is your place. It is far from Lake Superior, but surrounded by hundreds of lakes and streams, and miles of forest. White River has gained some fame in a most unusual manner. In 1914 a veterinarian in the Canadian Army on his way to Europe and World War I bought a bear cub he named Winnie at White River as a mascot for his unit. The bear was left in the care of the London Zoo in England where a certain A.A. Milne and his son Christopher Robin noticed it and fell in love with it because of its playful ways and personality. That bear of course became the basis for the famous lovable bear known by children everywhere— Winnie-The-Pooh. In mid-August each summer the town celebrates the annual Winnie's Hometown Festival.

Upon leaving White River Route 17 begins its westward march, far inland at this point as it skirts around Pukaskwa National Park, a huge wilderness park on the shore of the lake south of the highway. In this region you can add Woodland Caribou to the large wildlife that roam the wilderness.

Lake Superior curves north to meet the road near the village of Marathon. Shortly west of there is Terrace Bay and just west of Terrace Bay is Aquasabon Falls and Gorge. They're just off the highway and definitely worth the stop. Water

*Magpie Falls, south of Wawa, Ontario, is typical of the hundreds
of spectacular waterfalls in the Lake Superior basin.*

roars over a cliff that is more than one hundred feet high and crashes into a gorge that then makes a sharp angled turn relative to the falls.

It is about 185 miles from Marathon to Thunder Bay. It is in this portion of the trip that I think a person has to keep an open mind. Though I personally believe that this region is remarkable for its beauty and raw natural power, I have heard a few folks complain of the emptiness and the lack of comfort and amenities. In some stretches, there isn't much of anything except more of nothing. If this bothers you then you should be aware of the fact that it is a reality. Personally, I find it comforting to know that in the 21st century there are still place that haven't been completely paved over and altered by mankind. In those long miles where the landscape might begin to look the same (but only if you lose your sense of awe of what you are seeing), I find that I am refreshed by the fabulous wildness of it all. Some may consider it boring, some might consider it heaven on earth—you decide for yourself. There are things to see all along the north shore; too many to list here. Watch for the signs as there is much to be discovered by the inquisitive traveler. But perhaps most enjoyable are the many instances where rock formations, views of the lake, or the scene ahead of you when cresting a hill will leave you breathless and lacking in the words to adequately describe what you are seeing. It is a region of superlatives.

The town of Nipigon is nestled at the northwest corner of Lake Superior, just before the shoreline starts angling southwest. Southwest of Nipigon the next must see stop is Ouimet Canyon. This marvel of nature was formed by rock faulting and is a spectacular sight. It is located six miles on a paved road off Highway 17 near the town of Dorion.

Continue following Route 17 to the City of Thunder Bay (previously Port Arthur and Fort William prior to their 1970 amalgamation). Make time for a visit to historic Old Fort William—billed as the world's largest re-created fur trading post—for a look at late 18th and early 19th century Upper Canada. Thunder Bay sits in a region of great natural beauty. It is surrounded by high hills on one side and the Lake on the other.

Route 17 joins Canada Route 11 near Thunder Bay and these two roads are combined through the city. In the southwest portion of Thunder Bay Routes 17 & 11 intersect with Route 61, and Routes 17 & 11 continue straight west through western Ontario and all points west. From Thunder Bay southwest along the coastline you'll ride Route 61 for the remainder of the Ontario portion.

By good planning or just serendipity the road remains numbered as Route 61 after you enter Minnesota so you will stay on Route 61 from Thunder Bay to Duluth. The "arrowhead" country of Minnesota is perhaps even more spectacular than the Ontario portion of the trip. Lake side cliffs, waterfalls, forests, hills, light traffic and a wonderful riding road make this a stretch you will want to come back to time and again.

Shortly after entering Minnesota you'll find yourself in Grand Portage. An enjoyable stop here is the Grand Portage National Monument, a restored Northwest Company depot that tells the story of the fur trade in this region. Also nearby is Grand Portage State Park with its High Falls—the state's highest waterfalls. Not far down the road in Magney State Park are the Devil's Kettle Waterfalls on the Brule River. Next comes the city of Grand Marais and a bit further the small town of Lutsen, located in the Sawtooth Mountains (okay, we're talking about Midwestern mountains here, not the Rockies). Lutsen Mountain Ski Area offers the longest and tallest ski runs in the Midwest and the gondola on Moose Mountain or the chairlift on nearby Eagle Mountain offer rides to the top in the summer for spectacular views of the surrounding area. South of the town of Beaver Bay are two more highly recommended attractions; Split Rock Lighthouse and Gooseberry Falls State Park. The lighthouse is perched high above the lake on a cliff that offers a tremendous view of the water, and the Gooseberry Falls are actually a series of several falls that roar over ancient lava cliffs into a gorge. They are just plain spectacular. South of Two Harbors route 61 has been widened and straightened quite a bit, but for those who like a sexier road with lots of curves and character, head onto CR-61. It is closer to the water's edge and more enjoyable, if a bit slower.

As I noted earlier, the attractions on this route are just too numerous to write about them all. Just be willing to take the time to explore sites as you pass them on the road, and I guarantee you won't be disappointed. The only way you will be let down is if you just keep riding and don't stop to enjoy the natural beauty and sights (which is tempting because the riding is so great!).

Duluth, MN is the next large town on the tour. This port city, located in the heart of the continent, looks like it was custom made to fit in this part of the country. There is nothing pretentious or phony in the town or the people. One of the quickest ways to learn about this area and its history and culture is a stop at The Depot. Technically it's the St. Louis County Heritage and Arts Center Historic Union Depot. You can understand why it's known locally simply as The Depot. The Depot houses everything from old railroad cars and locomotives to historical and cultural artifacts and displays that span two centuries. The Depot once served seven different rail lines and 5,000 people per day walked through its doors. It has been beautifully restored and is a recommended stop on your journey through the Superior region. There are so many other things to see here that the city deserves a chapter of its own. A Leif Erikson Viking ship, a beer museum, a World War II tugboat, and much more await your exploration. If you can arrange to be in Duluth in early July you're in luck because that's when they hold the annual Classic Car Show and Harley Revue. Check out downtownduluth.com for information on all of the activities hosted in this historic port city.

Finally, before leaving Duluth ride the Skyline Parkway, which forms a 38-mile long semi-circle around Duluth on the high lands on the edge of town. You'll drive on a cliff high above the city and the lake, with stupendous views being your reward. A ride by the waterfront to see the landmark aerial lift bridge is also recommended. This very unusual bridge design spans a canal and raises vertically to allow boats to pass underneath.

In the city of Duluth Route 61 will merge into I-35 for a short distance until its juncture with US-2 where the tour turns east toward Superior and the end of a marvelous trip around a truly superior lake. Depending on how many of the side trips one takes, the total tour will be in the range of 1,500 miles in length. Scheduling a week-long trip around Lake Superior makes for a very enjoyable tour with time to do some additional things such as boat rides, waterfall excursions, exploring historic lighthouses and museums, short hikes, and much more.

This is definitely a trip you will recount with your riding buddies for years to come.

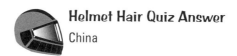

Helmet Hair Quiz Answer
China

The Door Peninsula

Helmet Hair Quiz

True or false—Beer is the official state beverage.

NO COMPREHENSIVE TOURING or vacation guide of Wisconsin would be complete without including the beautiful and unique Door Peninsula. The state has several discrete regions, and this is one of them. Any way that you look at it—land cover, agricultural specialty crops, geology, the fact it is a peninsula, or its maritime flavor and history—this part of the state is distinctive.

The ride starts in the Lake Michigan port city of Two Rivers, at the southeast corner of the peninsula. The origin of the name of this city is easy; the West Twin River and the East Twin River converge here, with the harbor being the river mouth. Start the ride by going east on route 42, and when it turns north just keep heading east on 22nd Street. In just a few blocks you will come to the well marked Sandy Bay Road / county road O. Turn left onto CR-O and we'll follow it along the shoreline for a bit over six miles to county road V. Between these two points is the large Point Beach State Forest (which is more like a park than a forest). As you ride through the park on CR-O you'll see a sign that states Entering Fee Area—don't worry, that's for entry to the park, not to ride on CR-O! The Rawley Point Lighthouse is the main attraction here, unless you want to camp, picnic, or play on the beach. Turn right onto Park Road to see the lighthouse and keeper's house if this is your thing. A 113-foot high steel tower, the Rawley Point light is one of the tallest on the Lakes, and with good reason. Prior to its construction, there were 26 wrecks off this point of land. The light is part of an active Coast Guard base so it isn't open to the public, but the facility can be easily viewed from the beach.

The second half of CR-O is real nice, though a slow posted speed limit keeps the fun to a sedated level. CR-O ends at CR-V, and the pavement only goes to the west. However, if you want free access to the beach there is a short drive to the east at this corner that goes to school property and open beach access.

We are on 'V' a very short distance when we arrive at state route 42. Turn right onto 42 and it will guide us all the way to Algoma. Highway 42 is an enjoy-

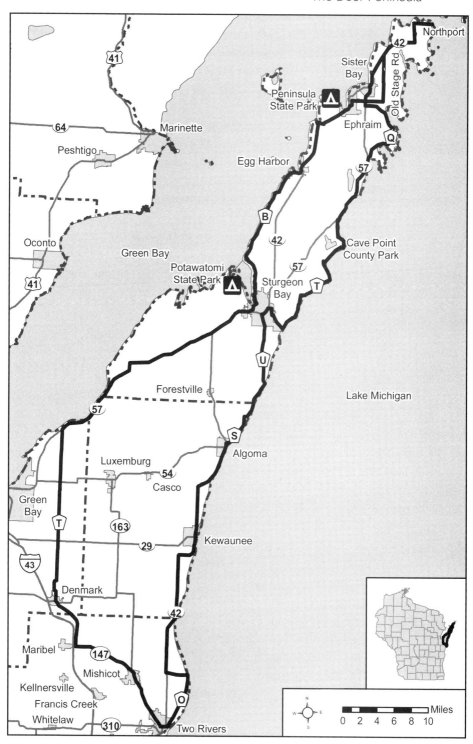

DOOR PENINSULA 225 MILES		
Miles	**Destination**	**Total**
00	Two Rivers	00
26	Kewaunee	26
29	Sturgeon Bay Ship Canal Bridge	55
22	Jacksonport	77
33	Northport	110
29	Egg Harbor	139
19	Sturgeon Bay Bridge	158
28	County Road T	186
19	Denmark	205
20	Two Rivers	225

able road to ride. It's fairly laid back, with a lot of farmland rolling by as one rides north. The route has quite a few graceful curves and some gently rolling hills, and occasionally you are treated to wonderful vistas with Lake Michigan in the distance as hilltop curves are rounded.

Kewaunee is the first town you will come to. It is a popular base for sport fishing excursions and also has a couple of attractions that might be of interest. On the waterfront *The Ludington,* an Army Corps of Engineers tug boat is berthed in the mouth of the Kewaunee River, which forms a harbor where sportfishing boats enter the big lake. There is a small park on the south side of the harbor where a person can walk out to the point and relax while viewing the lake and watching boat traffic and shore fishermen trying to catch dinner. If you have Otis Redding's *The Dock on the Bay* on your IPod, this would be a good time and place to listen to it.

If touring old jails piques your interest you may want to explore the Kewaunee Jail Museum, located at 613 Dodge Street, one block west of route 42 in town, on a high hill adjacent to the very cool old courthouse. The building dates from 1876 and back in the day it served as the sheriff's residence, office and jail. The original 1876 cellblocks with their tiny 5' x 6' cells are intimidating enough to have kept even the wildest hard drinking lumberjack on the straight and narrow.

Interestingly, the museum has a scale model of the *USS Pueblo,* a ship built in Kewaunee in 1944 and captured by North Korea in 1968 while it was in interna-

*The pier at Kewaunee's waterfront is a great place to relax and watch
a sunrise or a moonrise over the calm waters.*

tional waters. Allegedly, the Soviet Union wanted a new cryptographic machine
that was on board to go with the decoding key they had recently obtained from a
spy. One sailor was killed in the attack and North Korea held the crew for eleven
months. They still hold the ship, which the Navy continues to consider as a commissioned American naval ship.

Between Kewaunee and Algoma are many miles of the same sort of pleasurable riding as south of town. Traffic isn't a hassle and the ride is very tranquil,
with the same occasional wonderful views of the big water. The shoreline north
of Two Rivers is a pleasant surprise in its light state of development. A wooded
shoreline or farm fields almost to the water's edge are the rule, rather than condos
and resorts.

Algoma is a pleasant town of about 3,500 souls. It dates back to 1851 and has
been known by three names. The Pottawatomie called the site Ahnapee, meaning
Land of the Great Gray Wolf, a legendary beast of Indian lore. The first settlers
named it Wolf River, a loose translation of the Indian name. It was later called
Ahnapee, and finally in 1879 the name was officially changed to Algoma—an
Indian term meaning Park of Flowers. Perhaps early Algoma boosters thought
that 'park of flowers' was a much more pleasing and agreeable nickname that
could attract business and tourists, as opposed to being known as the site of a

bloodthirsty oversized wolf. Algoma has an attractive waterfront that is an enjoyable pause on the trip.

In Algoma we leave forty-two after many miles of pleasurable company. Immediately after crossing the Ahnapee River turn right onto Water Street, which becomes Lakeview Drive and finally county road S outside of town. It is well marked and very easy to follow. We will be on 'S' for 4 miles, then turning right onto CR-U. County road U will be our host all the way north to the city of Sturgeon Bay. The first several miles are along the coast and then it moves inland as it works its way north. Both 'S' and 'U' are very nice roads and will provide miles of enjoyable two wheeling.

County road U rejoins with state route 42 again in Sturgeon Bay, and we will use the highway 42 bridge to cross the Sturgeon Bay Ship Canal. It took ten years to dig the 1.3 mile canal, connecting Sturgeon Bay with Lake Michigan. The shipping channel was originally dug by a railroad company, which later sold the canal to the U.S. government. It is currently operated by the Army Corps of Engineers. The canal effectively turned the northern portion of Door County into an island, connected by bridges to the mainland.

Our ride has us motoring along the north shore of the canal to the Lake Michigan shore. To accomplish this we need to turn right onto Utah Street less than a half-mile after crossing the bridge. (Watch for signs for the Coast Guard facility and CR-Tt). After just a few blocks we turn south on Cove Road which then curves east as CR-Tt. This lightly traveled county road provides 2 or 3 areas to pull over to view the canal if you wish before it swings north at the mouth of the canal, and the location of the Coast Guard station. The Sturgeon Canal lighthouse is at this point, but it is not accessible. A small public parking area is available just outside the USCG station if you want to view the light and canal from a short distance.

County road Tt runs north from the canal along the lake as a designated Rustic Road, and it earns that title with full honors. The road is narrow and twisty asphalt through a heavily forested area resulting in a very nice ride for its 3.5 mile distance. When Tt makes a ninety-degree swing west, we are going to make a very short jog to the east, then following Lake Michigan Drive north along the shoreline to county road T. County road T is also a designated Rustic Road and it is just great. The narrow roadway twists and turns its way north along the shoreline through dense forestland. Just like CR-Tt, county road T will eventually turn due west. At that point, however, we turn right and continue following the coastline on Cave Point Drive. We will pass through Whitefish Dunes State Park, but our destination is Cave Point County Park—a jewel of a park that must be seen to be appreciated.

The road to the county park turns into a very narrow and tightly twisting drive and you will suddenly find yourself at a parking area near the shore. A short walk

Rock formations and small sea caves at Cave Point Park are compelling reasons to take a break from the road to marvel at nature's handiwork.

will take you to a series of small sea caves and rock formations that are beautiful to behold. The waves of the lake crash amongst the tree covered rocks resulting in a visual and audio treat that makes this trip worth every mile ridden. I have been to this park a couple of times on a bike and have yet to see another person there while I was present. If the weather is cooperative, sitting on the rocks overlooking the water for an extended period will soothe your troubled spirits better than any-thing else I've ever found. Like many of the destinations I discuss in this book this is best done as a small group ride. The road into the park, and the limited parking area really weren't made for dozens of bikes, or for large RVs for that matter.

Follow the drive north out of the park and it will eventually join with route 57 at the tiny town of Jacksonport. A sign in Cave Point Park clearly points the way to this town.

We will ride 57 for a bit over eight miles, to the north side of Baileys Harbor. This small town was the first village to form on the peninsula, and that came out of necessity when Captain Justice Bailey sought refuge in the harbor during a fierce Lake Michigan storm in 1848. Signs for CR-Q and North Bay clearly point out our next turn. We will follow 'Q' as it goes east to the shoreline, and then after several miles it will swing back west again to re-join highway 57. For the period where it goes north along the shore it is a very nice, and easily followed, motorcycling path. The qualities that we are becoming accustomed to—curves, light traffic, heavily forested stretches—they are all here, making for wonderful biking.

The Cana Island lighthouse is along this stretch. However, it is a fairly long and somewhat confusing ride out to the island, and once there you must park and walk across the island to the tower. It is a nice diversion but it will require parking your bike in an unprotected sand lot after following a confusing road system from 'Q' out to the island. Definitely doable, but you should really want to do it, as opposed to doing it just for the hell of it.

Once CR-Q joins route 57 it is a short ride north to the town of Sister Bay, where we pick up SR 42 northbound. We will follow 42 through Ellison Bay, Gills Rock, and finally Northport, which is literally at land's end.

Sister Bay and Ellison Bay are both high-end resort areas, blessed with great natural beauty, waterfront locations, and well-established resorts and restaurants. Gills Rock and Northport are much smaller. From Gills Rock a person can take a cruise boat out to the islands north of the point, and the Washington Island ferry leaves from the dock, located at the end of route 42, in Northport.

The seven-mile wide strait between Northport and Washington Island is where the Door Peninsula derives its name. Long before the arrival of the first Europeans, the local Native Americans learned the hard way of the danger of crossing this strait. Unpredictable winds, currents and waves made the passage treacherous, and the Indians called the passageway the door of death. It earned this name following a battle between local Pottawatomie Indians who lived on the island, and Winnebago Indians who had planned a surprise attack. Many braves died when their canoes were swamped, and the natives pledged that they must never attempt the passage again. In turn, early French explorers gave it the name *Porte des Morts*. The name stuck and Door Peninsula was named.

Washington Island is a favorite getaway for those seeking some low keyed R&R. It is easy to assume that the island was named in honor of George Washington, but there is a bit more to it than just that. In 1816, the captain of the U.S. schooner Washington paused here in a sheltered bay while waiting for the rest of his small flotilla of ships that were enroute to present day Green Bay to establish Fort Howard. He named the island Washington in recognition of the ex-president's many accomplishments.

We of course don't want to retrace our steps on the way south from the tip of the peninsula so we will take a different route as much as possible. Follow 42 back south to just west of Ellison Bay, to Old Stage Road. At this corner there are several tall antennas to mark the location for us. Old Stage Road is a pleasant ride

Stately Rock Mill is a beautifully restored water powered mill. Grist mills played a vital role in the lives of pioneers.

through a region of newly regenerated woodlands, and quite a few abandoned farms and orchards that are reverting back to natural cover. Old Stage Road makes a westerly turn eventually and crosses route 57 just east of the town of Ephraim. West of fifty-seven the road's name changes to Settlement Road, but it's the same alignment. Follow Settlement Road into town where it eventually joins with state route 42 on the waterfront. We will follow 42 as it works its way southwest along the shore to Egg Harbor. This stretch is probably the least pleasant of the entire trip because of the likelihood of heavy recreational traffic during the peak vacation period. It isn't too bad, but I have had occasion to get caught behind large RVs or trucks pulling large boats, making passing difficult because of traffic density and curves. If you encounter this type of traffic just be patient, as you will soon leave it all behind.

In Egg Harbor watch for the sign for county road G (aka Horseshoe Bay Drive). CR-G will angle off to your right front, following the water's edge while 42 skirts inland. We will ride CR-G four miles, when it will turn east, but CR-B will continue straight south along the shoreline. It is very easy to follow, as we just want to stay on the waterfront pavement, regardless of name change. CR-B will be our partner for many miles, in fact all the way south to Sturgeon Bay and the Michigan Street bridge across the shipping canal to route 42 on the south shore. County road B is a fun ride. Though it is near the water the views of Green Bay are not constant because of trees. Just north of the town of Sturgeon Bay notice the large stone quarry and high cliff wall on the east side of the road; quite impressive!

We are going to follow routes 42, then 57, southwest many miles toward the city of Green Bay. Eventually you will cross into Brown County at a wide spot in the road called Dyckesville. A mile further you will pass Bayshore County Park, and about two miles further along you will come to county road T. We turn left onto 'T' and work our way south across many miles of fertile green farmland to the village of Denmark. Route 29 bisects this region, with the land north of 29 being intensively farmed and quite flat, but south of 29 the scenery becomes more interesting, with more wooded land and a nice rolling character.

◄◄◄◄◉►►►►

Denmark is an interesting small town, which, true to its name flies the Danish flag. Obviously a pocket of ethnic history. On the south side of Denmark we pick up county road R, which runs southeast from town. Our next stop is a few miles down the road at historic Rock Mill, located on private land in the Devils River Campers Park. This is a very nice stop where a person can view the 1848 stone barn and original milling equipment. Nearby is the scenic rocky gorge where falling water once powered the water wheel to turn the mill's stone. It is a great place to camp should that be on your agenda.

After leaving Rock Mill continue south on CR-R just a mile or so and you will come to Maribel Caves County Park and some very scenic rock formations in a rugged river valley. On the near side of the river are bedrock cliffs of fifty feet or more in height, and on the other is a flat lowland. The cliff line marks a geologic demarcation, separating the erosion resistant Niagara escarpment Dolomite from a region that was eroded and made flat through glacial action and subsequent erosion. Over the centuries water has carved several caves in the lower cliff faces for added interest. It is a short walk from the paved parking lot to the cliff face, and a wood walkway has been built along the base of the cliffs to make access very easy.

Just south of Maribel park CR-R takes us to highway 147, which we follow back to the starting point of Two Rivers. Along the way we ride through the small town of Mishicot, named in 1847 in honor of the Pottawatomie chief who ruled in this region. The town's opera house, which still stands on Main Street, speaks to the once bustling nature of this small town.

From just west of Mishicot to the city of Two Rivers, Route 147 closely follows East Twin River as it flows toward Lake Michigan, marking the end of this delightful ride.

Helmet Hair Quiz Answer

False (it is milk)

Lake of the Clouds in Porcupine Mountains Wilderness State Park is definitely worth a stop.

Historic homes with beautiful architectural styles are abundant in towns and cities across Wisconsin. Many are open for tours, whether publicly or privately owned.

Wrapping It All Up

I HAVE LONG ENJOYED concocting tours that took me completely around the perimeter of a state. This is a great way to see all that a state is made of; the different physical regions, the urban and rural sections, the differing social and cultural influences, and the many historical events and their continuing impacts.

Wisconsin is no different. Taking a roughly circular tour around the state sheds light on what the state is all about. And of course, as is key in my books, the tour is on the best roads possible, with almost no duplication from other tours discussed in the book.

It is a long ride, and with the many things to see and do I suggest making it a four-day event. That way you can really see and experience Wisconsin.

Even if you don't take a tour of the fascinating House on the Rock, located south of Spring Green, it is worth exploring the grounds to see the landscaping, gardens and sculptures.

The Great Circle Tour

Helmet Hair Quiz

What is the oldest continually operating automobile racetrack in the world?

WE BEGIN THIS EPIC TOUR of Wisconsin at the rapidly developing city of Sun Prairie, located just north of Madison on route 19. The town got its start in 1837 when President Van Buren ordered an assemblage of men to build a capitol in Madison. The group departed from Milwaukee and traveled for two weeks in the rain. They finally emerged at the edge of the prairie with the sun shining for the first time since leaving Milwaukee. A member of the group carved the words "Sun Prairie" into a tree.

Fifty years later Sun Prairie's most famous daughter was born in a local farm family. Georgia O'Keeffe attended rural schools and studied art in this area until she was sixteen, when the family moved to Virginia. Eventually O'Keeffe went on to broaden her obvious artistic talents at various academies and by the late 1920s she began painting in the southwestern style in New Mexico, for which she is best known.

This immediate locale is representative of suburban Wisconsin, with all the positive and negative repercussions of a sprawling urban area being evident. Commercial and retail businesses are booming, and those who build infrastructure are doing very well. Persons who remember a more rural and bucolic town surrounded by farmland and quiet two-lane roads might have a different impression of all this progress. Nevertheless, traffic congestion and cookie cutter subdivisions are a sign of the times. Every urban center in the state, from Beloit to Superior, struggles with how to protect things such as open spaces and a high quality of life while planning for and managing the inexorable growth that will come to the edges of their cities seemingly without regard to what local residents may wish.

In Sun Prairie we have to make a jog to the north to stay on 19 and then commence westward. The first few miles west of Sun Prairie is predictably not the best motorcycling to be found, but once west of U.S. 12 conditions improve rapidly with highway 19 becoming narrow and curvy, and the land around us much more hilly and wooded. State highway 19 joins forces with highways 78 and 14 for a bit,

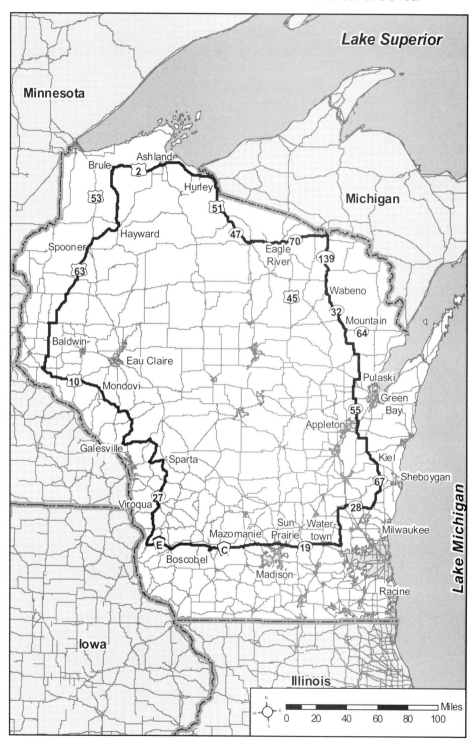

	THE GREAT CIRCLE 950 MILES	
Miles	**Destination**	**Total**
00	Sun Prairie / Madison	00
71	Muscoda	71
66	Viroqua	137
79	Galesville / U.S. 53	216
55	Mondovi / U.S. 10	271
102	Turtle Lake / U.S. 8	373
62	Hayward	435
75	Ashland	510
40	Hurley / U.S. 51	550
78	Eagle River	628
62	Laona	690
76	Pulaski	766
81	Plymouth	847
77	Watertown	924
26	Sun Prairie	950

taking us to the historic village of Mazomanie. This town has several nicely preserved old buildings, including the oldest wooden railroad depot in the Midwest, built in 1857, during the towns railroading glory days.

Highway U.S. 14 will be our guide west toward the Wisconsin River, first passing through the small town of Arena and Arena Cheese Company, with the large cheese eating mouse statue out front.

About five miles west of Arena you will see county road C and signs pointing toward Tower Hill State Park. Turn left on CR-C, which we will follow west along the south shore of the Wisconsin River to route 130. After departing highway 14 CR-C runs along the south boundary of Tower Hill State Park. The park's name gives a description of some of what can be found in the park—a tower and melting house where lead shot was made in the 1800s from an adjacent deep tunnel mine. The south part of the park has nice bluff trails as well as campgrounds.

Wisconsin's scenic farm country provides mile after pleasant mile of enjoyable motorcycling through a bountiful and bucolic landscape.

CR-C jogs south on route 23 for less than a half-mile before continuing west. At state route 23 you will need to decide if you wish to take a short side trip several miles south on 23 to see the amazing House on the Rock. Even if a person doesn't actually take the tour of the House it is interesting going through the parking area to view the outdoor sculptures and the overall lay of the land. Near the intersection of C and 23 are the Frank Lloyd Wright Visitor Center, and his famous Taliesin retreat. For more information go to www.taliesinpreservation.org or call 608.588.7900.

Continuing west on C from highway 23 is a joy. To the right is the floodplain of the Wisconsin River and immediately left are forested hills and rock formations. Follow this scenic road to route 130, turning right, and following it until it joins with route 133. Highway 130 will turn north and cross the river but we want to continue straight west on 133 many scenic and enjoyable miles to the town of Boscobel and U.S. 61. It is roughly twenty-eight miles across this stretch, all of it following the south shore of the Wisconsin River. The scenery is much like we've become used to, with the flat flood plain alternating between farm land and woods to our right, and hills and more densely wooded lands to the south. West of Muscoda watch for an unusual display on your left consisting of a variety of old motorcycles and parts and pieces thereof, on exhibit in a farm yard and adjacent field. Quite unusual but it certainly makes a statement; just not sure what the statement is meant to be. I'm sure there is a fascinating story behind this outdoor motorcycle art museum.

At Boscobel we pick up highway 61 and cross the river. Before leaving the wild turkey hunting capital of Wisconsin, however, there are a few sites in Boscobel worth seeing. The 1857 Boscobel Depot Museum at 1005 Wisconsin Avenue is interesting, and the meeting hall of Civil War Veterans—the Grand Army of the Republic Hall—still stands at its location at 102 Mary Street. It has many Civil War artifacts and memorabilia. It is open Saturdays and by appointment. Call ahead to 608.375.5693.

Once across the river we immediately turn left on county road E and twist and turn on this fabulous road through the hills and valleys to route 131 where we turn left and follow it into Steuben to pick up highway 179. Route 179 will continue west in the same fashion as CR-E; following forested stream valleys as they meander through the hills in a very pretty setting to route 27 and the town of Eastman, where we begin our northward leg of the trip.

We will be on route 27 for many miles—all the way up to Sparta just north of I-90. Highway 27 is a very nice biking road. It has very few straight sections, is quite hilly for the most part, and the scenery ranges from pleasant to very nice. From Eastman north to Mt. Sterling the roadway often follows a ridgeline, providing wonderful views of the distant hills, valleys, farms and woods fading into the horizon. North of Mt. Sterling quite a ways and just a bit south of Liberty Pole is Monument Rock—an interesting geologic formation. The rock is on private property and parking is limited on the narrow road shoulder, so if you pull over use care.

Viroqua, the self-proclaimed capital of the driftless area, has an attractive and historic downtown area, though sprawl is crawling out north of town in the form of a lot of strip development. North of Viroqua route 27 joins with U.S. highways 14 and 61 for several miles to the town of Westby, where 27 splits off on its own once again. North of Westby route 27 continues its fun motorcycling character all the way to Sparta. The land in general gets a bit more wooded as one travels north, though never completely forested as it is further north. For much of the distance between Westby and Sparta 27 follows a scenic valley formed by the Little LaCrosse River, creating not only a very scenic panorama but also providing the usual great motorcycling that one finds when tailing a river.

In Sparta we head west on route 16 to northbound 162. If you have an interest in our country's space program, especially as it concerns native son and astronaut Deke Slayton, or if it's antique bicycles that get you excited, then by all means visit the

Brats and cheese make up two of the primary food groups in Wisconsin.

Deke Slayton Memorial Space & Bicycle Museum. It's located in downtown Sparta a block north of the courthouse.

Sixteen is enjoyable because of light traffic and decent surroundings, but things really improve on 162. This road traverses a heavily wooded region, and is a blast to ride. We will take it northwest to route 108 and Melrose, where we pick up route 54 and continue our temporary westerly ride.

Route 54 is great—woods, hills, curves, light traffic—what more can I say? Fifty-four follows the Black River as we journey west, so enjoy the ride all the way to Galesville where we head north again, this time on U.S. 53. From Galesville we're going to cruise on 53 as it carves its way through various stream valleys north to Whitehall; a lot of scenic and very enjoyable miles. Most of 53 is newly paved and provides wonderful motorcycling. The last few miles south of Whitehall are older pavement but the road and scenery lose little of their charms, even if the landscape does open up a bit.

In Whitehall get on route 121 and head northwesterly for about twenty miles. You will be grinning a lot on this road as it meanders merrily on its way, seeming not to care if it arrives today or tomorrow. For much of this area we are riding on the eastern edge of the Mississippi River bluff country. To our right the landscape is more open and farmlands predominate, while to the left is the hillier and more forested coulee region. Many roads, route 121 being no exception, follow stream valleys in this area, which results in above average motorcycling opportunities. About twenty miles northwest of Whitehall, just beyond the tiny town of Lookout, turn right onto county road-H, taking it north to Mondovi. CR-H is another characteristically fun Wisconsin county road.

In Mondovi link with U.S. 10 and take it west a long way—in fact, forty-four miles to its junction with U.S. 63 where we begin our 'up north' portion of the tour in earnest. U.S 10 between Mondovi and Ellsworth is enjoyable riding. The road has surprisingly light traffic and it is clear that heavy trucks and long distance travelers utilize nearby I-94, leaving this once major highway to a status of handling local traffic, which is just fine with us bikers. The road goes through a very pretty area of rolling land made up of a good mix of forest and farm. There are continual broad curves to keep things from getting boring. There is an especially enjoyable stretch midway where the highway passes through the Rush River valley area. In Durand, where 10 crosses the Chippewa River, several taverns are located just south of the highway on Main Street, on the shore of the river. They make a good lunch stop.

We will get to know route 63 very well as it carries us over the countryside all the way north to Hayward. It is a great road from which to see the changes in Wisconsin's geologic, cultural, and economic facets as one travels from south to north. Farmland, lake country, and the big woods; we will pass through all of it. Once again, having major highways relatively close by means that we won't be fighting heavy truck traffic. I-35 to the west and U.S. 53 to the east carry the heavy load, leaving 63 to handle local and recreational traffic.

On busy summer weekends highway 63 can get congested with RVs and pickup trucks pulling boats, but if you time your travels to miss the predictable weekend rush it is an enjoyable road to ride. There are many attractions along the way, just watch for signs and be willing to pull over to check out the various places of interest. In Clear Lake there is a nice veterans memorial and just beyond Clear Lake is where the 'up north' look really begins. In Spooner there is a very cool railroad museum and the Great Northern Railway, on which rides into the surrounding countryside can be had. Check them out at http://www.spoonertrain-ride.com/ or call 715.635.3200. They even have a dinner train—what a great way that would be to conclude a day of motorcycling!

North of Spooner highway 63 merges with U.S. 53 for about four miles, and then splits off again at the town of Trego. East of Trego 63 follows the beautiful Namekagon River, which is part of the St. Croix National Scenic Riverway. It is a very scenic and enjoyable ride from Trego to Hayward along this winding stream.

I discuss Hayward in another chapter, but by all means if this is your only trip here be sure to check out the fishing museum. Look for the giant Muskie just south of the main intersection of 63 and 27. North of Hayward it is state highway 27 that will be our partner. This road goes essentially straight north, albeit with lots of twists and turns through the forests, hills and lakes of this region, depositing us onto highway U.S. 2 at the village of Brule. Route 27 will offer mile after pleasing mile of laid back relaxing riding through the kind of landscape that most of us conjure up in our mind when we think of northern Wisconsin.

<<<<●>>>>

One of my favorite long distance riding roads—U.S. 2—will carry us across the top of Wisconsin. I like roads that run through the wide-open spaces that we enjoy in North America. Highway 2 is typical of that kind of road; whether it is through the forests along the north shore of Lake Michigan or the south shore of Lake Superior, the big sky country of the Great Plains, or the mountains of the west, along highway 2 you will see it all. And there is certainly a lot to see along seventy miles that this road carries us across northern Wisconsin.

Just west of Ashland, I recommend a stop at the Northern Great Lakes Visitor Center. This is more than a museum. It includes interactive displays of the natural and cultural history of this region, an impressive observation tower, theater, and a trail to walk through the new wildlife refuge.

In historic Hurley we start on the long southward leg of our ride. U.S. highway 51 will take us a bit less than thirty miles south to the town of Manitowish, where we pick up state route 47. Highway 51 traverses a land of forests, and in the Mercer and Manitowish areas, lakes. A lot of Wisconsin's nearly 15,000 lakes can be found along 51 in this area. Route 47 continues south through a magical countryside of more forests and water, including a long stretch through the Lac Du Flambeau Indian Reservation. A historical marker at Flambeau Lake tells the historical significance and origins of the lake of the torches. If Casinos are the kind of nightlife you seek, the very large Lake of the Torches Casino should keep you happy.

We depart forty-seven at the town of Woodruff, and head east on route 70 (which requires a northerly jog of a couple miles in town). We will be on 70 east bound for about fifty-five beautiful miles, so you don't have to worry about checking your map—just concentrate on the ride and the scenery. While 99% of the ride is through wonderful open spaces, there are a couple of spots that, in comparison, seem a bit congested. One is at the resort town of St. Germain, where recreational traffic can sometimes be a bit heavy. The other is the city of Eagle River where U.S. 45 delivers traffic from the south to the many nearby lakes. East of Eagle River we ride through the huge Chequamegon Nicolet National Forest for many miles. Traffic and congestion will be the last thing on your mind in this wild and beautiful region.

Just after crossing the Florence County line we pick up state route 139, which becomes our next southward route. One thirty nine carries us many more miles through the national forest. If anything, this road is even better than route 70. Traffic is lighter, winding curves more common, and road conditions overall being very good.

When riding roads such as route 139 I feel that I understand why dogs stick their heads out of car windows. They understand; they get it! If they could, I am certain that most dogs would ride motorcycles. Canine or human, it is a wonderful ride south down to U.S. 8, which we follow west and then almost immediately south again to the town of Laona at the intersection of U.S. 8 and state route 32. The town was named after Laona Johnson—the first white child born in the new settlement.

⤜⤛⬥⤛⤚

In this tiny town nestled in the forest, the big attraction is the Camp 5 Logging Museum and the Lumberjack Steam Train. The train uses a refurbished logging company steam engine to pull passenger cars through the forest to the Camp Five Farm. Check them out at www.lumberjacksteamtrain.com or 715.674.3414. The train is located at the corner of U.S. 8 and highway 32, which just happens to be the road we take south of Laona to continue the trip.

Route 32 takes us all the way to Pulaski; nearly to Green Bay. But there is much to see and do before we leave the north woods. This road continues to dissect the national forest for numerous miles. Along the way watch for attractions such as the logging museum in Wabeno, with its out of the ordinary outdoor displays that make for interesting photo opportunities. Many more exhibits and authentic artifacts await in the museum building. The Wabeno Lions Club built the logging museum in 1941, using authentic methods of construction to make the building itself a replica of buildings one would find in a logging camp circa 1890. In June 1880 a massive tornado tore through the forests in this location. The Native Americans referred to the damaged area as waubeno, loosely meaning 'the coming of the winds'. When a logging company established a camp and mill there a few years later, they retained the Indian name for the place.

The Lumberjack Steam Train transports riders back to the 1890s when timber was king and lumberjacks lived as hard as they worked.

The landscape starts to change south of route 64. We can observe the obvious changes as we ride south to a land that has been converted to almost pure farmlands in the Pulaski area.

At Pulaski take a short jog west on route 160 to state highway 55, on which we continue our southward ride. Route 55 travels through the productive farmlands north of Lake Winnebago until we reach the urban areas lining the Fox River east of Appleton. Fifty-five will carry us through Kaukauna, one of the most historic places in Wisconsin. Jean Nicolet was the first white man to see this location in the 17th century when he was searching for a water route to China. There was a series of three waterfalls at this site, called KeKaling by the Indians, because it was a place where they had to portage their canoes. In time it became an important fur trading station. Its name is derived from the original Indian name for the portage site.

Cross the Fox River and continue south on route 55 to just beyond the town of Sherwood where we pick up route 114 east bound five miles to the town of Hilbert. In Hilbert join routes 32/57 and ride through the farmlands to the town of Kiel, where we pick up route 67. Upon entering the region of the Kettle Moraine south of Kiel the motorcycling and scenic potential rises. SR 67 carries us south

A Paul Bunyan–sized statue of Larry the Log Roller depicts the larger than life mythical nature of the logging era in northern Wisconsin.

through Elkhart Lake, past Road America, and on to the busy town of Plymouth, where we will want to spend some time.

Plymouth is one of those small towns that have retained an active and healthy downtown section. There are some good places in town to stop to eat or take a break, and afterwards just to walk around a bit.

A required stop in my opinion is on the east edge of Plymouth's downtown section at Veterans Memorial Trail. This small park, situated on the south side of the millpond, puts an interesting spin on the need to remember our history and veterans. A flag and marker commemorate each war the country has been involved in, from the Revolutionary War to Iraq and Afghanistan. What is very cool is that each flag is identical to the flag of the time; in other words, the flag that flies over the Revolutionary War stone has 13 stars, the War of 1812 flag has 15 stars (and 15 stripes—the only flag in our history to stray from the standard number of stripes). The Mexican American War flag has 28 stars, and so on. Only the flagpoles over the monuments for Vietnam and Iraq / Afghanistan fly the current 50-star flag. A 'trail' connects the many monuments, carrying the viewer through time from the 1770s to the present. It is very nicely done, and being situated alongside the pond and stream below the spillway adds to the overall ambience. Picnic tables under a couple of large trees are another nice touch.

Just south of Plymouth route 67 turns directly west, and just after that turn you will see county road E going straight south. We want to take E four miles south to route 28, where a right turn will start our westward ride.

Route 28 entertains for many miles as it cuts through the Kettle Moraine State Forest, delivering us to the town of Mayville. In between are loads of enjoyable hilly and curvy miles of very good motorcycling. Mayville's claim to fame (besides being a very pleasant small town) is that it was the site of Wisconsin's first iron smelter.

From Mayville, which is also the east gateway to the Horicon Marsh, we ride south again on route 67. The riding gets better as we proceed south, with some high hills to add variety and enjoyment to the ride. At a wide spot in the road called Old Ashippun keep any eye out for Pribnow's Maple Inn. This is a great place to dine if you have developed a large appetite. Their Friday fish fries are legendary.

Two miles south of Ashippun we turn west on county road CW, taking this pleasant country road over to Watertown. County road CW becomes Division Street in Watertown, and intersects with route 109. Turn left onto 109, taking it south a short distance to route 19, where we turn right and head west once again. You may recall that route 19 was the road on which we started this epic journey. The final leg takes us through typical and pleasant southern Wisconsin country-side, a mix of well-tended farms and woodlots, through the small towns of Water-loo and Marshall, and finally Sun Prairie.

I hope you are able to take the time to complete this trip the way it is meant to be done—over at least four days, and with the intent of not just riding, but rather by exploring and learning about the marvelous people and places that make up this great state.

 Helmet Hair Quiz Answer
The Milwaukee Mile—begun in 1903!

Turn the clock back a century by staying at the many hotels still in use in smalll towns across the state. Old-fashioned small town hospitality and friendly service at locally owned hotels and restaurants enhance the travel experience.

Some Suggested Safe Riding Tips

These tips are not official rules copied from motorcycling safety manuals— they are lessons I have learned by experience from over 35 years and more than 250,000 miles on the seat of a bike. I also encourage you to study safety manuals printed by various motorcycle training and regulatory organizations as they have many valuable suggestions for safe riding. Even the most experienced riders need reminders of some very basic techniques and skills, perhaps especially the experienced rider. It is a human tendency to get a bit overconfident and even arrogant as we become comfortable with the task at hand. The most important training tool is experience and perhaps the most dangerous trait is overconfidence. As motorcyclists, we are responsible for our own safety and we can never let our guard down.

> *Always* assume you are not being seen by car and truck drivers. The approaching car that is about to make a left turn in front of you doesn't see you; the pizza delivery kid who's in a hurry and driving an unfamiliar vehicle on a strange road doesn't see you; and the soccer mom driving the minivan full of kids who's about to pull out of her driveway doesn't see you. None of the above drivers gives a damn about you at that particular point in time. They are all deep in thought and probably doing 3 or 4 other things besides driving their vehicle. If you want to survive the encounter with these and every other vehicle it's entirely up to you to take the necessary precautions and defensive actions. Being in the right means nothing when it is a contest between a motorcycle and a four-wheeled vehicle.

> Leave a margin for error in curves, on wet pavement, or other potentially dangerous conditions and situations. I find that if I ride just below my limits, rather than at or above them, I actually have more fun, and at much less risk to myself and others.

> If you find that competition takes over when you ride in a group and you end up taking chances or often ride over your head to impress your friends, then ride alone.

> When the light turns green for you, *always* look each way before proceeding. Cars routinely run red lights during that couple second period after it turns green for you and red for them. This defensive tactic has kept me out of serious trouble many times in my driving and riding lifetime.

> When stopping at a traffic light or stop sign pay as much attention to what is happening behind you as to what is going on in front of you. Make it a habit

to flash your brake light as you are slowing and even when stopped, until the car behind you is also at a dead stop.

- When stopped at a traffic light or stop sign, I suggest leaving your bike in gear and leave room in front of you and to your side to take evasive action if necessary. Always have an escape route planned in the event it is needed. Watch your rear view mirror to spot any vehicle approaching rapidly from behind that will be unable to stop in time. While you are stopped is not a time to relax—vigilance must continue even when at a standstill. Danger at this point is more likely approaching you from behind rather than from ahead or the sides. Moreover, it is not just at stop signs or red lights where you need to watch your behind. On open country roads the danger is potentially even greater. If you have to stop for any reason on a stretch of open road, cars coming behind you aren't expecting it and represent a very real threat. Monitor your mirrors and be ready to take appropriate action if a vehicle approaches at a speed that tells you the driver is not seeing what's occurring up ahead and won't be able to stop in time. Of course this is also a situation when you want to be flashing your brake light to help get the attention of someone closing on you from behind.

- Riding through an intersection where oncoming traffic is present always poses potential danger. Is that car coming at you going to decide to turn left in front of you without warning? There is no magical solution to this problem except extreme awareness on your part. Have a couple fingers on the brake pedal and formulate a plan in your mind as to what you will do to avoid a collision if a car driver does turn across your path. Slow down to allow more time to react and evade the danger should it arise at the last second. Change positions within your lane from one side to another as appropriate to enhance your visibility to others, and to provide greater vision distance for yourself. Maneuvering for maximum visibility within your lane is one of the most fundamental aspects of motorcycling safety. It is virtually impossible to fully describe because of the countless variables that can occur within a short time and distance, but nonetheless should be a skill that is constantly put into motion.

- One of the most maddening habits that many car drivers have is approaching a stop sign or stop light at a high rate of speed and hitting the brakes hard at the last second to stop. They may have intended to stop all along but from the motorcyclist's perspective it sure as hell looks like they're going to run the stop sign. At every intersection where I have the right of way or green light— whether it's a country road with very light traffic or a typical urban intersection—I watch vehicles that are approaching on the side road very carefully to ensure they're showing indications that they are in fact going to stop. When I see a car approaching a stop sign at a rate of speed that seems too fast I assume they're not going to stop and I've been known to almost come to a stop myself while ascertaining their intent.

▶ When riding a motorcycle with a single headlight I ride with my headlight on the high beam during the daytime when on open roads. Visibility to others is of extreme importance. In heavy urban traffic or if I am right behind someone I lower the beam out of courtesy. Of course if your bike is equipped with multiple lights or accessory lighting fixtures running your high beam isn't necessary, and in fact can be distracting and annoying to oncoming traffic.

▶ If you ride at night remember that the odds against you are significantly increased. Not only are you even less visible, you are also more likely to encounter impaired drivers, debris on the road that can't be seen, and wildlife. The populations of large wildlife, ranging from coyotes to bears, have increased all across North America. From dusk to dawn is when you are most likely to encounter one of these animals. Deer of course represent the greatest danger to motorcyclists. Scan the area of the shoulder and ditch for deer and at night search for the reflection from deer's eyes in the area adjacent to the pavement. Most importantly, slow down between dusk and dawn.

▶ Speed Kills. Ironically, it is riding fast on enticing and enjoyable back roads that will kill us—not speed on boring uninspiring superslabs. Expressways are designed for high speeds and few surprises (such as a car suddenly deciding to turn left in front of you) but you never know what is just around the next curve on a fun two-laner in the boonies.

▶ Never follow behind a loaded pickup truck, or any kind of open or uncovered loaded trailer. It doesn't matter if it's a boat trailer or flatbed trailers. I have seen everything from ice chests to two-by-fours fly off trailers or out of pickup trucks as they're driving down the road. You do not want to be the vehicle right behind a truck or trailer when this occurs!

▶ We have long been reminded to keep adequate space between us and the vehicle in front of us to allow a safe stopping distance. There is another reason for maintaining a safe distance and it has nothing to do with stopping distance, however. Bikers also need to leave enough room between themselves and the car ahead of them so that they can spot debris or a large pothole in the road in time to take evasive action. While a four-wheeled vehicle will nonchalantly drive over a muffler or piece of wood or a large hole, straddling it with their wheels, a biker has problems if he or she suddenly sees such an object in their path. Keep a healthy distance between you and the vehicle ahead of you not only for safe stopping ability, but also to be able to see road conditions ahead of you relative to your speed.

▶ Maintain your cool. No matter what moronic move a car or truck driver made that infringed on your space and caused your blood to boil, keep in mind that motorcycles are at the bottom of the pecking order in contests with larger vehicles. The old saying about never playing games with 18-wheelers is applicable to every other vehicle on the road if you are on two wheels. Take a deep breath, put some space between yourself and the guilty driver, and get on with your ride.

▶ Pay attention to brake light action in front of you on open roads. If a driver touches their brakes there is usually a reason, even if it isn't immediately apparent to you. Maybe it is a large pothole, perhaps it is a radar car, debris on the road, or deer just out of your sight in the ditch. If you see brake lights up ahead slow down and anticipate the possible need to stop or take evasive action.

▶ Most of us would agree that motorcyclists have qualities and traits that lead us into this activity in the first place. One of these is a feeling of independence and separation from the crowd, and another is a sense of confidence in our ability to handle situations that arise. As a result too many of us eschew advice or training, with an attitude of 'I don't need no stinking training, I learned how to ride motorcycles the old fashioned way—I just got on and rode'. The reality is that while this approach may have worked 30 or 40 years ago when traffic was lighter and roads much less developed, and there were far fewer hyper-caffeinated, cell phone talking and texting distracted car drivers on the road than today, it is a recipe for disaster given current realities. Everything has changed—roads, traffic, power and speed capabilities of our machines, congestion, distractions, far more unskilled car drivers out there, you name it. Bottom line—take a training class, and if you are already an experienced rider continue your training with constant skills practice or formal classes. Piloting a motorcycle is much like flying an airplane—both types of pilots need constant training and practice.

▶ Wear proper gear. I know I am going to alienate myself with some readers by saying this, but when given the choice as to wearing a helmet or not—wear one. It can and likely will save your life in an accident. I too believe in choice. I would not force anyone to wear a helmet, or seat belts for that matter, and in fact I think it stinks that police now spend a large amount of their time on seat belt enforcement patrols instead of focusing on crime. I have nothing but disdain for know-it-all safety radicals who want to impose their standards on me and other citizens. I choose to wear a seat belt because I think it is the smart thing to do, but I resent being forced to and getting a ticket if I should somehow forget. Many years of trail and street riding, and an active imagination with which I can vividly envision what will happen if my head strikes a tree, the pavement, or a car bumper at even low speed, causes me to wear a helmet even when it isn't required. I shudder when I see riders in T-shirts, shorts and beach thongs passing me on the highway. Bikers don't have to dress like Darth Vader, but for your own sake please do wear protective gear—at a minimum a jacket, helmet, gloves, proper footwear, and long pants. The Hayden Brothers, Rossi, DuHamel, Mladin, Carr, Stewart, and other professionals would never consider racing without proper gear. And they're riding on a controlled course where there are no cars, deer, mufflers laying in the road, or impaired drivers likely to do something stupid in front of them. If it is good enough for them, it ought to also make sense for those of us that are far less skilled. Motorcycle apparel has made tremendous gains in the last 20 years, both in form and function. It is actually more comfortable, and thus the ride more enjoyable, to wear proper motorcycling apparel than to ride with skin exposed to the sun and the various flying debris that is encountered on the road.

▷ Despite the aura of the hard-drinking biker as an American icon, the reality is alcohol and motorcycles do not mix. I don't know how many bikers are killed due to drinking or drug use, but I'm afraid it is a statistic that would shock us if we knew. Even one beer can influence the fighter pilot-like responses needed to safely and skillfully operate a motorcycle. Leave the alcohol for the end of the day.

▷ I find myself using the airplane pilot comparison often when talking about operating a motorcycle. Like pilots, bikers must be at the top of their game while riding because even a small error or mishap can quickly turn tragic. A prime example of this comparison exists before the motorcycle is even started. Make it a habit to check out your bike before every ride, ensuring that the tires haven't lost air, that your various lights work, and that everything is securely attached. Pilots and bikers both need pre-flight checklists.

▷ I have seen and heard many motorcycle enthusiasts, including instructors, make the comment that there are two kinds of motorcyclists; 'those that have crashed and those that haven't crashed yet', implying of course that sooner or later everyone will crash. I think this attitude is unfortunate and plays directly into the hands of those who believe motorcycling is a dangerous antisocial activity that needs to be tightly regulated. I know many veteran motorcyclists who have never had an accident or gone down, because they operate their machine in a skillful manner that minimizes that possibility. It might sound macho to make statements about the inevitability of crashing but it harms our sport and sends the wrong message. Instead, let's talk about how safe riding habits and skill at piloting a motorcycle greatly reduce the possibility of an accident. Crashes are NOT inevitable.

▶ *Always* expect the unexpected—it will happen!

▶ Last but not least—Have Fun. We are participating in the most enjoyable and exciting activity in the world. I could not imagine life without it.

Wisconsin Motorcycle Operation Laws

Laws and regulations can and do change on a regular basis. Contact state governmental agencies listed below for the latest regulations and to obtain copies of laws, pamphlets or training manuals. This section provides only a brief outline of laws as they were when this book was being written and is not meant to be a definitive, complete, or official guide for motorcycle operational or licensing requirements.

Motorcycle Types
- **Type I:** Two-wheeled cycle with integral power source capable of speeds of at least 30 miles per hour. Includes standard motorcycles with sidecars.
- **Type II:** Three-wheeled vehicles.

Operation Requirements / Laws
- Safety helmet required by law under age 18 and required for instructional permit holders. Motorcycle safety training available for all eligible applicants—required under age 18. Wisconsin accepts motorcycle endorsements from other states.
- Eye Protection—No person may operate a motorcycle on any highway without wearing any of the following eye protection: A protective face shield attached to the headgear, glasses, or goggles. Except for prescribed photosensitive corrective glasses, eye protection worn during hours of darkness may not be tinted or darkened. If the motorcycle is a Type 2 motorcycle equipped with a windshield or a Type 1 motorcycle equipped with a windshield that rises a minimum of 15 inches above the handlebar, the use of other eye protective devices is not mandatory.
- Daytime use of headlight required by law. Modulating headlight permitted.
- Passenger seat required if carrying a passenger and passenger footrests required if carrying a passenger. There are no passenger age limitations.
- No restrictions on helmet speakers.
- Rear view mirrors required on both sides of motorcycle.
- Turn signals are required on both sides and front and rear of motorcycle.
- Radar detectors are legal at this time.
- Mufflers: No person shall operate on a highway any motor vehicle subject to registration unless such motor vehicle is equipped with an adequate muffler in constant operation and properly maintained to prevent any excessive or unusual noise or annoying smoke.

No muffler or exhaust system on any vehicle shall be equipped with a cut-out, bypass or similar device nor shall there be installed in the exhaust system of any such vehicle any device to ignite exhaust gases so as to produce flame within or without the exhaust system.

No person shall modify the exhaust system of any such motor vehicle in a manner which will amplify or increase the noise emitted by the motor of such vehicle above that emitted by the muffler originally installed on the vehicle, and such original muffler shall comply with all the requirements of this section.

▶ State Insurance Requirements—compulsory liability (Minimum Limits) (25/50/10.- Financial responsibility required.

▶ Handlebar height maximum of 30" above seat

▶ Motorcycles may operate two abreast in same lane. All motor vehicles including motorcycles and mopeds are entitled to the full use of a traffic lane and no vehicle may be driven or operated in such a manner so as to deprive any other vehicle of the full use of a traffic lane. With the consent of both drivers, Type 1 motorcycles may be operated not more than 2 abreast in a single lane. Lane splitting is not referenced in the Administrative Code or Statutes.

Wisconsin Motorcycle Program Contact Information

DMV Service Centers
http://www.dot.wisconsin.gov/about/locate/dmv/scmap.htm

DMV Web Site
http://www.dot.wisconsin.gov/drivers/index.htm

Motorcycle Crash Facts
http://www.dot.wisconsin.gov/safety/motorist/crashfacts/docs/motorcyclefacts.pdf

Motorcycle Licenses
http://www.dot.wisconsin.gov/drivers/drivers/apply/types/motorcyc.htm

Motorcycle Safety Course information
http://www.dot.wisconsin.gov/safety/vehicle/motorcycle/index.htm

Motorcycle Training Sponsors and Locations
http://www.dot.wisconsin.gov/safety/vehicle/motorcycle/training.htm

Motorcyclists' Handbook
http://www.dot.wisconsin.gov/drivers/drivers/apply/cycle-handbook.htm

Scheduling Skills Test Appointments
http://www.dot.wisconsin.gov/drivers/drivers/schedule.htm

WIDOT Web Site
http://www.dot.wisconsin.gov/

Wisconsin Government Sites
http://www.dot.wisconsin.gov/

Wisconsin Sheriff Departments

Adams County
301 Adams Street
Friendship. 608.339.3304

Ashland County
220 East 6th Street
Ashland. 715.685.7640

Barron County
1420 State Hwy 25 North
Barron. 715.537.3106

Bayfield County
117 East 6th Street
Washburn. 715.373.6120

Brown County
300 East Walnut Street
Green Bay. 920.448.4200

Buffalo County
407 South Second Street
Alma 608.685.4433

Burnett County
7410 City Road K #122
Siren 715.349.2121

Calumet County
206 Court Street
Chilton 920.849.2335

Chippewa County
32 East Spruce Street
Chippewa Falls. 715.726.7719

Clark County
517 Court Street
Neillsville 715.743.3157

Columbia County
723 East Cook Street
Portage 608.742.4166

Crawford County
224 North Beaumont Road
Prairie Du Chien 608.326.0241

Dane County: Public Safety Building
115 West Doty Street
Madison 608.284.6100

Dodge County
141 North Main Street
Juneau 920.386.3726

Door County
123 South 5th Avenue
Sturgeon Bay 920.746.2400

Douglas County
1316 North 14th Street, Suite 100
Superior 715.395.1371

Dunn County
615 Stokke Parkway
Menomonie 715.232.1348

Eau Claire County
728 Second Avenue
Eau Claire 715.839.4709

Florence County
501 Lake Avenue
Florence 715.528.3346

Fond du Lac County
180 South Macy Street
Fond Du Lac. 920.929.3391

Forest County
101 East Polk
Crandon 715.478.3331

Grant County
1000 North Adams Street
Lancaster. 608.723.2157

Green County
2827 6th Street
Monroe 608.328.9400

Green Lake County
486 Hill Street
Green Lake 920.294.4000

Iowa County
1205 North Bequette Street
Dodgeville 608.935.3314

Iron County
300 Taconite Street
Hurley. 715.561.3800

Jackson County
30 North Third Street
Black River Falls 715.284.5357

Jefferson County
411 South Center Avenue
Jefferson 920.674.7310

Juneau County
200 Oak Street
Mauston 608.847.5649

Kenosha County
1000 55th Street
Kenosha 262.605.5100

Kewaunee County
620 Juneau Street
Kewaunee 920.388.3100

La Crosse County
333 Vine Street
La Crosse 608.785.5942

Lafayette County
626 North Main Street
Darlington 608.776.4870

Langlade County
840 Clermont Street
Antigo 715.623.4111

Lincoln County
1104 East First Street
Merrill. 715.536.6272

Manitowoc County
1025 South 9th Street
Manitowoc 920.683.4200

Marathon County
500 Forest Street
Wausau 715.261.1200

Marinette County
2161 University Drive
Marinette 715.732.7600

Marquette County
67 Park Street
Montello 608.297.2115

Menominee County
3269 Courthouse Lane
Keshena. 715.799.3357

Milwaukee County
821 West State Street
Milwaukee 414.278.4726

Monroe County
210 West Oak Street
Sparta 608.269.2117

Oconto County
301 Washington Street
Oconto 920.834.6900

Oneida County
2000 East Winnebago Street
Rhinelander 715.361.5100

Outagamie County
410 South Walnut Street
Appleton 920.832.5605

Ozaukee County
1201 South Spring Street
Port Washington 262.284.7172

Pepin County
740 7th Avenue West
Durand 715.672.5945

Pierce County
432 West Main Street
Ellsworth. 715.273.5051

Polk County
1005 West Main Street
Balsam Lake 715.485.8300

Portage County
1500 Strongs Avenue
Stevens Point 715.346.1400

Price County
164 Cherry Street
Phillips 715.339.3011

Racine County
717 Wisconsin Avenue
Racine 262.636.3211

Richland County
181 West Seminary Street
Richland Center. 608.647-2106

Rock County
200 East US Hwy 14
Janesville 608.757.8000

Rusk County
311 East Miner Avenue, Suite L100
Ladysmith. 715.532.2189

Saint Croix County
1101 Carmichael Road
Hudson 715.381.4320

Sauk County
1300 Lange Court
Baraboo. 608.356.4895

Sawyer County
101 East 5th Street
Hayward 715.634.4858

Shawano County
405 North Main Street
Shawano 715.526.3111

Sheboygan County
525 North 6th Street
Sheboygan 920.459.3112

Taylor County
224 South 2nd Street
Medford 715.748.2200

Trempealeau County
36245 Main Street
Whitehall 715.538.4509

Vernon County
1320 Bad Axe Court
Viroqua 608.637.2124

Vilas County
330 Court Street
Eagle River 715.479.4441

Walworth County
W4054 City Road NN
Elkhorn 262.741.4400

Washburn County
421 Hwy 63
Shell Lake 715.468.4700

Washington County
500 North Schmidt Road
West Bend 262.335.4378

Waukesha County
515 West Moreland Boulevard
Waukesha 262.548.7117

Waupaca County
1402 East Royalton Street
Waupaca 715.258.4466

Waushara County
430 East Division Street
Wautoma 920.787.3321

Winnebago County
4311 Jackson Street
Oshkosh 920.236.7300

Wood County
400 Market Street
Wisconsin Rapids 715.421.8715

Wisconsin State Patrol

Emergencies: Call 911

Wisconsin State Patrol Division Headquarters
Hill Farms State Transportation Building
4802 Sheboygan Avenue, Room 551
Madison, WI 53705 ▪ 608.266.3212

SOUTHWEST REGION
Wisconsin State Patrol DeForest Post
911 West North Street
DeForest, WI 53532-0610 ▪ 608.846.8500
Counties: Columbia, Dane, Dodge, Grant, Green, Iowa, Jefferson,
Lafayette and Rock

Wisconsin State Patrol Tomah Post
23928 Lester McMullen Drive
Tomah, WI 54660-0604 ▪ 608.374.0513
Counties: Crawford, Juneau, La Crosse, Monroe, Richland, Sauk and Vernon

NORTHEAST REGION
Wisconsin State Patrol Fond du Lac Post
851 South Rolling Meadows Drive
Fond du Lac, WI 54936-0984 ▪ 920.929.3700
Counties: Brown, Calumet, Door, Fond du Lac, Kewaunee, Manitowoc,
Marinette, Oconto, Outagamie, Sheboygan and Winnebago

NORTH CENTRAL REGION
Wisconsin State Patrol Wausau Post
2805 Martin Avenue
Wausau, WI 54401-7172 ▪ 715.845.1143
Counties: Adams, Florence, Forest, Green Lake, Iron, Langlade, Lincoln,
Marathon, Marquette, Menominee, Oneida, Portage, Price, Shawano,
Vilas, Waupaca, Waushara, and Wood

SOUTHEAST REGION
Wisconsin State Patrol Waukesha Post
21115 East Moreland Boulevard
Waukesha, WI 53186-2985 ▪ 262.785.4700
Counties: Kenosha, Milwaukee, Ozaukee, Racine, Walworth,
Washington and Waukesha

NORTHWEST REGION
Wisconsin State Patrol Eau Claire Post
5005 Highway 53 South
Eau Claire, WI 54701-8846 ▪ 715.839.3800
Counties: Buffalo, Chippewa, Clark, Dunn, Eau Claire, Jackson, Pepin,
Pierce, St. Croix and Trempealeau

Wisconsin State Patrol Spooner Post
7102 Green Valley Road
Spooner, WI 54801 ▪ 715.635.2141
Emergency: 715.635-7725
Counties: Ashland, Barron, Bayfield, Burnett, Douglas, Polk, Rusk,
Sawyer, Taylor and Washburn

Hotel and Motel Contact Information

Adam's Mark Hotels 800.444.2326

Americinn 800.634.3444

AmeriHost Inn. 800.434.5800

Baymont Inn 866.999.1111

Best Inns and Suites . . . 800.BESTINN

Best Western. 800.780.7234

Cambria Suites. 877.424.6423

Clarion Hotels 877.424.6423

Comfort Inns 877.4CHOICE

Comfort Suites. 877.4CHOICE

Courtyard by Marriott . . 800.321.2211

Days Inn 800.329.7466

Doubletree Hotels 800.222TREE

EconoLodge 877.424.6423

Embassy Suites. 800.EMBASSY

Fairfield Inn 800.228.2800

Four Seasons Hotels 800.819.5053

Hampton Inns 800.HAMPTON

Hawthorn Suites 800.527.1133

Hilton Hotels 800.HILTONS

Holiday Inns. 800.HOLIDAY

Howard Johnson 800.446.4656

Hyatt Hotels 888.591.1234

Knights Inn 800.843.5644

La Quinta Inns. 866.725.1661

Lees Inn & Suites 800.SEE-LEES

MainStay Suites 877.424.6423

Marriott 888.236.2427

Microtel Inns 888.771.7171

Motel 6 . . . . .800.4MOTEL6

Omni Hotels. 888.444.6664

Quality Inns 877.424.6423

Radisson Hotels 888.201.1718

Ramada Inn 800.2RAMADA

Red Roof Inns 800.REDROOF

Red Carpet Inn 800.251.1962

Regent International 800.545.4000

Renaissance Hotels 800.HOTELS1

Residence Inn. 800.331.3131

Rodeway Inns. 877.424.6423

Sheraton Hotels 800.598.1753

Shoney's Inn 800.552.4667

Signature Inn 800.822.5252

Sleep Inn. 877.424.6423

Suburban Inns 877.424.6423

Super 8 Motels 800.800.8000

Suisse Chalet 800.5CHALET

Travelodge 800.578.7878

Westin   Hotels

& Resorts 888.625.5144

Wyndham   Hotels/

Resorts 800.822.4200

Contact Information for Credit Card Companies

American Express ▪ 1.800.668.2639

Chase Customer Service ▪ 1.800.334.0601

Diner's Club ▪ 1.800.2DINERS

Discover ▪ 1.800.DISCOVER

Mastercard ▪ 1.800.MASTERCARD

VISA ▪ 1.800.847.2911

Motorcycle Dealers and Repair Shops

AMERICAN IRONHORSE

Jamie's Customs
S6925 Enterprise Drive
Big Bend 262.662.4511
www.jamiescustoms.com/

APRILIA

Racine Motor Sports
2005 Lathrop Avenue
Racine 262.632.4000
www.racinemotorsports.net/

Corse Superbikes
700 E. Milan Drive
Saukville 262.284.2725
www.corsesuperbikes.com/

BIG DOG

Jamie's Customs
S6925 Enterprise Drive
Big Bend 262.662.4511
www.jamiescustoms.com/

Vandervest Harley-Davidson & Big Dog
810 Frontage Road
Peshtigo. 715-582-8843
www.vandervestharleydavidson.com

BMW

Mischler's BMW / H-D
N8131 Kellom Road
Beaver Dam 920.887.8425
http://www.mischlersbmw.com/

Nick's BMW
2246 Mid Valley Drive
Depere. 920.347.9144
www.nicksbmw.com/

BMW Motorcycles of Milwaukee
7016 North 76th Street
Milwaukee 414.358.2465
www.bmwmotorcyclesof
  milwaukee.com

BOSS HOSS

Milwaukee Boss Hoss Cycles
Hartland: Phone: 262.538.2677
www.milwaukeebosshoss.com

CUSTOM BUILT MOTORCYCLES

Chopper Zone
203 Pleasant Street
Beloit. 608.364.9844

Impact Cycle
2537 Riverside Drive
Beloit. 608.368.1111
www.impactcycle.com/

MJ Customs, LLC
Corner SR 12 / 18
Cambridge 608.423.1392
www.mj-customs.com

Hard Time Cycles
Darlington 608.482.2414

Black Widow Chopper Company
Highway 25 West
Durand 715.672.3504
www.blackwidowchoppers.arebad.com

Signature Cycles
S8710 Route 93
Eleva 715.878.4800

Todd Curtis Customs
1338 Velp Avenue
Green Bay 920.490.0070

Vandervest Custom Cycles
1800 Velp Avenue
Green Bay 920.498.8822

Rock Lake Customs
704 East Lake Street
Lake Mills 920.648.4353

Mad Town Choppers
Madison 608.206.3845
www.madtownchoppers.com

Pistol Pete's Custom Cycles
2010 Stout Road
Menomonie 715.235.3659
www.pistolpetesusa.com/

Outpost Custom Cycles
24522 Route 35 / 70
Siren 715.349.7637
www.outpostcustomcycles.com

Osborne Pro Street
9051 Highway 13 South
Wisconsin Rapids 715.325.6464

Hollywood's Chop Shop
1216 Old Highway 51
Woodruff 715.355.5816

DUCATI

Bob Barr's Kawasaki
1701 South Stoughton Road
Madison 608.222.6800
www.barrskawasaki.com

Corse Superbikes
700 ast Milan Drive
Saukville 262.284.2725
www.corsesuperbikes.com/

HARLEY-DAVIDSON / BUELL

Harley-Davidson Appleton, WI
5322 Clairemont Drive
Appleton 920.757.1651
www.h-dappleton.com

Northern Lights Harley-Davidson
1700 Hwy 51
Arbor Vitae 715.358.5054
www.northernlightshd.com/

Mischler's Harley-Davidson BMW
N8131 Kellom Road
Beaver Dam 920.887.8425
www.mischlershd.com

Al Muth Harley-Davidson
N 6630 County Road A
Black River Falls 715.284.4725
www.almuth-harleydavidson.com

Doc's Harley-Davidson of Shawano
W2709 State Highway 29
Bonduel. 715.758.9080
www.docshd.com

Sport Motors Harley-Davidson
2452 Hallie Road
Chippewa Falls. 715.723.7433
www.sportmotorsharley.com/

Open Road Harley-Davidson
24 S. Rolling Meadows Dr
Fond du Lac 920.921.2344
www.openroadhd.com

McCoy's Harley-Davidson
2728 Manitowoc Road
Green Bay 920.406.3900
www.harleydavidsongreenbay.com

House Of Harley-Davidson
6221 West Layton Avenue
Greenfield 414.282.2211
www.houseofharley.com

Hartford Harley-Davidson Shop
427 Sumner St. (Hwy 60)
Hartford 262.670.1000
www.hartfordhdbuell.com

Kutter Harley-Davidson
3223 North Pontiac Drive
Janesville 608.757.0880
www.kutterharley.com

Uke's Harley-Davidson
5995 120th Avenue
Kenosha 262.857.8537
www.ukeshd.com/

Capital City Harley-Davidson
6200 Millpond Road
Madison 608.221.2761
www.capitalcityhd.com

Stock's Harley-Davidson
2433 Hecker Road
Manitowoc 920.684.0237
www.stockshd.com

Bala's Harley-Davidson
N 4833 Highway 58
Mauston 608.847.7702
www.balas-hd.com/

Milwaukee Harley-Davidson
11310 West Silver Spring Road
Milwaukee 414.461.4444
www.milwaukeeharley.com

House of Harley-Davidson
Mitchell Internatinoal Airport
5300 South Howell Avenue, WC-1
Milwaukee 414.747.5384

Kutter Harley-Davidson Shop
129 West 6th Street
Monroe 608.329.4884

Hal's Harley-Davidson
1925 South Moorland Road
New Berlin 262.860.2060
www.halshd.com

St. Croix Harley-Davidson
2060 Highway 65 North
New Richmond 715.246.2959
www.stcroixhd.com/

Wisconsin Harley-Davidson
1280 Blue Ribbon Drive
Oconomowoc.......... 262.569.8500
www.wishd.com

LaCrosse Area Harley-Davidson
1116 Oak Forest Drive
Onalaska.............. 608.783.6112
www.lacrosseharley.com/

Vandervest Harley-Davidson
810 Frontage Road
Peshtigo.............. 715.582.8843
www.vandervestharleydavidson.com

Racine Harley-Davidson
1155 Oakes Road
Racine............... 262.884.0123
www.racinehd.com

Rice Lake Harley-Davidson
2801 South Wisconsin Avenue
Rice Lake 715.234.5400
www.ricelakehd.com

Harley-Davidson of Wausau
1570 County Road XX
Rothschild 715.355.4464
www.hdwausau.com

Sauk Prairie Harley-Davidson
836 Phillips Boulevard
Sauk City............. 608.643.3735
www.saukprairiehd.com

Route 43 Harley-Davidson
3736 South Taylor Drive
Sheboygan 920.458.0777
www.route43hd.com

Suburban Motors Harley-Davidson
139 North Main Street
Thiensville 262.242.2464
www.suburbanharley.com

West Bend Harley-Davidson
2910 West Washington Street
West Bend............. 262.338.8761
westbendhartfordharleydavidson.com

Bala's Harley-Davidson
524 Wisconsin Dells Parkway
Wisconsin Dells........ 608.253.2252
www.balas-hd.com/

HONDA

Kawasaki Suzuki Honda of Antigo
N2804 Highway 45
Antigo............... 715.623.2379

Beaver Dam Honda Kawasaki
N8309 Kellom Road
Beaver Dam 920.887.2709
www.beaverdamhondakawasaki.com/

Beloit Honda-Yamaha-Suzuki
2210 Whipple Street
Beloit................ 608.362.9344
www.beloithonda.com/

Don & Roy's Motorsports
17740 Bluemound Road
Brookfield............ 262.786.7928
www.donandroys.com/

Brule Sport Shop
Highway US 2
Brule 715.372.4849

Cedar Creek Motorsports
7518 State Route 60
Cedarburg. 262.377.5700
www.cedarcreekmotorsports.com/

Zacho Sports Center
2449 South Prairie View Road
Chippewa Falls. 715.723.0264
www.zachosports.com/

Team Motorsports
1890 Mid Valley Drive
DePere. 920.983.8326
team-motorsports.com/team
    motorsports/

Pro Motorsports
86 Rolling Meadows Drive
Fond Du Lac. 920.922.8521
www.promotorsportsinc.com/

Rob's Performance Motorsports
601 Highway Y
Johnson Creek 920.699.3288
www.robsperformance.com/

Ace Powersports
8124 Sheridan Road
Kenosha 262.654.3090
www.acepowersports.com/

Two Brothers Powersports
124 Rose Street
LaCrosse 608.781.3360
www.twobrothershonda.com/

Midwest Action Cycle
251 Host Drive
Lake Geneva. 262.249.0600
www.midwestactioncycle.com/

Mad City Power Sports
5110 High Crossing Boulevard
Madison 888.623.2489
www.madcitypowersports.com/

The Engelhart Center
1589 Greenway Cross
Madison 608.274.2366
www.engelhart.com/

Badger Cycle
1351 South Rapids Road
Manitowoc 920.682.2127
www.badgercycle.com/

Craft's Trading Center
Highway 10 East
Marshfield. 800.606.2723
www.craftstrading.com/

North Honda Motorsports
3711 10th Street
Menominee 906.863.5592

Airtec Sports
1714 Freitag Drive
Menomonie 715.232.8590
www.airtecsports.com/

Southeast Sales
6930 North 76th Street
Milwaukee 414.463-2751
www.southeastsales.com/

Monroe Honda
502 10th Street
Monroe 608.325.3071
http://monroehonda.com/

Sportland 2, Inc.
7221 South 13th Street
Oak Creek. 414.764.2800
www.sportland2.com/

Two Brothers Powersports
1241 Oak Forest Drive
Onalaska 608.785.1077
www.twobrothershonda.com/

Ecklund Motorsports & Marine
2794 Marine Drive
Oshkosh 920.233.3313
www.ecklundmotorsports.com/

Racine Motor Sports
2005 Lathrop Avenue
Racine 262.632.4000
www.racinemotorsports.net/

Northwest Honda
1230 South Main Street
Rice Lake 715.234.7557
www.nwhondawi.com/

Vetesnik Power Sports
27475 Highway 14
Richland Center. 608.647.8808
www.vetesnik.com/

Tomahawk Sports Center
693 North 4th Street
Tomahawk 715.453.5373
www.tomahawksportscenter.com/

Action Power Sports
202 Travis Lane
Waukesha 800.640.6729
www.actionps.com/

Wausau Motorsports
4101 Rib Mountain Drive
Wausau 715.355.6120

Country Sports, Inc.
10520 South Highway 13
Wisconsin Rapids; 715.325.5381
www.countrysportsinc.com/

HYOSUNG

Motorcycle Performance
5205 University Avenue
Madison 608.238.1195
www.motorcycleperf.com/

Kickstands Motorsports
W5750 Stub Road
Trego 715.635.2647

INDEPENDENT SALES
& REPAIR SHOPS

Underground Cycles
W5543 County Road West
Adell 920.994.9499

MG Cycle
601 Ogden Avenue
Albany. 608.862.2302

Precision Saw Cycle
6211 Blueberry Road
Allenton 262.629.9949

Sport Rider
1504 Highway 12
Altoona 715.834.0244

Mid-America Cycles
1134 W. Wisconsin Avenue
Appleton 920.830.1903

Tommy's Custom Cycle
5625 French Road
Appleton 920.739.9242

Bob Stadler Motors
1002 South US 12
Baraboo. 920.261.3717

Mike's Bike Shop
117 East Huron Street
Berlin. 920.361.3565

Road Track & Trail
W228 South Enterprise Drive
Big Bend 262.662.1500
www.roadtrackandtrail.com/

Ironhorse Trading Company
2520 Eastwood Lane
Brookfield. 262.938.2348

MJ Customs, LLC
Corner SR 12 / 18
Cambridge 608.423.1392
www.mj-customs.com

Dane County Cycle
139 North Main Street
Cambridge 608.423.1392

Flying Eagle Cycle
W4304 Highway 67
Campbellsport 920.533.5595

Indianhead Motors
2022 State Route 53
Chippewa Falls. 715.720.1700

Triple R Motorsports
14058 Wildcat Road
Darlington 608.776.8230

Westside Cycle
1620 Westgate Road
Eau Claire. 715.832.8300

Eau Claire Cycle
3620 Mall Drive
Eau Claire. 715.835.1442

Signature Cycles
Hwy 93 @ I-94
Eleva 715.878.4800

Cycle Plus, Inc.
701 North Lincoln Street
Elkhorn. 1.888.743.1415

Del's Cycle Service
2229 Shawano Avenue
Green Bay. 920.494.7069

Cycle City
2661 Industry Court
Green Bay. 920.499.4488
www.cyclecity.biz/201.html

Mike's Motorcycle Service
1690 Lime Kiln Road
Green Bay 920.465.1762

Sinister Bike Works
1734 Main Street
Green Bay 920.406.0900

Title Town Cycles
711 Potts Avenue
Green Bay 920.435.1121

NAEF Cycle
2380 O'Connor Road
Green Bay 920.434.8189
www.naefcycle.com/

Milwaukee Bike Works
10700 West Parnell Street
Hales Corners 414.427.1155
(American V-Twins Only)

The High Rpm Speed Shop
3506 Route 5
Hazel Green 608.748.4405

K-Towne Motorcycles
Cor. 30th Avenue and 63rd Street
Kenosha 262.925.8990

Firehouse Performance
4502 22nd Avenue
Kenosha 262.656.0773
www.firehouseperformance.com

S&S Cycle
235 Causeway Boulevard
LaCrosse 608.627.1497
www.sscycle.com

Gopher's Cycles Repair
110 Tama Street
Livingston 608.943.8533

Madison Motorsports
2421B South Stoughton Road
Madison 608.221.1000
www.madisonmotorsports.com/

Motorcycle Performance
5205 University Avenue
Madison 608.238.1195
www.motorcycleperf.com/

Motorcycle Solutions
2613 South Stoughton Road
Madison 608.268.6780

Suter's Speed Shop
3333 Femrite Drive
Madison 608.221.8865
www.sutersspeedshop.com/

DWD Motorcycle Service
8302 Lisbon Avenue
Milwaukee 414.445.7402

Brunkow's Performance V-Twins
N2615 Coplien Road
Monroe 608.325.1300

Hauri's Cycle Shop
633 1st Avenue
Monroe 608.325.9952

Rev Motorsports
W27545 National Avenue
Mukwonago 262.363.7381
http://revdeals.com/index.html

Maximum Output Speed & Custom
3090 Oregon Street
Oshkosh 920.303.5956

Tin Pan Alley
108 Dover Street
Princeton 920.295.6987

Shoreline Motorsports
321 Sheridan Road
Racine 888.752.9679

Jones New World Sports
28526 Highway 14 East
Richland Center. 608.647.4131

Rosholt Motorcycle Company
East Hwy 66
Rosholt 715.677.4738
www.rosholtmotorcycle.com

Dodge County Cycle & Sport
N4220 Highway 67
Rubicon. 920.625.2999

Shanedrives LLC
Sauk City. 608.643.8429
www.shanedrives.com

Motorcycle Riders Depot
639 Grand Avenue
Schofield 715.359.0989

American Marine & Motorsports
830 Green Bay Street
Shawano 715.526.4300
www.americanmarina.com/

Rerun Motorcycles
527 North 13th Street
Sheboygan 920.208.0894
www.reruncycle.com/

Outpost Custom Cycles
Hwy 35 North
Siren 715.349.7637

Blackhawk Motorsports
101 State Route 11
South Wayne 608.439.2222

Advanced Cycle Machining
1171 Winter Street
Superior 800.844.3200
www.advancedcyclemachining.com

Zandis V Twin Service
W229n8996 Colgate Road
Sussex 262.246.4266

Lincoln County Cycles
851 North 4th Street
Tomahawk 715.453.2300
www.lincolncountycycles.com/

One Powersports
406 Madison Street
Walworth 262.394.5663

All Pro Motorsports
S4130 Pine Hollow Court
Waukesha 262.542.4848
www.allpromotorsportsinc.com/

Vintage Classics
1330 E Main Street
Waukesha 262.549.4009

Wausau Motorsports
1815 Stewart Avenue
Wausau 715.355.6120

INDIAN
Indian Motorcycle of Chippewa Falls
2022 State Highway 53
Chippewa Falls. 715.720.1700

Indian Motorcycles Green Bay
1988 East Mason Street
Green Bay 920.465.4185

Puma's Cycle
1129 Washington Avenue
Racine 262.637.1313

KAWASAKI
Kawasaki Suzuki Honda of Antigo
N2804 Highway 45
Antigo 715.623.2379

Beaver Dam Honda Kawasaki
N8309 Kellom Road
Beaver Dam 920.887.2709
www.beaverdamhondakawasaki.com/

Don & Roy's Motorsports
17740 Bluemound Road
Brookfield 262.786.7928
www.donandroys.com/

Cedar Creek Motorsports
7518 State Route 60
Cedarburg. 262.377.5700
www.cedarcreekmotorsports.com/

Maxxx Motorsports
690 Gerry Way
Darien 262.882.6299
www.maxxxmotorsports.com/

Central Kawasaki
2247 Shawano Avenue
Green Bay 920.498.1212

Midwest Action Cycle
251 Host Drive
Lake Geneva 262.249.0600
www.midwestactioncycle.com/

Bob Barr's Kawasaki
1701 South Stoughton Road
Madison 608.222.6800
www.barrskawasaki.com

The Engelhart Center
1589 Greenway Cross
Madison 608.274.2366
www.engelhart.com/

Craft's Trading Center
Highway 10 East
Marshfield. 800.606.2723
www.craftstrading.com/

Southeast Sales
6930 North 76th Street
Milwaukee . . . . (414.463-2751
www.southeastsales.com/

Sportland 2, Inc.
7221 South 13th Street
Oak Creek. 414.764.2800
www.sportland2.com/

Team Winnebagoland
5827 Mid Valley Road
Oshkosh 920.233.3070

Prairie Motor Sports
1100 East LaPointe Street
Prairie du Chien 608.326.8682
www.prairiemotorsports.com/

Shoreline Motorsports
321 Sheridan Road
Racine 262.552.7911
www.shorelinemotorsports.com/

Vetesnik Power Sports
27475 Highway 14
Richland Center. 608.647.8808
www.vetesnik.com/

KTM

Xtreme Motorsports
9443 Highway 124 North
Chippewa Falls; Ph; 715.723.2237
www.xtrememotorsportsllc.com/

Team 2 Racing
2160 Holmgren Way
Green Bay 920.498.2449
www.team2racing.com/
    KtmMotorcycles

Bob Barr's Kawasaki
1701 South Stoughton Road
Madison 608.222.6800
www.barrskawasaki.com

Corse Superbikes
700 East Milan Drive
Saukville 262.284.2725
www.corsesuperbikes.com/

KYMCO

Mischler's Power Center
N8077 Route 33
Beaver Dam 920.885.6552
www.mischlers.com/

Reina International
12730 North Capital Drive
Brookfield. 262.781.3336
www.reinaintlauto.com/

Miller Supply
9804 North U.S. 45
Clintonville. 715.823.6263

Cycles Plus, Inc.
701 North Lincoln Street
Elkhorn. 262.723.1415
www.cyclesplusinc.com

Two Brothers Powersports
124 Rose Street
LaCrosse 608.781.3360
www.twobrothershonda.com/

Metro Motorcycles, Inc.
1020 American Drive
Neenah 920.722.0700
www.Metromotorcycles.com

Two Brothers Powersports
1241 Oak Forest Drive
Onalaska 608.785.1077
www.twobrothershonda.com/

Advanced Landspeed
N5584 Luey Lane
Plymouth 920.893.3114
www.alandspeed.com/

Prairie Motor Sports
1100 East LaPointe Street
Prairie du Chien 608.326.8682
www.prairiemotorsports.com/

Kickstands Motorsports
W5750 Stub Road
Trego 715.635.2647
kickstandsmotorsports.com/

Neinfeldt Cycle
4811 Plover Road
Wisconsin Rapids 715.423.1903
www.neinfeldtcycle.com/

Romanowski Auto & ATV Sales
2004 Cutoff Road
Weston 715.355.8768

MOTO GUZZI
Reina International
12730 North Capital Drive
Brookfield. 262.781.3336
www.reinaintlauto.com/

Vespa Milwaukee
715 North Milwaukee Street
Milwaukee 414.271.3336
www.reinaintlauto.com/

Racine Motor Sports
2005 Lathrop Avenue
Racine 262.632.4000
www.racinemotorsports.net/

Sharer Cycle Center
7685 Highway PD
Verona. 608.845.6768
http://www.sharercycle.com/

MV AGUSTA
Corse Superbikes
700 East Milan Drive
Saukville 262.284.2725
www.corsesuperbikes.com/

SUZUKI
Kawasaki Suzuki Honda of Antigo
N2804 Highway 45
Antigo 715.623.2379

Beloit Honda-Yamaha-Suzuki
2210 Whipple Street
Beloit. 608.362.9344
www.beloithonda.com/

Black River Powersports
W10120 Highway 54
Black River Falls 715.284.2600

Zacho Sports Center
2449 South Prairie View Road
Chippewa Falls. 715.723.0264
www.zachosports.com/

Maxxx Motorsports
690 Gerry Way
Darien 262.882.6299
www.maxxxmotorsports.com/

Team Motorsports
1890 Mid Valley Drive
DePere. 920.983.8326
www.team-motorsports.com/

Pro Motorsports
86 Rolling Meadows Drive
Fond Du Lac. 920.922.8521
www.promotorsportsinc.com/

TA Motorsports
525 American Drive
Francis Creek /
    Manitowoc 920.682.1284
www.tamotorsports.com/

Ace Powersports
8124 Sheridan Road
Kenosha 262.654.3090
www.acepowersports.com/

Midwest Action Cycle
251 Host Drive
Lake Geneva. 262.249.0600
www.midwestactioncycle.com/

Mad City Power Sports
5110 High Crossing Boulevard
Madison 888.623.2489
www.madcitypowersports.com/

The Engelhart Center
1589 Greenway Cross
Madison 608.274.2366
www.engelhart.com/

Badger Cycle
1351 South Rapids Road
Manitowoc 920.682.2127
www.badgercycle.com/

Southeast Sales
6930 North 76th Street
Milwaukee 414.463-2751
www.southeastsales.com/

Sportland 2, Inc.
7221 South 13th Street
Oak Creek. 414.764.2800
www.sportland2.com/

Ecklund Motorsports & Marine
2794 Marine Drive
Oshkosh 920.233.3313
www.ecklundmotorsports.com/

Vetesnik Power Sports
27475 Highway 14
Richland Center. 608.647.8808
www.vetesnik.com/

Corse Superbikes
700 East Milan Drive
Saukville 262.284.2725
www.corsesuperbikes.com/

Action Power Sports
202 Travis Lane
Waukesha 800.640.6729
www.actionps.com/

Country Sports, Inc.
10520 South Highway 13
Wisconsin Rapids 715.325.5381
www.countrysportsinc.com/

TRIKES

Impact Cycle
2537 Riverside Drive
Beloit 608.368.1111
www.impactcycle.com/

Majestic Trikes-N-Cycles
306 Washington Street
Horicon 920.485.3330
www.mtrikes.com/

Badger Cycle
1351 South Rapids Road
Manitowoc 920.682.2127
www.badgercycle.com/

Midwest Motor Trike
S109 Main Street
Nelson 715.673.4079

Steve's Service Center
N7431 Highway 13
Phillips 715.339.4656

Northwest Honda
1230 South Main Street
Rice Lake 715.234.7557
www.nwhondawi.com/

Torbleau Trikes
501 Business Park Circle
Stoughton 608.873.0200
www.torbleautrikes.com

TRIUMPH

Sport Rider, Inc.
1504 Hillcrest Parkway
Altoona 715.834.0244
www.sportriderinc.com/

Team Triumph of Wisconsin
4747 East US Highway 14
Janesville . . . . (608.741-9900
www.triumph1.com/

Mike's Cycle Shop
1114 Valley Road
Menasha . . . . (920.734-3363
http://mikescycle.hondamcdealers.com/

Southeast Sales
6930 North 76th Street
Milwaukee 414.463-2751
www.southeastsales.com/

Shoreline Motorsports
321 Sheridan Road
Racine 262.552.7911
www.shorelinemotorsports.com/

Shambeau's Lawn & Recreation
4621 East Hillcrest Road
Two Rivers . . . . (920.793-4536

Sharer Cycle Center
7685 Highway PD
Verona 608.845.6768
http://www.sharercycle.com/

UM / UNITED MOTORS

Countryside Lawn & Sport
N21926 US 141
Niagara 715.251.1300
www.countrysidelawnandsport.com/

Romanowski Auto & ATV Sales
2004 Cutoff Road
Weston 715.355.8768

URAL

Allen's Sales & Service
111 East Main Street
Eagle 262.594.3524
www.allens-sales.com/

St. Croix Harley-Davidson, Inc.
2060 Highway 65 North
New Richmond 715-246-2959
www.stcroixhd.com/

Steve's Service Center
N7431 Highway 13
Phillips 715.339.4656
www.stevesservicecenter.com/

VENGEANCE

GhostRiders, Inc.
16450 Kenrick Avenue
Lakeville, MN. 952.898.2453
www.ghostridersinc.com

VENTO

Mischler's Power Center
N8077 Route 33
Beaver Dam 920.885.6552
www.mischlers.com/

TA Motorsports
525 American Drive
Francis Creek /
    Manitowoc 920.682.1284
www.tamotorsports.com/

MJ's Motorsports
1809 Allouez Avenue
Green Bay 920.465.9800

Town & Country Motorsports
5813 Bluemound Road
Milwaukee 414.453.5045

Voodoo Motorsports
700 North Progress Drive
Saukville 262.284.2222
www.voodoomotorsportscorp.com/

Puma's Cycle
1129 Washington Avenue
Racine 262.637.1313

VICTORY

Sport Rider, Inc.
1504 Hillcrest Parkway
Altoona 715.834.0244
www.sportriderinc.com/

Ken's Sports
W2520 County Road JJ
Kaukauna 920.788.0220
http://polaris.kenssports.com/home

Ace Powersports
8124 Sheridan Road
Kenosha 1.877.414.0879
www.acepowersports.com

Cozzy's Polaris
W1740 US 41
Marinette 715.732.6501
www.cozzyspolaris.com

G&G Power Sports
W191 57757 Racine Avenue
Muskego 262.679.9036
www.ggpowersports.com

Team Winnebagoland
5827 Green Valley Road
Oshkosh 920.233.3070
www.teamwinnebagoland.com/

Vetesnik Power Sports
27475 Highway 14
Richland Center. 608.647.8808
www.vetesnik.com/

Bill's Service Center
801 North Weber Avenue
Stratford 715.687.3128
www.billsservicecenter.com/

Hanley Company, Inc.
641 West Main Street
Sun Prairie 608.837.5111
www.hanleycompany.com

Erv's Sales & Service
1598 North 4th Street
Tomahawk 715.453.2824
www.ervssales.com/

Shambeaus Lawn & Recreation
4621 East Hillcrest Road
Two Rivers 920.793.4536
http://polaris.shambeaurec.com/

Midcities Motorsports
7515 Friendly Drive
West Bend. 262.338.1118
http://polaris.midcitiesmotor
   sports.com/

VIPER

Majestic Trikes-N-Cycles
306 Washington Street
Horicon. 920.485.3330
www.mtrikes.com/

YAMAHA

Powersports of Abrams
2667 East Frontage Road
Abrams 920.826.6000
www.powersportsabrams.com/

Antigo Yamaha
119 Superior Street
Antigo 715.284.2600
www.ncy-antigoyamaha.com/

Appleton Powersports
4497 Converters Drive
Appleton 920.734.7134
www.appletonpowersports.com/

Johnson Sales
N1255 Highway 51
Arlington 608.635.7381
www.johnsonsalesinc.com

Beloit Honda-Yamaha-Suzuki
2210 Whipple Street
Beloit 608.362.9344
www.beloithonda.com/

C & R Yamaha
714 Rosevale Drive
Belleville 608.424.3211

Don & Roy's Motorsports
17740 Bluemound Road
Brookfield 262.786.7928
www.donandroys.com/

Zacho Sports Center
2449 S. Prairie View Rd.
Chippewa Falls 715.723.0264
www.zachosports.com/

Maxxx Motorsports
690 Gerry Way
Darien 262.882.6299
www.maxxxmotorsports.com/

Team Motorsports
1890 Mid Valley Drive
DePere 920.983.8326
www.team-motorsports.com/

Pro Motorsports
86 Rolling Meadows Drive
Fond Du Lac 920.922.8521
www.promotorsportsinc.com/

Iron River Sports
8030 Highway 2
Iron River 715.372.5252

Rock River Powersports
365 E Racine Street
Jefferson 920.674.9280
www.rockriverpowersports.com

Ace Powersports
8124 Sheridan Road
Kenosha 262.654.3090
www.acepowersports.com/

Two Brothers Powersports
124 Rose Street
LaCrosse 608.781.3360
www.twobrothershonda.com/

Midwest Action Cycle
251 Host Drive
Lake Geneva 262.249.0600
www.midwestactioncycle.com/

The Engelhart Center
1589 Greenway Cross
Madison 608.274.2366
www.engelhart.com/

TA Motorsports
525 American Drive
Francis Creek / Manitowoc
Phone: 920.682.1284
www.tamotorsports.com/

Airtec Sports
1714 Freitag Drive
Menomonie 715.232.8590
www.airtecsports.com/

Mukwonago Yamaha
970 Greenwald Court
Mukwonago 262.363.6480
www.mukwonagoyamaha.com/

Two Brothers Powersports
1241 Oak Forest Drive
Onalaska 608.785.1077
www.twobrothershonda.com/

Team Winnebagoland
5827 Mid Valley Road
Oshkosh 920.233.3070

Yamaha of Port Washington
540 West Grand Avenue
Port Washington 262.377.5480
http://portyamaha.com/

Vetesnik Power Sports
27475 Highway 14
Richland Center. 608.647.8808
www.vetesnik.com/

Wausau Motorsports
4101 Rib Mountain Drive
Wausau 715.355.6120

Donahue Super Sports
6821 Highway 54 East
Wisconsin Rapids 715.424.1762